Advance praise for *Overcoming Passive-Aggression*

"Murphy and Oberlin have written a practical, straightforward book on overcoming hidden anger. Through the use of numerous real-life examples, they weave a path through the pain, stress, desire, and control that are associated with passive-aggression. They offer solid wisdom, guidance, and advice for uncovering it in family, school, and workplace relationships. Most importantly, they offer and discuss valuable tools for easing it in oneself and others, including mindfulness, forgiveness, laughter, praise, and effective listening. Written for both a lay and professional audience, readers will come back to this book time and again as a resource for managing their overall mental health and well being."

—PAUL GIONFRIDDO, President and CEO, Mental Health America;
author of *Losing Tim: How Our Health and Education
Systems Failed My Son with Schizophrenia*

"Chronically irritable, blaming, undermining, and downright toxic, the passive-aggressive's concealed anger is destined to wreak havoc in relationships, in families, and on the job. Murphy and Oberlin shine the light of hope on this personality style and show readers the antidote to passive-resistance and malignant anger. This book is certain to be a game changer for passive-aggressive people, those who love them, and the mental health professionals who struggle to help them."

—W. BRAD JOHNSON, PhD, author of *Crazy Love:
Dealing with Your Partner's Problem Personality*

"This book shines the spotlight on passive-aggression, which lives below the radar. Well researched and loaded with up-to-date examples, practical strategies abound in this outstanding book."

—JEFFREY BERNSTEIN, PhD, author of
10 Days to a Less Defiant Child

"The revision of the excellent *Overcoming Passive-Aggression* is most welcome, providing a comprehensive understanding and coping strategies for passive faces of anger, while also addressing hostile and aggressive teens, intimate relationships, and passive anger that is threatening to children and divorce. I will continue to recommend this book to my angry patients with even more enthusiasm."

—W. ROBERT NAY, PhD, author of *Taking Charge of Anger, Second Edition*

"Tim Murphy and Loriann Oberlin have written an informative and lucid description of a prevalent and insidious psychological mechanism. Passive-aggression is maladaptive and detrimental, not just for the person manifesting this behavior but, for those toward whom it is directed. Understanding how to recognize, manage, and ultimately resolve such behaviors can be, not just therapeutic but, liberating."

—JEFFREY LIEBERMAN, MD, Chair of Psychiatry, Columbia University College of Physicians and Surgeons; Psychiatrist in Chief, New York Presbyterian Hospital; past President, APA; author of *Shrinks: The Untold Story of Psychiatry*

Praise for the previous edition

"Murphy, a psychologist and member of Congress, and Oberlin (coauthors of *The Angry Child*) closely examine how this kind of anger, called passive-aggressive, can undermine sufferers and their relationships and make life generally miserable. . . . While acknowledging the complexity of the problem, the work provides ample opportunity (and exercises) for personal growth regardless of whether you are on the giving or receiving end of passive aggression."

—*Publishers Weekly*

"*Overcoming Passive-Aggression* is not just a clear, concise description of a common problem; it's an invaluable tool to help you deal with it."

—MARGUERITE KELLY, family advice columnist for the *Washington Post*

" . . . scientifically well-grounded, beautifully written, and eminently practical in its discussion of . . . the expression of anger, direct and hidden."

—THEODORE MILLON, PhD, DSc, Professor of Psychiatry, Harvard University, author of *Personality Disorders in Modern Life*

"*Overcoming Passive-Aggression* helps passive-aggressives deal with their hidden anger and offers their targets ways to cope and manage."

—MARTIN KANTOR, MD, author of *Passive-Aggression: A Guide for the Therapist, the Patient, and the Victim*

OVERCOMING
PASSIVE-AGGRESSION

REVISED EDITION

OVERCOMING PASSIVE-AGGRESSION

*How to Stop Hidden Anger
from Spoiling Your Relationships,
Career, and Happiness*

Tim Murphy, PhD
and
Loriann Oberlin, MS, LCPC

Da Capo
LIFE
LONG

DA CAPO LIFELONG BOOKS

Copyright © 2016 by Tim Murphy and Loriann Hoff Oberlin

Designed by Linda Mark
Set in 11 point Electra LT Std by Perseus Books

Cataloging-in-Publication data for this book is available from the Library of Congress.
Revised Da Capo Press edition 2016
ISBN: 978-0-7382-1918-9 (paperback)
ISBN: 978-0-7382-1919-6 (e-book)

Published by Da Capo Press, an imprint of Perseus Books, LLC, a subsidiary of Hachette Book Group, Inc.
www.dacapopress.com

Note: The information in this book is true and complete to the best of our knowledge. This book is intended only as an informative guide for those wishing to know more about health issues. In no way is this book intended to replace, countermand, or conflict with the advice given to you by your own physician. The ultimate decision concerning care should be made between you and your doctor. We strongly recommend you follow his or her advice. Information in this book is general and is offered with no guarantees on the part of the authors or Da Capo Press. The authors and publisher disclaim all liability in connection with the use of this book. The names and identifying details of people associated with events described in this book have been changed. Any similarity to actual persons is coincidental.

Da Capo Press books are available at special discounts for bulk purchases in the United States by corporations, institutions, and other organizations. For more information, please contact the Special Markets Department at the Perseus Books Group, 2300 Chestnut Street, Suite 200, Philadelphia, PA 19103, or call (800) 810-4145, ext. 5000, or e-mail special.markets@perseusbooks.com.

10 9 8 7 6 5 4 3 2 1

About the Authors

TIM MURPHY earned his PhD from the University of Pittsburgh and has spent four decades as a psychologist and advocate for a better healthcare system. In January 2015, he began serving his seventh term in the US Congress, representing the 18th District of Pennsylvania. He is co-chair of the Mental Health Caucus, a founding member of the GOP Doctors Caucus, and chairs the Oversight and Investigations Subcommittee of the House Energy and Commerce Committee, which encompasses healthcare matters, food and drug safety, public health research, environmental quality, energy policy, and much more.

Congressman Murphy's subcommittee began a multi-year investigation in 2013 into the nation's broken mental health system in the wake of school shootings and mass acts of violence, homelessness, victimization, and other problems associated with untreated mental illness. His landmark reform legislation, called the Helping Families in Mental Health Crisis Act, HR 2646, of 2015 was written to solve the shortage of psychiatric hospital beds and mental health providers, improve research, allow families to have a helpful role in care, and provide treatment before tragedy. Praise for this has come from esteemed groups such as the American Psychiatric

Association and the National Alliance on Mental Illness as well as from na-
tional media from coast to coast, including CNN, *The Wall Street Journal,*
The Washington Post, The Seattle Times, San Francisco Chronicle, and
Pittsburgh Post-Gazette.

Dr. Murphy has an active license as a psychologist and serves as a commander in the Navy Reserve Medical Service Corps at Walter Reed National Military Medical Center in Bethesda, Maryland. He works as a Navy
psychologist with service members undergoing treatment for traumatic
brain injury and posttraumatic stress. Prior to joining the House of Representatives, Murphy served as a Pennsylvania State Senator from 1997 to
2002, where he was responsible for writing and passing the state's historic
Patient Bill of Rights, among other achievements. He serves as an associate
adjunct professor at the University of Pittsburgh School of Public Health
and was an assistant professor in the School of Medicine. For more than
twenty years, Dr. Murphy worked with children and families in private
practice and at Children's Hospital of Pittsburgh.

LORIANN OBERLIN earned both a master's degree and a post-master's cer-
tificate in clinical counseling from Johns Hopkins University. Currently,
she maintains a private practice as a licensed clinical professional counselor
(LCPC) in Maryland with two offices—one outside Washington, DC, and
the other on Maryland's eastern shore. In her practice, she treats children,
adolescents, adults, couples, and families, using evidence-based cognitive-behavioral and family systems modalities. She also provides coaching
and consultation services and has spoken before colleagues, employee assistance groups, the community, and at workplace seminars.

Ms. Oberlin has completed mediation, child-access, and collaborative
law training as well as Gottman Method Couples Therapy workshops. She
has worked in Maryland's second-busiest emergency department and in
community mental health prior to establishing her own practice. Oberlin
spent more than thirty years as a writer of nonfiction books, magazine and
newspaper articles, and most recently fiction, writing under the pseudonym

Lauren Monroe. She's a member of the Eastern Shore Writers Association, assists in planning the Bay to Ocean Writers Conference, and presents at other conferences. Her website is www.loriannoberlin.com. Ms. Oberlin manages this book's Facebook presence at www.facebook.com/OvercomingPassiveAggression.

The insights presented in this book stem from previously published literature; the former psychological practice of Tim Murphy, PhD; the current clinical practice of Loriann Oberlin, MS, LCPC; and our own observations of human behavior.

All anecdotes in this book are composites crafted to illustrate certain concepts. Fictitious names and details have been added, and thus any similarities between the anecdotes presented in this book and any actual person, living or deceased, is entirely coincidental.

We wish to make it clear that this book is not meant as a substitute for professional counseling or psychological help. We hope to raise awareness of problematic behaviors such as hidden anger, and we encourage healthy coping strategies as well as the appropriate self-expression of thoughts and feelings, including anger. We hope that you will learn a great deal and perhaps recommend this book to others who may benefit as well.

To Thomasina and Luca, my grandchildren,
and to the next generation for whom
we must make this a better world.
—Tim

To my sons, Andy and Alex,
with thanks for their support and
pride in all that they achieve.
—Loriann

Contents

Introduction

I'VE PRACTICED PSYCHOLOGY NOW FOR MORE THAN FORTY YEARS, served as a Pennsylvania legislator for six, been a member of the US House of Representatives for fourteen years (as I write this), and I've contributed numerous articles and books along these journeys. In this second edition of a hidden anger book, I'm saddened to say that many interpersonal interactions are not only just dysfunctional but now that dysfunction is even more pervasive. Hiding anger in an underhanded, hurtful, gotcha-now manner has become the go-to choice for a society that's losing its ability to know how to identify a problem and solve it in a respectful way. People confuse getting even with getting results and in so doing feed their own dysfunction. It's childish . . . and ugly. It's no wonder that the first edition of *Overcoming Passive-Aggression* sold well and has become a guide for many in dealing with personal, relationship, and work messes.

I sometimes joke that this book should be the field guide to surviving politics and Congress. Here's a glimpse into that world: people will say to a bill's creator that they support a particular piece of legislation only to tell leadership "please don't run that bill." Mixed message? You bet it is. Sometimes staff or other members won't read a bill but will criticize it anyway. A member may declare to be a friend in public but then raise millions to get the supposed buddy out of office. I call this high-stakes passive-aggression. Most people in government are there for the right reason, but it takes a few to make a mess of a good institution.

Yet Congress, like any system or group of people, is a mirror of society. If you elect someone running on a platform of "I'm mad as hell and headed to the Capitol just to yell more about it," you should not be surprised when that official spends more time picking fights instead of finding solutions. In these pages, we'll show how to use your passion for betterment and effectively put an end to future ugliness. As we outline in the ten traits we have created in our books, angry people make their own misery. End making yours.

—*Congressman Tim Murphy, PhD*

A UTHORS LOVE IT WHEN THEIR BOOK INFLUENCES THE READING public. *Overcoming Passive-Aggression* hit psychology shelves at bookstores years ago, and became popular with readers who saw themselves, their colleagues, and their loved ones in its pages.

Working as a licensed mental health counselor, I know that if you dig deep enough into any group of people, you will find very disparate communication styles and coping mechanisms. Since this book's debut, poor behavior has been showcased even more frequently on reality shows and situation comedies that millions tune in to, often after exposure to the same poor behavior at work or in school. For these people, it's no laughing matter.

What's sad, however, is the occasional journalistic attention granted to media where nasty barbs, indirect innuendo, and even explosive rants make the newsfeed each evening or are posted on social media. Sensationalizing invites more embellishing, and as we know, doing the same thing and expecting a different result gets us no place productive. Counterproductive communication is all around us. In my work, I've seen schoolchildren tormented enough by the sly bully that they end up truant, teens who ponder suicide rather than face the vicious rumors social media exposed them to, and couples who censure each other with a diet of disrespect only to become defensive when called out on such ineffective behavior.

This book is written in both of our voices, and for clarity, we will sometimes insert one of our names when needed. Because we write about both genders, we'll alternate pronouns, sometimes using *he*, other times *she*. This new edition of *Overcoming Passive-Aggression* is updated throughout, with two new chapters. One chapter focuses on how hidden anger takes root in childhood and flourishes in adolescence. Another addresses failed relationships, which are often dissolved in divorce. The battlegrounds created prove costly to people's money and happiness, and often children become the innocent casualties. We've also added a section for clinicians and lay people alike. We know that your time is valuable. This revised edition has quick take-away tips you can implement immediately. New material explains how not to put your health and happiness at risk.

Because much bitterness exists on the periphery of people's lives, we know that this book will aid readers daily; most of you put up with difficult, seething souls either in your personal lives, work, or school.

If any of our composite sketches resonate with you personally, it's likely because your struggle is the same as someone else's. If something strikes a chord, we hope you'll recommend this book to others and follow us online for additional opportunities to connect and learn about this topic.

—*Loriann Oberlin, MS, LCPC*

PART 1

Passive-Aggression & Hidden Anger Explained

one

What Is Passive-Aggression Anyway?

N ICK CONTRIBUTED CONSISTENTLY TO HIS DEPARTMENT AND ENJOYED working alongside Brendan, a colleague turned friend. When Travis replaced Brendan in a reorganization, however, Nick wondered if Travis had nudged Brendan aside. Nick and other members of his team got tired of hearing Travis say, "Where I worked before, we did *this* . . ." or "*that* worked out better."

"Give Travis a try," Louisa, the boss, directed, not justifying her hiring decision. Yet the team criticized via text messages and e-mails: "Look how that guy dresses. And that *annoying* ring tone!"

One day, Travis offered suggestions on a project that the team knew would never work. Rather than tell Travis when he asked for feedback, teammates showered him with praise, and thus, he wrote up his plan.

The day Travis presented the project, it fell completely flat. Travis's jaw dropped when not one of his colleagues came to his aid. The presentation was so off the mark that even the boss said, "Maybe check with your team rather than reinvent the wheel."

In this office, good enough never had the chance to become great. The team would never see crowning accolades, nor bonuses. They maintained their mediocrity via rejection, resentment, and revenge. No one really won, but in some sick way, that doesn't matter to the passive-aggressive person for whom even a morsel of revenge outweighs a lack of success.

On the surface, this passive-aggressive team camouflaged sabotage with public compliments that turned bitter privately. Throughout this book, we'll show you how to raise your radar and distinguish between people who hide anger and those who back their words with action. Whether at work or in your personal life, we'll help you change or end the passive-aggression that's within your grasp and cope with it when mired in it.

Anger, always triggered by some other powerful emotion, resides in everyone. You can choose to work through it, control it, and move past it. Decades of research concludes: happy people live longer, more productive and satisfying lives. Unremitting, anger can even be deadly.[1]

If you or someone you know harbors more than temporary anger, even as a semi-permanent trait, count upon looming, dark clouds and storms, clashes with other people, more than the ordinary challenges at work, and, in romance, forget a dozen roses, except maybe for the thorns. Intimate relationships will likely become quicksand or constant struggle. Anger can precipitate the decline of one's mental and physical health.

We will unravel the differences between open anger and forms so under the radar that the NSA might face challenges in finding it. We'll define, explain, and unpack passive-aggression, citing its weary hold on friendships, marriages, and families; within the workplace and school; even behind the doors of therapy sessions. Hidden anger encompasses much more than passive-aggressive behavior, but by far that's the most familiar form, so we provide it center stage. Self-absorption, chronic depression, strong personality traits, and other conditions equally sidetrack relationships, career success, and overall contentment. We will help you see inside the mind of a bitter person anchored in criticism and negativity, entwining themselves—and you—in the dock lines as their tide rises. Most struggle to stay above water. We'll show you how to swim toward calm waters.

AGGRESSIVE ANGER VERSUS HIDDEN ANGER

It's sometimes okay to be angry, but it's never okay to be mean. Aggressive anger is powerful, visible, and immediate. Aggressive anger takes the form of a threat, scream, physical blow, or broken or destroyed object. It's an in-your-face attack. There is another type, however, that's subtle, covert, and not easy to spot. Hidden anger, cloaked and disguised, may take time to effect true damage, since it's shrouded in other words or deeds.

The immediate consequences of hidden anger aren't often apparent, especially with passive-aggression, where anger is secretly expressed but in an outwardly docile, consequence-free way. Passive-aggression often manifests in *not* doing some required or helpful action. Someone might forget to pick you up on time, not put money in the meter so that you get a fine, lose your keys so that you're inconvenienced, or delay giving you a report until you have no choice but to present material unrehearsed. Hidden anger might be a late child support payment, silence when someone awaits an answer, or not filling the car with gas. It might also look half-right, half-wrong, like filing a report in the wrong drawer so it's as good as lost or withholding information that someone needs or requests.

The tenet we cited—that anger is sometimes okay but should never be mean—is important to bear in mind. As a psychologist and licensed counselor, respectively, we have often used that reminder with children and adults alike. Whether in a political campaign, the corporate boardroom, your cubicle, at the dinner table, or in the school cafeteria, our anger expressions are meaningful barometers of what's going on in our lives.

DEFINING HIDDEN ANGER

Not always the demon most of us might think, anger is a powerful response triggered by another negative emotion, which results in an attack of variable intensity that is not always appropriate. That triggering emotion could be sadness, jealousy, fear, embarrassment, or another difficult feeling. Hidden anger has some of these components, but to truly embrace this concept we see it as the following:

- Indirect, incongruent, and unproductive behavior
- Subtle, manipulative actions, inactivity, or even crimes of omission
- Consciously planned, intentional, or slyly vindictive; or it can be unconscious
- Part of a dysfunctional pattern of dealing with and diminishing others in a shrewd way
- Often payback for a grudge or pain inflicted out of envy or perceived unfairness
- Allowing the perpetrator to deny responsibility for it and often to appear as the victim
- Stalling because it doesn't move toward resolution; it blocks resolution
- Motivated by the intent to hurt, annoy, or destroy
- Triggered by needs that haven't been met or based on irrational fears/beliefs
- Never positive because of its manipulative and indirect nature
- Toxic to relationships and groups of people, especially over time
- Self-perpetuating, powerful, and rarely, if ever, appropriate
- A power play to establish pecking order

If hidden anger is unleashed upon you, you'll potentially feel like the bad character. You can sense a problem, only you're not sure who is responsible, why it's happening, or what to do about it. Often, it's socially acceptable, excused because it's so covert. You may wonder if you made some mistake.

Passive-aggressive people possess keen skills: manipulation tops the list. They can have handy alibis and display a cunning charm. Ignorant of what's truly happening, others grant free passes for the behavior until they catch on and challenge or hold the person accountable. Teachers, bosses, doctors, judges, coworkers, even loved ones essentially give passive-aggressors the benefit of the doubt. Not until they slip up, forget to cover their tracks, or simply accrue too much reasonable doubt are they taken to task. They can redirect their contempt no further. Never wishing to fall from others' graces, they offer further explanation to keep socially masking their true intent with "You should have told me," or "I can't get over how sensitive you've become."

Since this phenomenon was first identified, mental health researchers have revised their theories and nomenclature to explain why those on the receiving end of this maddening behavior have trouble determining whether it's intentional or not. Words such as *ambivalent, negative,* and *oppositional* have appeared within the definition of passive-aggression. Actually, they all describe what happens. For instance, the passive-aggressor vacillates between wishing for independence and depending upon others. The person may say he'd like to take a more active role at work (or at home) but veers away from responsibility when given the opportunity for action. The "dirty trick" or underhanded tactics used by this person account for the negativity. The retaliatory "get back" behavior of obstruction or resistance, much like Nick and his colleagues displayed in our example, is most assuredly oppositional.

Passive-aggression, in the bigger hidden-anger picture, can look like some or all of the following:

- Chronic irritability and chronic depression
- Self-absorption/narcissism/vanity (an entitlement personality)
- Low self-esteem, weak boundaries, and family enmeshment
- Self-destructive behavior or acting out
- Aggression that gets redirected onto a safer target or scapegoat
- Substance abuse and addictive behavior
- Social immaturity
- Unacceptable conduct that's excused for many reasons

Something else incites or sparks anger because anger is always a reaction to some other event or emotion. We're not built with some invisible button that, when pressed, causes anger. Rather, our emotional reactions are shaped and directed by our experiences, thoughts, and interpretations. Two different people may react in two entirely different ways to the same word, gesture, or action.

Here's how it works: Someone makes a statement. We interpret it based upon who says it and what that person and their statement mean to us. Our interpretation triggers our emotional reaction. Let's say your friend reports, "I'd have called you sooner, but I didn't get your message until today." That sentence can provoke two different reactions depending upon whether you think your friend wasn't telling the truth or had been genuine—perhaps traveling and unavailable.

At times, the thoughts and feelings that trigger anger can serve a valuable purpose and have a positive intent and outcome. When the world seems out of control, you can channel the spikes in cortisol, hormones, blood pressure, and heart rate to fuel your own focus, cooperation, leadership, creativity, and ambition for good. This fosters optimism, hope, empathy, and understanding. Indeed, the frustrations that could lead to anger, when channeled appropriately, can instead lead you to catch yourself, pause, rethink the situation, and then engage in the higher emotional intelligence of healthy, honest, and direct communication, which is far more useful (productive anger).

As well, if you manage yourself and your reactivity for fear that too much honesty will spark someone's explosive anger, tucking away your angry feelings, at least temporarily, focuses on problem resolution. This reflects a positive motive and outcome rather than manipulation, passivity, or avoidance (unproductive anger). Ignoring rather than counterarguing or venting provides better long-term results.

Let's put human faces and circumstances to this new definition of hidden anger, looking at intent and outcome. Watch for our key words and portraits that possibly describe people you know.

CASE #1 PROFESSIONAL JEALOUSY

Three law school classmates—Wade, Crystal, and Shannon—agreed on a four-step process. Graduate, pass the bar, gain experience, and set up their law practice. Wade and Crystal, graduating a year earlier, led the plan. Wade clerked for a judge while Crystal worked as a paralegal. Then they set up shop. As Shannon stored away her cap and gown, her friends had a job ready where she could gain experience and offset their rent, split three ways. The trio worked well for ten months, until Shannon got chosen by a local TV reporter to comment upon a news-making case and the daily paper asked her to pen a weekly Q&A column. Wade whispered to Crystal, "What gives?"

Both Wade and Crystal said they were happy for Shannon, but their downturned looks convinced otherwise. Each Thursday, the same day the column appeared, the newspaper mysteriously disappeared from the waiting area, and the lunchroom copy cradled the morning's coffee grounds in the trash.

CASE #2 REDIRECTED GRUDGES

Overwhelmed parents, Jan and Lester, along with five children comprise the Smith household. Twins (Morgan and Michael) are significantly older, with a sixteen-year gap between them and the youngest child. Whenever Jan or Lester asks the twins to do chores or to shuttle a younger sibling, Michael complies whereas Morgan forgets or follows through so very begrudgingly—sarcastic or critical of her siblings—that the family is driven to tears from her subtle hostility. Home from college, Morgan reaches into a cabinet, hiking her sleeve, to reveal cut marks on her arm. Shocked, Jan confronts Morgan about the thin scars, which Morgan at first denies. Later, the girl tearfully breaks down, admitting that she does this to herself to hide feeling abandoned by their mom. She says that her younger siblings remind her of those disregarded needs.

Many children become resentful if nudged out of special attention. Most family members adapt to their new roles, but the attention once showered upon Morgan and Michael abruptly shifted as their brothers and sisters were born, and this may have led to Morgan's present-day grudges. Deepseated indignation self-perpetuates to toxic levels if not talked through. While the perceived unfairness gets targeted to the siblings, we'll detail how the parents may be the primary, albeit inconvenient and less safe targets.

CASE #3 BACK HOME ON THE COUCH

Elena, the only child of Mateo and Marcela, recently completed her college degree at age twenty-five. Her South American parents knew struggle and valued the education and hard work that brought success. But Elena faced the Millennial generation's graduation gift: recessionary unemployment. Following graduation, her parents had funded Elena's passion—the visual arts—providing even more courses. They clipped classifieds and browsed career websites for her now that she was home. They did this after long work days and transit commutes, though they'd find Elena sprawled on the family room sofa, smartphone in one hand and remote control in the other, a toppled bowl of chips half-stomped into the carpet.

"I texted you to do chores today," Marcela scolded. "You can't help out but can count LIKES on Facebook."

"What happened to 'Hi, how was your day?'" Elena mumbled. "You make me feel like crap."

Did Mateo and Marcela unwittingly set up a bothersome blame trap? Keep reading to find out.

CASE #4 DIVORCING THE ENTITLED SPOUSE

Sunita and Deepak had an arranged marriage. Educated in the United States, their values reflected high family expectations. Decades later, Deepak had twice cheated on Sunita, belittled her nursing career, and stepped into fatherhood mostly to show off their four kids on trips to India. He constantly reminded everyone about his doctoral degree in philosophy. For as much as he professed to his university classes, his actions lacked the wisdom that should have come with education.

Two of their children sought therapy after striving for straight As in AP classes and the loud arguments that ensued when they fell short. Another saw a GI specialist for an upset stomach. Sunita had had enough. Her saved bonuses funded a divorce attorney. Predictably, Deepak turned more manipulative, accusing her of having someone on the side (she didn't; he did). Even her family pleaded: "How could you disgrace the family?"

Threatening to never give Sunita a dime—even from marital property— Deepak took a sabbatical to lower his wages. When questioned, he used his Dr. title, often making third parties believe he was a medical doctor or a psychologist, whichever fit his purposes. He would "pay back" Sunita by depriving her, because he felt entitled to her, his children, and the perfect life she had disrupted. To Deepak, the lost income was worth the revenge.

These scenarios—jealous colleagues, a resentful teen, overfunctioning parents and an immovable daughter, as well as the entitled, vindictive spouse—illustrate hidden anger with persistent patterns of indirect, often manipulative, behavior. Sometimes this is very intentional; other times, it remains hidden even from the perpetrator, who is unaware of his redirected anger. In most of these examples, the perpetrator escapes blame or responsibility. "Aren't all families frazzled?" some could claim, or "I just forgot," or "I'm saving my kids from divorce." Yes, there can be sensible excuses for behavior, but when the need for revenge, self-pity, and jealousy overshadow reason, trouble ensues.

With our legal colleagues, what did Shannon's success mean for her two supposed friends and mentors who had each agreed to establish the office and work collegially?

Families routinely add siblings and most reestablish a cohesive bond. It's not uncommon that parents have the benefit of higher income and the school of scraped knees and sleepless nights to change both their perspective and how they subsequently parent younger children. In other words, older sibs often have it tougher than younger ones. Yet how did Michael become more easygoing than his aggrieved sister Morgan, whose noncompliance and sarcasm made her discontent manifest?

The couch-confined daughter could retract her snarky comments with "I was *just* joking" or "I didn't *really* mean it." In a divorce, people aim to differentiate themselves, sometimes to uncooperative extremes, because they failed at this developmental task during adolescence. People who conceal their inner angry feelings say things to save face, to be socially accepted, because recognition is a core need for them, and very often they do this within their families of origin.

Passive-aggressive people slickly brush off blame. You react, and they are the misunderstood victims. They win on two counts, so they gain attention twice and dump anger on you, to boot. Even if they are not totally aware of how and why they behave as they do, it's a well-rehearsed outcome that achieves results.

Vacillation is a key component. Too often a person who hides anger does so because he can't really make up his mind whether he should depend on or need the other person. His uncertainty gets channeled into a power move: "I'm independent, free at last, and better than him, too!" With our frazzled family, it might be hard for Morgan to speak to her parents. Years ago, she didn't feel she could safely tell them that she wasn't ready for "big girl" caretaking duties, that she still needed her parents' guidance. To have spoken up then—or now—feels threatening. Every time Morgan is asked to cooperate, her overlooked inner child cries out to prove something to her parents. She can't possibly alienate them, so Morgan redirects her frustration onto her siblings, the household, even her own skin.

AN UNWELCOME TARGET

Anger never exists in a vacuum. There's usually a target. Victims of another person's wrath know how unsettling veiled hostility can be, how it can cause an adult to finally differentiate from a family whose goals and values are dissimilar; a worker to want to change jobs; or a spouse to leave a marriage. We have both counseled enough children to know the true hurt and confusion this causes when divorcing parents use passive-aggression. We believe that when children are old enough to gain their own insights, they see any negative light parents may conceal. That became evident when a teenage girl named Nina came close to the breaking point because her divorced parents couldn't communicate. Dad worked long hours. Her mother pretended her e-mail was down—except when her boyfriend or office messaged. "Tell your mother your uniform payment is due Friday," Nina's father would say. Her mom would retort, "See, he doesn't even support your cheerleading." This infuriated Nina. She quietly seethed inside and quit the sport when her pent-up voice could have been cheering on her school's team. Instead, every practice, every Friday night game that Nina stayed home reminded her of what she tried to escape. To survive, Nina must learn how to calmly and assuredly take a stand, even within her fractured family.

Nina has to end the faulty pattern. She will not quickly forget how their lack of skill made her feel uncomfortable, yet she will have to work at trusting them in the future. Not only did Nina's parents' passive-aggression damage their bond with her, but Nina is also at risk for mismanaging her own anger if she doesn't learn to develop her own assertiveness.

How do you know when someone is being passive-aggressive or when he truly is overwhelmed and forgetful or maybe honestly miscalculated and made a mistake? There's no easy answer.

Say a staff member not only made your airline reservation too late, placing you in a back middle seat, but also forgot to order the necessary materials for an important meeting. Days before the event, her mistake means wasted hours spent gathering last-minute, makeshift supplies.

Is this person really incompetent? Forgetful? Well, if you know she's got proven job talents, excellent references, and received your request months ago, then you have reason to believe she might have silently exerted power or discharged hidden anger. But even then, you may not know unless you debrief and simply ask what happened. An honest employee would come right out with the reason, such as "I wrote down the wrong date," and tell you how it would not happen again. Even then, did she intentionally inconvenience you? Get overwhelmed with other problems? Time will tell.

As you read, you'll learn about different actions and behaviors that, all told, might help you to draw faster conclusions; however, psychology is not a coherent, linear science. Too often pop psychology allows us to believe that the cause of something leads pretty easily to a closely related effect or conclusion. It's simply not a smooth transition; our own temperaments, personalities, environments, attitudes, and interpretations play big roles in shaping us. How we interpret a situation can have a bigger impact upon determining our reaction than the situation itself. A few incidents of forgetfulness might mean something entirely different from passive-aggression.

In the classroom, if a teacher spots a student displaying forgetfulness, as well as impulsivity, blurting out answers, and falling off task, it might mean that student has attention-deficit/hyperactivity disorder (ADHD) and is not passive-aggressive at all. When an especially organized adult whose mind would ordinarily be on top of many details forgets information, might this sudden lapse have something to do with an accident she suffered? Traumatic or other brain injuries slow and sometimes overwhelm a person's thinking. Veterans adjusting to combat traumas may be distracted by troubling memories. Forgetfulness in older adults frequently raises suspicions of dementia, and stress interferes with everyone's memory, attention, and learning.

At work, low morale could indicate hidden hostility such as the disgruntled worker who isn't happy with his current position. He might be afraid to conduct a job search. Remaining passive and staying with the known versus the unknown circumvents his taking risks. "The certainty of misery is preferable to the misery of uncertainty," the late Virginia Satir, a pioneer of family therapy, once said.

Because the worker is stuck and doesn't feel he can openly express his anger, he might intentionally do a lousy job or let mistakes slide until he infuriates or trips up his boss or coworkers. Ambivalence begets errors, the cost of which can be terribly expensive, even deadly. Imagine important safety measures left off products or hazards created by consciously careless employees who have a "get back" attitude. When employees stage a work stoppage by calling in sick in droves, it's a passive-aggressive way of making a point, and could well backfire against their intentions.

Often, inciting anger in another is the conscious or unconscious goal of people disguising their own anger. Why? Anger is so uncomfortable to them that they cast it onto another person, thereby getting to experience it vicariously, so that they don't have to take any responsibility for it. With no direct expression of anger, they can live comfortably without risking consequences. They hold fear in check by having it both ways—they remain passive, but by pulling off a slick move, they show their aggression.

We can apply this same premise to any anger concealer caught red-handed. She might use the common retort "I'm *not* angry!" Yet you've determined mean-spirited intent and have seen (maybe felt) the poor outcome. Sure she was angry, but she denies it. To do otherwise stirs too many fears and forces her to confront what she puts great energy toward avoiding. If she admits openly to her true feelings, she might risk the relationship, and well . . . she can't, because she's dependent upon you.

When a person doesn't deny his concealed aggression, he sometimes retracts an angry response with fence-mending words, contrition, or both. Occasionally, it's too late to repair the damage and the dreams gone astray. Unless there is new insight and a commitment to change, hidden anger can often be the root of life's disappointments that lie shrouded in excuses and a lifetime of blame. Sadly, with passive-aggression, disappointment can become a recurring theme or self-perpetuating prophecy.

WHOSE PROBLEM IS IT?

Try to remember a time when you started out having an ordinary discussion. You offered an opinion or broached a topic only to meet suddenly with fierce resistance or defensiveness that was way out of proportion to your remark. In an honest discussion of a time you felt hurt, your retelling the story takes a person back to a time in her own life, when perhaps she caused a similar problem for someone else. It hits close to home, triggering embarrassment, guilt, or another powerful feeling, as it did for the two women described here.

Marianne chatted with neighbor Barbara about life and people they knew. As the conversation shifted, as it often does, Marianne mentioned how hurtful her ex-husband's infidelity had been to live through. A passing remark—nothing more. But Barbara suddenly became defensive and curt. Why did she turn on Marianne?

Without either woman realizing it, Barbara identified with Marianne because Barbara was once "the other woman" causing similar sorrow (to another female). She simply couldn't stand listening to Marianne. To squelch the discomfort (since Barbara felt she couldn't be honest without risking further embarrassment), she could become defensive, change the topic, or remain standoffish and mask her feelings.

This is not about Marianne; it's about Barbara. Whoever is on the receiving end of icy tension feels annoyed because the reason remains hidden—the proverbial elephant in the room that no one dares to notice.

When people go to a therapist's office because they are dealing with passive-aggressive, entitled, or just plain difficult people, they may have complaints about anxiety and worry. In some cases, the redirected anger has been cast upon them, as the passive-aggressor says, "You need therapy," or some other condescending comment. This is the passive-aggressor's way of convincing herself, by persuading other people that they are the problem, not the other way around. If this happens to you, and you buy into the blame, then you vindicate the passive-aggressor.

Even if an angry person never changes, by gaining insight, you can change *your* approach. Victims of anger often become anxious and try diligently to fix things and make problems go away. When another person's reaction to your actions doesn't make sense, realize that resolution may be elusive. If you made a mistake or were insensitive, try to clear that up. You can't control what has happened to you in the past, but you can control how you think, feel, and act in the present.

When someone reacts strongly to something you did with innocence, and the reaction seems way out of proportion to your actions, you can ask what happened. "I'm sorry, but I'm confused about why you are upset. Did what I say upset you?"

If that doesn't work, remove yourself as a target until you find a better strategy. Your own valuable insight can extricate you from someone else's angry battle. Don't blame yourself for things you never did, and understand that people who exhibit hidden anger or passive-aggression could very well have more than momentary wrath. Their behavior may stem from:

- Low frustration tolerance
- Impulsivity
- Markedly different character traits or a personality disorder
- Emotional or verbal abuse
- Physical signs of "losing it" or barely containing hostility
- A locked-step, dysfunctional dance with someone else
- Chronic irritability
- Low energy, passivity, and resentment of those who have high energy, activity, and happiness
- Low self-esteem
- Lifelong struggles and unhappiness

In fact, hidden anger may seem so normal that passive-aggressors may resist any attempts to change. Healthy functioning remains a foreign concept, and they'd rather stick with what they know, because, sadly enough, passive-aggression often works. Their anger may also qualify as a deeper disorder.

ANTICIPATED, APPROPRIATE ANGER

Earlier we explained that the true indicator of whether hidden anger serves a purpose rests in its intent or whether it's developmentally expected. Here are some scenarios where hidden anger wouldn't be too surprising or out of the ordinary:

- Self-protection or problem solving could justify concealed anger. Silence may be the most polite or productive response. In a civil society, you don't always show your emotions to a clerk, coworker, or even a confidante. Self-control makes you a more pleasant person to be around. Feeling entitled to say or do whatever you feel is often just plain rude. How often has one person's impulsive, bad feeling been tweeted and re-tweeted before it went viral? How often do we get into trouble because we fail to engage thought before behavior?
- Sarcastic comments will be funny when mutually understood within a genuine, supportive relationship or standup comedy. Talk-show hosts lob remarks at the celebrity *du jour* to entertain. A study released in 2015 looked at the long overlooked psychological benefits of sarcasm, finding that it has the potential to catalyze creativity for those expressing and receiving it. Yet another finding from the same report says that sarcasm has the negative propensity to instigate conflict in parties with limited rapport.[2] Hence, use sarcasm sparingly, with good taste, and never to hurt.
- Unrelenting positions due to political debate or advocacy might appear as stubborn stances. Refusal to back down here doesn't reflect a personality deficit but instead reflects a commitment to debate what's important. Alternatively, if a person holds deep-seated resentments and acts to destroy others, especially when advocating a point isn't in the best interests of others, then it's angry, spiteful, and wrong. It is important to account for motive and purpose, among other key factors.
- For teenagers, a certain level of rebellion comes with the territory, including procrastination, withholding, and avoidance. A child's covert antagonism is often a passing phase. Teenagers notoriously exhibit that push-pull that exemplifies the passive-aggressive person's dilemma. No longer a child, not quite mature either, the teen sends mixed messages: "take care of me," but "leave me alone," or "I need the family cell phone plan," yet "why do I have to help around the house?" All this is akin to "give me responsibility, but

not too much, please." These are classic struggles between wanting the comforts of parental income without actively pitching in as parents earn it. If this isn't welcome news, remember, teens do mature beyond this stage. Most develop a better repertoire of skills, becoming more confident and proactive. Only when a continued pattern of passivity, ambivalence, obstructionism, or resentment carries into adulthood does it point to real problems.

HOW ARE THINGS IN YOUR LIFE?

When you were a student, how did you handle displeasure with your grades or a teacher? Anger's presence could have served as a catalyst for positive change and growth. It could have inspired you to get to know your teacher in a different way, so that you forged better relations and ultimately achieved better grades. If you discussed your performance, asked for guidance or tutoring, this could have had a more positive effect than lobbing an angry comment.

Now, replace *student* with *worker*. Then replace *teacher* with *boss*, and *grades* with *job performance* and quite possibly a raise or promotion. For that matter, replace *student* and *teacher* with *Democrat* or *Republican*. In any circumstance, the keys are productive, honest expression and problem solving, not the consequences of an angry agenda. In the grocery checkout both the exhausted child and the worn-out parent face the same problem as do adult siblings divvying up an inherited estate. Anger may be common, yet self-reflection that gets sparked clarifies who we are, how we feel about something, what we will or won't tolerate, and how we'll change things.

That's not to say that anger cannot motivate hard work. To provide insight into how you handle your own struggles and anger, try our brief questionnaire. Answer either "yes" or "no" to each question ("sometimes" is not valid here).

If you're really troubled in a relationship with a friend, family member, colleague, or someone else, and you know their background well, you can attempt to answer from their perspective. By doing this you may gain insight into the difficulties both of you experience.

1. Was expression of anger prohibited in your home as a child?
2. Did you (or do you) struggle to please your parents?
3. Did your parents deny or fail to value your fundamental needs and wants?
4. If you were appropriately assertive for yourself, did you feel afraid or punished?
5. Did the attachment to your parents change in any abrupt way or feel threatened?
6. Would you describe your parents as having a negative attitude when you were growing up?
7. Do you take actions to protect the status quo rather than try out new approaches?
8. Do you use brief answers or short phrases because you're afraid to speak up?
9. Does your smile disguise your truly frustrated emotions?
10. Do others tell you about an interpersonal problem they think you have that you don't see?
11. Are you ever intentionally slow performing a request?
12. Do you tell others that you don't understand their requests or concerns so that they'll leave you alone?
13. When you disagree, do you feel less anxiety by silencing your frustration?
14. Do others feel that you have all-or-nothing thinking, often misinterpret a situation, or read things into it?
15. If you see a coworker headed for a big mistake, do you keep quiet?
16. When afraid to share your opinion, do you later resent things not going your way?
17. Do you bristle when others criticize your work?
18. Do you soothe uncomfortable feelings with food, alcohol, drugs, sex, or gambling?
19. Do you often feel that problems you encounter are someone else's fault?
20. Do you continue an argument past its logical end?
21. Does the fear of rejection prevent you from taking action?
22. Do you feel that others can make better decisions than you can?

23. Have you ever turned in projects that contained errors or omissions that would cause problems for someone?
24. Do you yearn for more freedom in a relationship but at the same time wish to be close?
25. Have you had a hard time following the wishes of those in authority?
26. Do you resent someone telling you how to do a better job?
27. Do you experience a secret glee in maintaining an advantage over others?
28. Do you keep your feelings inside for so long that you eventually explode in unexpected outbursts?
29. When a person is too demanding of you, do you look for ways for him to fail?
30. Have you put your foot in someone's path because you resented that person's good fortune?

The purpose here is not to give you a definitive score, but rather to alert you to the presence of your own hidden needs, fears, and things you might be avoiding. The more "yes" answers you have tallied, the more likely it is that you're concealing emotions, including anger. These concealed emotions would render anyone more apt to respond inappropriately or passive-aggressively.

MISMATCHED THOUGHTS, FEELINGS, AND BEHAVIORS

Congruence—consistency between how you feel and the way you act—fosters honesty and communication. Thoughts, feelings, and actions should match and send similar messages. People who are incongruent may claim they feel or believe one thing and then act in an altogether different manner. Essentially, they hide their identity from others, and sometimes even from themselves. Feelings and actions need to be rationally connected to one another, but they also need to be appropriate (i.e., polite, mannerly) and within society's norms. The hungry screams of a young child are congruent (age linked with behavior), but the same behavior is terribly incongruent in a thirty-year-old man. Sending off mixed messages harms just about any relationship. It's like living a lie, and it is a key reason why some lack insight into their own behavior or feelings.

UNMASKING THE ANGER

This is vast territory we're covering, not a one-size-fits-all problem. As long as anger remains hidden, we can't change it. Our goal is to acknowledge what a lot of angry people go to great lengths to conceal—that is, core needs, what they fear or avoid, and what behavior manifests openly. Our visual blocks shed light on these complexities.

When we speak of a chronically angry person's core need, we mean a deep-seated requirement that is almost compulsive. With pervasively angry people, it borders on (or just plain is) a pathological need. For instance, angry people who really need to *control* things may act differently than those who are *depressed* or whose core need is to become the center of attention. In Part 1, the five basic needs we will outline are: control, manipulation, childlike immaturity, self-absorption, and depression.

Yes, you will find overlap in the characteristics. Passive-aggressive behavior is often born of the similar fears of being controlled or caught in confrontation, and the need to work *around* others more than directly *with* others. That same obsessive component applies to an angry person's fear and avoidance. We all have fears. Behaviorally, we may choose to avoid being near the guy on the bus who coughs and sneezes, because we don't want the flu (a rational worry). However, if we choose a distant seat solely because of different cultural attire, we're unnecessarily uncomfortable (a more irrational fear).

Avoiding discomfort doesn't necessarily mean you're an angry person. We're talking about the extremes—for example, doing just about anything to avoid expressing yourself because your faulty thinking convinces you that even a minor disagreement begets great conflict. Trauma survivors—battle-tested veterans or crime victims—may experience this. When the threat is long gone, and the person uses anger to keep others away, the behavior, thoughts, and emotions no longer match the reality of the moment.

We will also outline what behavior you might commonly see in an anger-concealing person. Reading our descriptions won't always be easy, but unmasking hidden anger provides a better chance to resolve, control, and change yourself. That said, not all of what we outline applies to every passive-aggressive, secretly angry person.

We hope you will have a few "aha" moments, when something in your life suddenly fits with theory. We'll also try to be sensitive with the wording, because we know that labels don't help matters. That's why we prefer the term *anger concealer* or *anger-concealing person* because not all hidden anger comes forth in passive-aggressive behavior.

THE NEED TO CONTROL

Douglas manages the regional branch of a nonprofit organization. As much as he'd like to have the top-performing chapter, Douglas hasn't made much happen. With donations down and a higher-than-normal employee turnover, the national office has sent a team of consultants to recommend improvements. Since he's afraid of being blamed for the problems, yet yearns to be successful, Douglas's response speaks volumes. Hopefully the audit gives him insight into his role in the problem.

CONTROL

When people yearn to control a situation, they rarely reflect upon what's really going on. Here, we've outlined the needs, fears, and things people are avoiding when they display controlling-type behavior.

Needs	Fears/Avoids	What You See
To have upper hand	Taking chances, risks	Black-and-white thinking
To be in charge or in control	Being hurt or blamed; losing control	Stalwart refusal, requests seen as demands, shut down; eating disorders
To be successful	Failure and competition	No progress, no promotions at work (sometimes but not always)
To be assured, certain	Dependence	Maintains safe status quo

If Douglas avoids feedback or feels weakened when he empowers others to grow, this can drive him to counterproductive behavior. This can cause faulty thinking. Douglas forgets that the nonprofit must succeed in order for him to advance his own agenda. He may feel that his very presence each day is altruistic enough.

We might think that people like Douglas, who needs control, would be proactive, taking on new challenges and climbing the organizational ladder. But if he cannot express himself and has learned to suppress his own needs, he may very well stick with the status quo. He may spend his time being reactive rather than proactive. When there's also an underlying fear of failure or of not measuring up, this person takes few risks. Why? The more risks he takes, the more chances he has of being disappointed or hurt.

People like Douglas are stuck. Remaining stuck for any length of time often fosters anger. Not the go-getters, these folks function best in jobs that require rules, steady structure, and repeated tasks. They don't manage risks well, nor do they step up if crisis occurs or remain open to new approaches. Rather, rigid thinking prevails. They often value just showing up and feel upper management should value this, too.

THE NEED TO MANIPULATE

Imagine being on a sales team where the all-important holiday campaign is unveiled. You earn possibly 50 percent of your income based on how well you sell from the time holiday decorations go on sale until January inventory. Your coworker, who has it in for you, forgot to e-mail you in the past.

His excuse: "You have a complicated name." This is the guy whom the boss entrusts to communicate to the entire office. Now your success—your income—lies in his hands. You double-check the location of the sales meeting and take the subway across town, only to realize when you walk into an empty room that the venue is all wrong. Infuriated, you call another coworker, who informs you that the meeting takes place now in the building you just left.

It's just like this guy, with his agenda and insecurities, to boost his own weak self-esteem at your expense. This colleague's need to win isn't about ordinary success; it's about causing enough trouble that he gets the lion's share of sales when there is plenty to go around. Your territories do not even overlap. His cavalier e-mail response has your blood boiling and leaves you to scurry back, walk in late, and miss information that is essential to your livelihood. You suspect this was far more than an oversight. He's so sly that you can't prove it. People like him cop excuses quite easily, and the sad part is that others actually believe them. There is nothing wrong with competition to motivate the sales team, but when the issue is not about performance and more about degrading others, neither the workers nor the company benefit.

This kind of work environment is toxic to everyone in it. Simon Sinek, author of *Leaders Eat Last*, reminds us that people have a basic need to feel safe. When they can't trust leaders in an organization, they hold back their performance and look for ways to either build their own security fence, or they imitate the leaders and undermine others. A good leader supports others, shows empathy for their work and lives, and builds a culture where everyone thrives. You can have healthy competition and a productive, supportive workplace. Without leadership backing, however, you won't see loyal employees willing to give it their all for fear that it won't be rewarded.

MANIPULATION

When people try to effect a certain outcome, others begin to feel swayed or pressured. It's easy to get angry in such a situation unless you can unravel what's behind the behavior—what the person needs, what she fears, or what she avoids.

Needs	Fears/Avoids	What You See
To manipulate or control the outcome or the process	Uncertainty	Sets up situations for selfish gain, engages in sabotage
To win, to have fun through fighting/ hurting	Having to cooperate, give and take; having to deal with others' expectations, needs, or concerns	Plots, schemes to win, demands
To push people's buttons, to exact revenge	Authority, perceived or real	Litigates not mediates

Needs	Fears/Avoids	What You See
To set agenda	Confrontation	Fights for sport of it, to win or to hurt
To hide true emotions	Being found out	Crafts others' responses
To blame, to find fault	Intimacy, dependency	Vengeance, often plays "get back"
To be intentionally ineffective or independent	Guilt, self-blame	Lacks internal brakes, impulsive
To keep responsibility at bay	Admission of the problem or any anger	Defies authority, resists, purposely stalls, thwarts preset plans, obstructs
To keep conflict at a distance	Responsibility	Displays lack of cooperation, problem solving
To be seen in a good light	Confrontation, responsibility	Denies, criticizes, harasses, "guilts" into
To remain on the fence	Assertiveness, accountability	Displays much incongruence (thoughts, feelings, words, actions do not match)
To have more immediate gratification	Time invested in cooperation and negotiation with others	"My way or the highway," not a-big-picture person or team player
To eschew accountability	Own emotions or role in problems	Evokes guilt or reactive anger in others

The worker who sabotages a product, "forgets" to grease the machinery, or allows a mistake to slip through the assembly line knowingly understood that the error would result in the machine's malfunction. If this is a lawn mower or automobile with safety compromised, imagine the ramifications. To the angry worker, someone else's injury or risk doesn't matter; getting even does.

Here, the employee takes revenge (his need) because he fears authority figures (his boss) and usually has trouble confronting or cooperating (the fear). The results are plotting, scheming, vengeance, defying authority, obstructing safe manufacturing, poor problem solving, and very much an attitude of "I'll show them." When angry, he's riled up with no internal mechanism to slow down his "get back" fury. Colloquially we call this lacking internal brakes or being impulsive.

What's the motive behind the Monday-morning migraine or a massive employee sickout? Why do people try to beat the system, abuse the Family Medical Leave Act, or find ways to get government benefits they may not deserve (taking away funds from those who do qualify)? Why does someone taint their own food, report it to the media, and sue the company? Why do people become intentionally slow when they know that their indecision stalls your forward movement on something vital?

Revenge? Anger? If it costs them their jobs, brings bad press, or plummets the company into bankruptcy, these counterproductive actions sabotage. Others might witness the "seriously injured" worker lifting her children into the car some evening when by day she claims a back injury and collects worker's compensation. To the manipulative person, getting a free ride prevails.

The college student who literally shuts down, pushing his parents' financial worry buttons is another saboteur. He may have needed to set a different agenda (overlapping with the desire to control), but because of his fear of confronting authority (perceived or actual), he has discharged his anger to avoid responsibility with plausible excuses ("The class was too hard" or "I took courses that my advisor pushed me into"). Maybe this student tries to be effective, but his way seems ineffective to everyone else. Direct, honest communication could have solved this student's problems.

Manipulation occurs daily. The cab driver takes the most circuitous detour while the meter costs you and benefits him; the bank teller closes her window for lunch as soon as you reach the front of the line; or a family member leaves your leftovers in clear view of the dog, knowing you were returning to your meal.

Not every frustrating action warrants negative light; there could be other reasons for what you witness. After you read various accounts, match up the behaviors with what you know about a person's needs or fears.

ANGRY/HAPPY PEOPLE COMPARISON

Ever wondered what anger looks like when contrasted with its more cheerful opposite? Life is not bleak. This chart depicts the flip side of the negative traits we discuss.

Angry People	Happy People
Irritated	Compassionate and empathic
Impulsive	Patient
Seek immediate gratification	Can delay gratification, require more of self
Demand	Ask
Blast or maintain silence	Openly and calmly discuss
Need to control or obstruct	Want to negotiate, cooperate, resolve problems
Criticize	Respect
Dig in heels	Accept change or differences
Immature, childish	Mature and possessing perspective
Tense, frowns, sighs	Relaxed, smiles, laughs
Blame	Take responsibility
Threaten, punish	Reward/praise
Put down	Inspire
Rely upon rage talk, swearing	Choose more inspiring vocabulary
Closed-minded, solitary	Open-minded, request help, reach out
Surrounded by negative people	Prefer positive people
Unhealthy habits and weight	Fit, trim, and healthy lifestyle
Harm or destroy relationships	Cultivate and build relationships
Focus on pessimism	Work at optimism
Sedentary, passive	Active, energetic
Destructive (sometimes actively so)	Constructive
Give up too easily	Persevere, push forward

LEARNING AND GROWING FROM ANGER

The face of anger wears many expressions, not all bad. We encourage you to use anger's potential to bring people closer instead of separating from them. Bad memories can hold us back or thrust us forward. We can learn to deal with them and survive or let them transform us to thrive!

Meet Will, a fourteen-year-old boy with a tsunami of testosterone and companion hormones flooding his adolescent brain. Surly and argumentative with his mother, he got his iPhone taken away to force homework into focus. Will loses his cool. Fist and foot both meet drywall. He screams from his lungs, "I hate my life. I ought to kill myself."

Shaken by the exchange, Mom rushes Will and his bleeding hand to the emergency room. While hospital staff can suture his injury, Will's meltdown may actually land him in a day treatment program or as an inpatient because Will is "a frequent flyer." The ER doc gave him counseling referrals the last two times. When Will yelled "I was kidding" down the ER hallway but collapsed in a puddle of tears, his emotional unraveling escalated treatment.

Had Will learned from past behavior, what would the scene at home have looked like? Our memories grant us growth opportunities or the ability to keep ruminating. Past experiences won't change. How we think about them—that can change!

Indeed, the pressure to succeed begins young. Teenagers may count among their healthcare providers a therapist, psychiatrist, and gastric physician all in an effort to fit in one more AP class, ace college entrance exams, star in the class play, and go to State with the basketball team. Some young people push themselves toward perfection; others internalize a parent's priorities and are unsure how to lead their own lives. We see the strains in adults and in relationships undermined by a demand for perfection. Tempers flare and anger ensues. Keep reading as we explore the mind-body connection and hidden anger's impact on our overall health.

two

Concealed Emotions Put People at Risk

D R. MURPHY ONCE HAD A CLIENT WHO SPOKE OF HER STRUGGLES being overweight. She told him how it impacted her marriage, how she tried to please her husband by dutifully attending Weight Watchers and dieting religiously, but that she just couldn't shed pounds no matter how hard she tried. Then one day, she brought in a bag from the convenience store, which slid off the chair. Out dropped half a dozen candy bars. After tearfully acknowledging that she ate a lot in between her restricted meals, she ran from her own responsibility and blamed a society that didn't accept overweight people. It was clear that her poor self-image and self-anger came long before her weight gain. Overeating gave her a passive excuse for self-pity. As a victim, she fought against the very goal she set, telling herself that she wasn't good enough to succeed.

Some people explode. Others seethe inside. Many do both. One person talks their problems through, while the next person harbors grudges. This client used food to achieve happiness. How do you express your anger?

We need only read news headlines to see despicable interpersonal incidents that grab our attention. This includes terror attacks, hostages taken and killed, school violence, assaults, murder, or the shock of intimate violence committed against a spouse or child. Our consciousness is so steeped that our memory recall makes tragedies as easily remembered as a brand name: 9/11, Columbine, the Nicole Brown Simpson murder, Sandy Hook.

According to the American Psychological Association, more than one in three women and more than one in four men in the United States have experienced physical violence, rape, or stalking by an intimate partner in their lifetime.[1] In the school setting, 22 percent of students ages twelve to eighteen were bullied during the 2012–2013 academic year. Kids who bully others are much more likely to become involved in criminal or antisocial behavior later in life as well as more liable to sexually harass others.[2] Many blatantly "external" crimes begin with unresolved internal emotional upset. Although untreated mental illness, such as schizophrenia or severe bipolar disease, can be the cause of such criminal and antisocial behavior, concealed anger can also be a trigger. Further, emotional upheaval blocks the awareness needed to change.

THE TIME BOMB PROBLEM

Continually buried emotions are like time bombs, ticking louder with each day, month, and year they accumulate. Very few people can keep up the façade of normalcy when they seethe inside. When authorities have thwarted a planned attack, it was because someone spotted behavior that seemed odd—awareness becoming the sentry to public safety.

In this age of heightened vigilance, everyone is more on guard against premeditated attacks. We're more skeptical of motives. Those knowledgeable about domestic violence and abusive behavior indicate that physical violence often follows months or years of concealed psychological attack. Let there be no mistake, people who hide their anger can be very dangerous, especially over time.

ORDINARY ANGST AND ANXIETY

These are extreme cases. We're far more likely—at work or school, in the shopping mall or grocery store, at home and with those we care for—to encounter ordinary, garden-variety hidden rage that doesn't make the nightly news but leaves us feeling powerless nonetheless. *Time* magazine shared a *Stress in America* survey in 2013. Here's one emerging trend: 53 percent felt that they did not handle their stress well and that the healthcare system did not help them either. "Unfortunately, our country's health system often neglects psychological and behavioral factors that are essential to managing stress and chronic diseases," reported Norman B. Anderson, PhD, American Psychological Association CEO. "We need to improve how we view and treat stress and unhealthy behaviors that are contributing to the high incidence of disease in the U.S."[3]

In Dr. Murphy's legislative work, he encounters many distraught individuals. If life was going swimmingly, he'd never hear from them. When life has dealt them a blow or when they perceive an injustice, they look to him for solutions. Sometimes they are just mad and turn to using public officials as verbal punching bags, fueled by angry talk shows who sometimes turn honest, reasonable debate into livid, unreasonable entertainment.

Today, fractured and frantic families tread water to survive a work culture that sometimes demands more of and promises less to individuals. It's now commonly accepted that most workers will experience more than two-dozen job changes within their careers. The workplace has changed. Sometimes this means working sixty hours a week at forty-hour pay. It's a 24/7 juggled commitment with less certainty as people deal with kids, carpools, and jobs simultaneously.

At home, families enroll children in private lessons, this team, that practice. Parenting is meted out in small doses, and kids get back at parents with attention-getting poor behavior. Children and adults walk around wounded from unexpressed anger.

In 2004 *Newsweek* reported on overindulging parents who set their kids up for anxiety, and possibly depression, when their children, once grown, failed at coping with daily disappointments.[4] "Helicopter parenting" has become a part of our vocabulary, and entitled kids appear on the Internet daily. Stress inoculation builds an ability to handle tough times. Resilience is the psychological strength that grows from facing tough problems, not running from them.

In the "I want" age, children find it hard to sit with their anxiety, so instead they ever-increasingly stew over how to get more "stuff" and how to be perceived as "cool." They lack limits and firm boundaries telling them where their needs and wants stop and other people's begin, and they haven't learned that giving something back to the world holds far more promise for the future than momentary self-absorption.

One might argue that children, lacking maturity, have it toughest. Kids who are bullied are more liable to develop low self-esteem and depressed mood, generalized anxiety and panic disorder, psychosomatic complaints (head and stomach aches, sleep disturbance, poor appetite), lower academic achievement, school avoidance, and drug- and alcohol-related problems. As we illustrated earlier, a child's impact upon the family doesn't end at age eighteen. The patterns of childhood become the personality of the adult. Others might argue that adults have a harder time because their ingrained responses and thinking become more difficult to change or correct with each passing year.

> The patterns of childhood become the personality of the adult.

HOW THE ANGRY MIND WORKS

Think about a time when you were angry. One or more negative emotions underpinned that frustration, triggering you to either openly express or stuff it. It could have been anxiety or depression, among other emotions, that triggered your upset, because anger never exists alone. If your mind felt as if it was filled with negative thoughts, faulty assumptions, and what psychologists call irrational beliefs, then you could have easily worked your way into a circular anger pattern.

Anger typically sparks faulty thinking or irrational beliefs. We might think "if only this could happen . . . ," "I should . . . ," or "This must . . ." Therapists hear irrational "shoulda, coulda, woulda" thinking regularly—all-encompassing, generalized thoughts, as in "I failed this test, so I'll never amount to anything"—instead of honest assessments, such as "if I'd partied less, I could have passed that test." Irrational beliefs build over time and cause people to lash or act out.

Positive consequences can fuel one's annoyance into the rewards of winning. Negative feelings or thoughts also cement faulty assumptions.

The angry person confirms, "See, I knew this would happen," or "Others are to blame for my problems." This circular process easily becomes self-sustaining as it avoids personal responsibility. Anyone in the midst of this negativity can also become emotional, anxious, or depressed over time, never knowing what to expect next.

FIFTEEN WAYS ANGER CAN HARM YOUR HEALTH—EVEN KILL YOU

Physicians and anger management researchers have found the following links between hot temper, harboring anger, and physical/emotional health:

1. Increased risk of high blood pressure and chronic inflammation (leading to many diseases)
2. Higher levels of homocysteine (amino acid), leading to arterial damage and an increased risk of coronary heart disease
3. Higher levels of C-reactive protein associated with heart disease and stroke risk
4. Escalated levels of cortisol and adrenaline (the body's fight-or-flight hormones)
5. Suppressed reproductive system, which can lead to sexual dysfunction and fertility problems
6. Greater risk of addiction with excessive smoking, drinking, or drug use
7. Weakened immune function (resulting from overactive hormones that stress the immune system)
8. Augmented body weight (from higher cortisol levels)
9. Elevated vulnerability to pathogens, everyday germs, viruses, or familial predisposition to cancer or heart disease
10. Increased risk of periodontitis (gum disease)
11. Enhanced vulnerability to eating disorders and self-injury
12. Persistent anxiety, depression, and somatic complaints (aches and pains)
13. Cellular deterioration, premature aging, and shortened life span
14. Escalated risk of committing or being a victim of road rage
15. Greater likelihood that angry patients will not comply with medical or psychological treatment, thereby putting their health at risk

THE UNHEALTHY ANGER PROBLEM

Lingering anger, veiled or not, leads to lasting health impediments, both physical and psychological. Physical complications can include high blood pressure, coronary heart disease, weakened immune function, increased hormone levels, weight gain, and vulnerability to germs and pathogens. Dr. Redford Williams at the Duke University School of Medicine has linked anger and poor physical health. He discovered that angry men are five to seven times more likely than their easygoing counterparts to die by age fifty.[5] Duke University research also found links between emotions of anger, hostility, and depression after testing blood for the substance called C-reactive protein (CRP).[6]

Janice Williams at the University of North Carolina found that anger-prone men and women, especially in middle age and with normal blood pressure, were nearly three times more likely to suffer a heart attack.[7] The *American Journal of Cardiology* reported that men with negative emotions (anxiety, pessimism, hostility) had a higher heart disease risk compared to peers who possessed positive outlooks.[8]

A study in the *Journal of Epidemiology & Community Health* reported that employees who covertly coped with unfair treatment at work (not telling or showing aggressors such unfairness) had an increased risk of hard-endpoint cardiovascular disease.[9]

Though emotional stress can cause physical health problems, according to the National Cancer Institute, the evidence that stress directly causes cancer needs further study.[10] Some researchers have explored the links between psychological factors and increased cancer risk as well as the progression of existing cancer growth and metastasis.[11] We do know that self-induced stress and anger can complicate medical problems, reduce compliance with treatment plans, and worsen symptoms.

An angry outlook is no better for one's mental state, since perpetually angry individuals often lapse into various forms of anxiety and depression. Eating disorders and addictions are more common in those with anger management problems. As well, physical and psychological issues are intimately linked: many people with psychological problems first contact their physician with physical complaints and pain. After a thorough and sometimes expensive workup, the wise doctor encourages the patient to seek counseling to tamp down chronic activation of the fight-or-flight response that jeopardizes good health.

Physiologically, the parasympathetic nervous system functions to calm people down. The sympathetic nervous system, its opposite, sparks arousal in one's anger response and floods the body with stress hormones (primarily adrenaline and noradrenaline). It was thought that since the parasympathetic nervous system response was weaker in Type A individuals—with repeated heart rate and blood pressure arousal—they didn't calm down as effectively and suffered bodily damage over time. Later research focused upon negative affectivity traits such as depression, anxiety, and anger/hostility. In fact, Johan Denollet, PhD, a professor at Tilbur University in The Netherlands, formulated the "Type D," or distressed personality, that may predispose people to depression and social isolation by combining two personality traits—the tendencies to experience negative emotions and to inhibit self-expression to others.[12]

Michael E. Kerr, MD, is the director of the Bowen Theory Academy and emeritus director of the Bowen Center for the Study of the Family in Washington, DC. Dr. Kerr suggests that anger is a substitute for dealing effectively with key relationships. When unable to solve a dilemma in an important relationship, the person's chronic stress response, although less intense, can generate mind, body, and behavioral dysfunction; for example, a chronic sublethal stress response stimulates chronic inflammation and additional factors. In a stressed person, cancer, atherosclerosis, Alzheimer's disease, psychosis, and other clinical conditions can flourish, according to Kerr.[13]

Finally, we often see characterological/personality disorders diagnosed in those who cannot come to grips with their inner hostility. Anger kills and it costs us plenty. It's terribly counterproductive and can only be untangled with awareness, assertiveness, and often, therapy.

The medical establishment and our lawmakers are beginning to address mental health. In *A Common Struggle*, Patrick J. Kennedy, a former member of the US House of Representatives, elaborates upon the cause he now supports full time, describing his goal as "nothing less than launching a new civil rights movement, to finally force medical equality for diseases of the brain." Kennedy was a key proponent of the Mental Health Parity and

Addiction Equity Act that Congress passed. "A check up from the neck up as regular as taking blood pressure" is Kennedy's goal.[14]

Dr. Murphy held hearings in Congress to discover breakdowns in the US mental health system. He introduced a bill to fix our nation's broken mental health systems and reduce the barriers to treatment for those who need it most.

THE ANGRY WEIGHT-GAIN PROBLEM

One of the most revealing findings in recent years is the link between hostility and unhealthy weight gain. Sue Ellen Browder calls this phenomenon "anger fat."[15] She cites a study of middle-aged, intensely angry women who gained more unhealthy fat over a thirteen-year period than less hostile women. They also had higher insulin levels.[16]

Males aren't exempt from angry weight gain. Biologically, weight gain occurs when adrenaline stimulates fat cells to empty their contents into the bloodstream. Your liver also converts fat into cholesterol, which is then absorbed into your arteries, attaching to artery walls, thus clogging your circulatory system. It's not just caloric intake but also smoking and alcohol consumption that can increase when stress levels rise. Even if you don't eat, smoke, or drink more, anger can redistribute your fat, storing more of it in the visceral danger zone, internally, around the body's vital organs (heart, liver, and others), where it's been linked to other serious medical problems. Your risk of heart attack, as well as weight gain, rises.

NATURE OR NURTURE

If your anger is out of control, your body descends on a downward spiral because one problem triggers another. Being too angry too much of the time can kill you. Dr. Redford Williams has studied the genetic link with anger, finding a tiny molecular variation of a gene that we all carry that may predict those more prone to anger.[17]

In 1996, University of Minnesota researcher David Lykken published a paper regarding the role genes play in determining people's overall sense of satisfaction or happiness in life.[18] Studying four thousand sets of twins born in Minnesota between 1936 and 1955, comparing the data from identical and fraternal twins, he concluded that about 50 percent of a person's satisfaction with life comes from genetic influence, including whether a person has a pleasant, sunny disposition, how he deals with stress, and how anxious or depressed he is. Genetic anger research is certainly worth exploring. Science is getting closer to identifying, on the basis of genetic characteristics, those people at higher risk for intense anger and rage. This finding wouldn't let an individual off the hook; in fact, having this knowledge would increase the importance of being able to actively control anger.

Our concern with this research is that some out-of-sorts people might use a link of anger to genetics as an excuse for a poor disposition or outlook. They might believe that "they are who they are." We believe we all have a responsibility to manage anger, channel it into something positive, or eradicate it, regardless of genetics, upbringing, or environmental contributors.

USING POPULAR EXCUSES

In *Payback: Why We Retaliate, Redirect Aggression and Take Revenge*, David Barash, PhD, and Judith Eve Lipton, MD, define their topic. "Redirected aggression—targeting of an innocent bystander in response to one's own pain and injury—seems not only absurd but also morally bankrupt and downright dangerous," they say, describing retaliation as direct; immediate revenge they describe as more complex. Many cultures urge us to forgo retaliation as payback.[19]

We've become accustomed to anger as a way of life since various experts have urged irate people to vent their emotions. Go ahead, blow off steam, break some dishes, punch a pillow, and visualize the one you're most angry toward. Wrong! More recent studies have backed the prevailing theory that venting anger only reinforces the connection between it and violence. The "I have to let it out" syndrome worsens matters, as people respond through attack the next time they're frustrated.

Dr. Brad J. Bushman, an associate professor of psychology at Iowa State University, led a study in 1999 on letting out aggression.[20] Study subjects were given the message to displace their aggression (they were told that hitting objects was an effective release). Later, they appeared to be more aggressive toward rivals or innocent third parties. Venting anger—by hitting, throwing, or kicking something—potentially keeps it alive rather than erases it, making it counterproductive.

Bushman's study found that exercise actually kept angry people at a heightened arousal level. "The arousal from the exercise could be misattributed as anger if the person is provoked after exercising," Bushman told us. Doing something incompatible to aggression or venting, such as reading, watching a funny movie, or listening to music might help to alleviate a person's anger. Others, however, have long felt that physical exercise dissipates anger and improves mood.[21]

OTHER WAYS HIDDEN ANGER AFFECTS US

Researchers Anwar T. Merchant, DMD, ScD, and his colleagues at Harvard School of Dental Medicine reported in the *Journal of the American Dental Association* that men who reported being angry on a daily basis had a 43 percent higher risk of developing periodontitis (gum disease) compared with men who reported seldom being angry.[22] In their study, they asked questions regarding whether the men argued with others, slammed doors, said nasty things, and lost their tempers, and they found that such anger expression was positively associated with gum disease.

Additionally, angry chronic pain patients may not recover as quickly as happier patients. We know that a positive, optimistic outlook can speed the healing process when a bone has been fractured, slow the progression of certain infections, and protect us against culprits like cardiovascular disease and stroke.

The last health implication we'll highlight is the noncompliant patient. One's own problematic behaviors—stalling, forgetting to take medication or adhere to treatment plans, and arguing with medical or mental health professionals—stand in the way of good health. If patients possess the irrational belief that the physician holds the miracle cure, they may even harbor anger toward the medical team. Sometimes they wish for healthcare practitioners to do all the work, eradicate their pain completely, or make things 100 percent perfect. Even patients who just bristle at the doctor's every suggestion potentially impede their progress.

Dr. Murphy once treated a boy whose mom usually brought him to sessions. One time, his dad brought him instead. The father's attitude: "Well, I guess you aren't as good as I thought. My son still isn't better and we've been coming here a whole month!" Trouble was, there was no "we." With his first visit, dad was determined to prove mom wrong and undermine his son's therapy.

Healthcare providers may need to pay extra-close attention to the behaviors we detail, because they may need to change their approaches with patients who react negatively to authority figures. Their stalled patients sure as heck won't budge. This applies to angry patients who refuse to give up smoking, take medicine as prescribed, exercise, or make lifestyle changes. For these patients, complying with treatment may mean giving up their own power by admitting that the healthcare provider is right.

It takes a lot of fortitude and persistence to work with such patients (see appendix). When healthcare providers gently educate and coach their patients rather than dictate to them, they back out of the authority figure role and give their patients much more of a personal stake in their own care. With persistence, you can turn a difficult patient into one much less liable to whine, resist, and hand you back a load of excuses. Everyone, including the doctor, should feel tremendously better.

MORE EFFECTS: ACADEMIC STRUGGLES AND THREATENED CAREERS

Academic achievement and/or career progression is often stymied or sabotaged altogether when anger lurks in the background. Passive-aggressive individuals are often considered more apt to be underachievers inside the classroom and in the workplace. Many passive-aggressive individuals adopt a "why bother?" attitude, never fully committing to a job they both love and loathe. So too, a passive-aggressive manager may unwittingly avoid hiring the best person for the job because deep down she fears that someone else's talent, drive, or determination—qualities this manager may desperately want—may eclipse hers. Reminded of her own deficits by a stellar résumé, the manager obstructs the applicant's career progression by refusing to interview or hire someone who might compete.

Other anger concealers have been mislabeled as having ADHD when actually their behavior is a deliberate choice to not pay attention as a way of manipulating others. Selective attention is a means of avoiding responsibility. When Johnny wants to drop out of school, it requires more time and energy to get him on track than to label him as having a disorder. The teenage brain is hard at work—literally—in a state of continued development. Research offered in *Scientific American Mind* indicated that irresponsibility may not fully explain what can easily look like rebellion. Bad decisions and risky behavior result from an immature prefrontal cortex.[23]

We see outright passive-aggression in higher education when parents send their offspring to college or graduate school, and their son or daughter simply shuts down. The passive-aggressive child would rather study another major, or perhaps do something entirely different with his or her life. Too frequently these children aren't able to openly express their true wishes; wasting hard-earned tuition dollars may seem like the way to "get back" at mom or dad for their control.

Maybe these children have justifiable anger, because if they did express themselves, it wouldn't do much good. Here, the parents may exert too much influence, yet the children need to disengage, learn how to be appropriately assertive, and improve their day-to-day functioning.

In *The Atlantic* (December 2015), journalist Hanna Rosin explored the ten-year suicide rate at Silicon Valley high schools, which was four to five times the national average. The article outlines how hard it is to maintain the narrative that these kids were social outcasts or that their suicidal ideation was the result of serious mental illness—in most cases it was not.[24]

Never underestimate how an angry student might take out his anger in the classroom.

Beyond presenting health and academic challenges, silently harbored anger in the workplace costs millions—sometimes billions—of dollars in lost contracts, reduced efficiency, and even worker safety. Planned mistakes equal sabotage. Faulty workmanship brings on lawsuits. Worker anxiety can lead to depression, and untreated, the cost of mental illness rises—for the worker in terms of both health and expenses, for the employer in lost productivity and premiums, and for anyone interacting with that employee. *Health* magazine reported in 2010 that depression in the workplace cost $23 billion in lost productivity, according to the National Institute of Mental Health.[25]

Not all depressed workers are bad workers. Many want to do a good job but are overwhelmed by this temporary setback. Anger can be a part of depression, but the two don't always go hand in hand.

All of this gives good reason for offering stress reduction seminars and anger management classes. The results of continuous anger certainly provide the impetus for superiors to listen to their employees. Working with people from all walks of life, each of us sees that when clients or constituents feel heard and listened to, it calms them a great deal, enough to let go of emotional reactivity and find real solutions.

Next, we explore how hidden anger forms, often early in life.

three

The Roots of Negative, Toxic Unhappiness

VAN AND SLOANE, STUDENTS IN AN ONLINE MBA PROGRAM, HAD A joint project due. Both had jobs, his for an environmental group and hers in school auditing. From two different coasts, Ivan and Sloane used e-mail, text, and FaceTime to work together. Until Ivan missed the last two sessions they scheduled. Sloane left a voicemail: "Ivan, we'll lose points if we miss the deadline. I feel you're not fully into this project."

"I'm busy saving thousands from pollution," Ivan e-mailed in response. "Everyone would understand, but I know, you had 'graduation' day for your twins. Oil spills are in the news, Sloane! Pull it together."

Sloane took a deep breath at that. Anything she typed back would be equally unkind. She shut down her computer and stalled all the progress she *had* pulled together so as to not instigate further aggression from Ivan—that would only make matters worse.

"Ivan e-mailed me a link to buy *How to Win Friends and Influence People*," Sloane told her husband.

"Isn't the first principle don't criticize and condemn?" he asked. "Tell me your topic again with Ivan the Terrible."

"Collaborative leadership." Sloane chuckled, though this project, their paper, and both of their grades hung in limbo.

What underlies Ivan's resentment? Is Sloane's life—immersed with a major milestone and different work/life balance—any less significant than Ivan's role as self-professed savior of clean water? For that matter, is our phrase "self-professed savior" and the husband's moniker of "Ivan the Terrible" righteous annoyance, understood sarcasm, or an intentional put-down?

IS IT ME OR EVERYONE ELSE?

How do we bring out the worst in others? Do we box others in so that their responses, actions, or lack of action seem too firm, like rebellion, when perhaps they are taking a stance?

Do our communication skills, or our need to refine them, plus one person doing more and one person doing less make passive-aggression flourish?

If you haven't experienced anger, then essentially you haven't lived. Part of the human condition, it's the intensity of that ire, the persistence or frequency of it, and the choices we make with it that matter more than its simple existence. It is when anger endures over many years that it truly becomes a drawback.

Carlos, at twenty-nine, complains. A lot, according to his wife, Rosa. His whining, fishing for compliments, and inability to make decisions reminds Rosa that she married a mama's boy. Strong father figure is what she had envisioned, as they plan to have a family soon. Instead, she sees a petulant little boy, still competing with his sister for his mother's attention.

If you've had a frustrating childhood and those past issues aren't resolved, you may be more susceptible to acting passive-aggressively or concealing bitterness. A family history of anger, addiction, or particular mental health problems put you at higher risk because of heredity or learned behavior. Very often, victims of abuse (physical, sexual, or psychological) who don't resolve their past experiences become increasingly angry over time, as these earlier wounds or traumas continue to fester.

A very bitter person may remember every slight, barb, humiliation, and physical blow, often laying the burden upon someone else, where it doesn't belong. Whenever he experiences a setback—death, divorce, or other loss; job complications; prolonged stress and anxiety—hidden anger can erupt so strongly that others may wonder why there's so much of it. Sure, the circumstances may be a problem, but the level of emotion just doesn't fit. Where else could it come from? Quite possibly from experiences long ago in childhood.

YOUR OWN CHILDHOOD

What do you remember from your childhood? Happiness? Sad times? Problems you overcame or ones that overwhelmed you?

If you felt your body tense at the mere thought of remembering your youth, perhaps the remembrances aren't so spectacular. For some, childhood wasn't a carefree time. In fact, it might have been anything but easy, reflecting sadness or pain.

Our memories are a two-way street. Who we are now influences what we recall, and what we recall influences how and exactly what we remember. The happy adult may recall pleasant memories and see them as more influential than the negative ones. The sad person, on the other hand, may give more weight to negative life experiences and allow these to cast a pall over what comes after. Every one of us has unpleasant memories that shape us. Once we realize that, these memories keep shaping us only if we allow them to; in other words, we can halt the transfer of old experiences into the present, and we should, because they cloud our ability to think clearly in the here and now. If you experienced failure or success as a child after taking risks or trying incredibly hard, your efforts may have been met with acceptance and love, or with rejection and anger. How they were met as a child may determine whether or not you are passive-aggressive as an adult.

Maybe the memories are wrapped up in so much misery that even though they are ten, twenty, or thirty years old, you still hide from them. Anger concealers often cannot express themselves because of childhood recollections (called childhood wounds). They're stuck, unable to break with the past and see the present. Sometimes people are aware of the influence ("my boss reminds me of my terrible stepfather!"), and sometimes people are unaware and get worked up over the slightest incident.

TOUCHING YOUR CHILDHOOD MEMORIES OF ANGER

To aid you as you remember how you handled anger as a child, here is a short list of questions. Try to answer them all. On a sheet of paper, jot your answers to the following:

1. What were the times/circumstances where anger typically erupted in your family?
2. How did your parents, siblings, or others in your home express their annoyance? Specifically, what did they say? How did they act? How did they react to anger in others?
3. If there was one button any of these people pushed on you most frequently, what was it?
4. What resulted when family members showed deep disappointment? Did it solve problems or make them worse?
5. Give examples of when you remember feeling most angry. How did you express that anger?
6. How was your expression of anger in your youth different from how you express anger today?
7. How different is your expression of frustrations from that of your family?
8. What would you most like to change about your way of surfacing annoyance now?
9. Despite any dysfunctional patterns, are there ways these have become sources of strength, insight, or better character in you?

THE ROOTS OF CHILDHOOD ANGER

We designed this nine-point quiz to provoke thought about your own angry roots. We explored how environment, parenting, family history, stress, addictions, and other problems contribute to anger management issues. But every family has its struggles. We have yet to meet one *perfect* family. Indeed, when people claim "My parents were never angry," we can make an educated guess that the emotion was there. But whereas some people can express it appropriately, some keep it hidden.

Where did it lurk? How did it surface? Coming out with it is not terrible, in and of itself, if expressed well and with resolution. The result depends upon the intent, what the anger looked like, what people's reactions were, and how it was dealt with after the fact. Did your family harbor resentment or take care of anger quickly so that it would not (or could not) linger and later be concealed?

In our practices and books, we characterize anger with four stages.[1] Here's a quick summary:

The Buildup is all the unresolved conflict, developmental stressors, poor problem solving, grudges recalled, and anger that got tucked away. Hidden. For a quick-tempered person, the buildup won't take long; for others, it amasses over many days, months, or even years. To prevent anger from becoming a problem, it's always best to prevent any buildup from ever happening.

The Spark, big or small, sets off the conflict. It's a situation or a thought, but is much like layers of candle wax. When ignited, it just might go up in flames. People either quickly extinguish it (swallowing any small impact) or they launch into immediate rage. An everyday spark could be a stubbed toe, lost keys, a remembered slight, a jealous feeling, or some other disappointment. Learn to recognize a hidden spark, defuse the problem, and prevent its smoldering. An angry, smoldering spark can flare over time.

The Explosion typically has lasting impact. We recognize the yelling, the fighting, the thrown dish, the threat, and then some. It can be a volcanic eruption or its subtler counterpart, an implosion.

The Implosion occurs when people hide the eruption and it becomes a slow underground rumbling. Buried inside, the implosion has no outward presence. It remains a mystery without notice except for indirect manifestations, such as sarcasm, unwarranted criticism, resistance, stalling, procrastinating, sabotaging, incongruent signals, or sad, anxious, or hypersensitive feelings. Indirect anger can also equal sneak attacks like vandalism, theft, computer viruses, and more. People often deny it's there in terribly unhealthy ways: smoking, drinking, using drugs, having eating disorders, injuring themselves, or cheating on a partner for revenge.

Just as a soda bottle can contain only so much fizz, people who implode often explode in ways that are recognizable, even with a pattern of anger concealment, because most people can only mask their anger successfully for so long. When you're about to explode/implode, the proper course is to contain and control it so that the anger doesn't harm anyone. Just because it is curtailed, however, doesn't mean the anger stages are over. There's one fourth and final step.

The Aftermath is the most overlooked yet most important stage. If you fail to address the incident and resolve what went wrong, it contributes to the next buildup. Yes, more layers, like sticks of dynamite, so then the spark ignites. You get the picture.

For prevention's sake, your goal is to solve the problem, warding off a cycle of hidden anger so that there are no trampled feelings, unspoken grievances, and anything else that the parties haven't shared. Put it out there on the table or in the space between you. Our good friend Fred M. Rogers, everyone's favorite neighbor and a man who was wise with regard to emotions, once said, "whatever is mentionable is manageable."[2] Remember this when tempted to skip this game-changing stage.

CHARACTERISTICS OF ANGRY PEOPLE

TEN TRAITS OF ANGRY PEOPLE

1. Makes his own misery
2. Can't analyze problems
3. Blames others for his misfortune
4. Turns bad feelings into mad feelings
5. Lacks empathy
6. Attacks people rather than solves problems
7. Uses anger to gain power
8. Indulges in destructive self-talk
9. Confuses anger with self-esteem
10. Can be nice when he wants to be

Excerpted from *The Angry Child: Regaining Control When Your Child Is Out of Control*, © 2001, by Dr. Tim Murphy and Loriann Oberlin.

Here's the vicious cycle, folks. Triggered emotions lead to acting out, which, in turn, leads to consequences and convinces a rankled person just how correct his (usually false) beliefs really were. When he relies on underhanded comments or tactics, and insulates himself from the very factors of change and any evidence to the contrary, guess what? He *makes his own misery.*

That process, where one *cannot analyze a problem,* contributes to faulty thinking. When an angry person operates from a worldview anticipating loss, she might hide her displeasure by acting out indirectly to minimize this loss—a preemptive strike. Doing so enables her to feel she's in control, and often this helps soothe her anxieties or other feelings.

The silent refusal to discuss what's bothering her, preferring to wallow in self-pity, is a classic example of this second trait. "I'm angry so I don't need to talk about it anymore" is also what we commonly see in clinical practice and what we call *feelthink,* or confusing feelings with fact. In other words, "I feel; therefore it is so." If the angry person's emotions are all the data he relies upon to draw a conclusion, he's operating under this faulty analysis.

A common defense people use when they want to disown anger is to *blame others* for their misfortune, and researchers concur that passive-aggressive people often resent others, thinking that everyone else has a sweeter deal, the easier life, and that they themselves have it toughest.

When something triggers or sparks negative emotions that characteristically turn into anger, *bad feelings become mad feelings,* with a limited range of expression. Anger concealers haven't mastered honest, open communication. Often, they can't even voice, "I'm mad," as nondescript as that is; they opt for silent attack instead.

Angry people *lack empathy,* and certainly children or adults who engage in "get back" behaviors create no-win situations. They feign innocence so that others are left bewildered or embarrassed. Chronically depressed people are short on empathy because they're too busy feeling sorry for themselves. Imagine Eeyore in *Winnie the Pooh.* Such people confuse help with meddling.

Indirect anger is all about the sneak attack, the snarky remarks, exacting revenge, or mastering the next setup to control a situation one can't otherwise handle successfully—*attacking people rather than solving problems.* Resolving issues requires respect for the other side, a belief that "I may not agree with you, but we can solve this anyway." Problem solving requires a belief that a future with an answer is worth more than hurting someone in the present. Those who disguise their indignation have little interest in compromise or resolution; with narcissism or self-centered thinking, it's usually a fight for any other reason than to solve a problem. It's to win, to destroy, or maybe even for the sport of being disagreeable and negative. All of these methods, and many others, help the angry person to indirectly *gain power.* As we've seen, passive-aggressive people seek control and power.

Destructive self-talk is similar to those irrational beliefs we mentioned in the self-perpetuating cycle of anger. Indirect anger manifests as a not-too-subtle dig, in complaints, in derogation, in denial, or when a person whines and feigns innocence. If she displaces her emotion, as is the case with blame or its close cousin projection, that's the polar opposite of direct expression, and to rationalize away responsibility lets oneself off the hook but snares someone else with its sharp point. Often, the angry person skill-fully crafts (in her own mind, that is) other people's responses, such as "I know my boss won't understand, so I'm going to come in late anyway."

Angry individuals *confuse anger with self-esteem.* Poor self-esteem under-mines school or work performance, interpersonal relationships, and future success. In severe cases, it can lead to anxiety disorders and depression. Healthy self-esteem drives our ability to navigate daily hassles while we re-spect other people. Because the person concealing anger shuns the risk of rejection or failure, he refuses to speak up, fails to be acknowledged, and obstructs his own chances of success. He pushes opportunities away and keeps them (and people) at a distance because he has trouble committing to anything or anyone. Never or rarely assuming responsibility for his actions makes him feel less competent, and then he often resents those who *can* use their talents to get ahead.

Self-esteem often gets confused because of the ambivalence inherent with indirect ire. The child or adult simply can't decide how he feels about himself. "I appear good if I keep quiet, but being silent I feel incompetent." Each appraisal vexes him.

Angry people with extremely high self-esteem can come across as so self-indulgent, so caught up in their own world, that others find it difficult to get close. The self-centered aren't accustomed to hearing "no" as a viable answer. Their behaviors and automatic thoughts can lead to a substantial reservoir of untapped gall. Having self-esteem is not the same as being psychologically healthy. Our prisons are filled with people who feel too good about themselves.

Finally, angry children and adults *can be quite charming, quite nice, when they want to be.* The angry smile epitomizes this incongruence. What one communicates is not one's true intent. If you claim, "Oh sure . . . fine," when you mean "Hell no, that won't stand," you cloak, swallow, and stuff negative feelings.

This trait seduces individuals into romantic unions where resentment wreaks havoc when fireworks fizzle out and employers into hiring what turns out to be the wrong employee. It's also what provides hope that angry people can get better.

Think here about the classic manipulator who is intent upon revenge. Think about the child who tells his teacher he'll help his classmate or stay after school to set up tomorrow's assembly. Sometimes these kids really want to be good, but if the child has no intention of assisting and purposely "forgets" to show up, he's manipulating the teacher, coming off as the good student when it matters, and perhaps thwarting something positive. Of course, many angry children do this unwittingly.

Let's return to Ivan and Sloane. Sloane used "I messages," owning what she said. Ivan trivialized Sloane's family responsibilities. Ivan's angry feelings evoked blame and guilt. He formed a triangle with "other professionals" and lobbed a dig about winning/influencing friends. Ivan used information completely out of context and for his own purposes. Sloane's husband used humor while listening and responding to his wife. A history of snarky remarks may signify a problem (though here this private utterance perhaps offered compassion).

"I MESSAGES": EASY ON THE EARS

When you hear the phrase "I statement" or "I message," you might think it leans to the selfish if you're unfamiliar with direct communication skills. But an "I message" is a statement about the beliefs,

continues —

— continued

feelings, and reactions of the person speaking: "I feel that remark is unfair. I can accept feedback but not when it sounds so mean." It's the opposite of the "you message," when people launch into attack mode with a litany of "You were supposed to . . ." or worse yet, "Why can't you? . . ."

What does it sound like when you're on the receiving end of a "You" or "Why" phrase? Most people feel their defensiveness kick into high gear. On the other hand, when we phrase things in an "I message," we take responsibility, and that welcomes the listener. An "I message" shows you are taking at least partial ownership in the communication. You're invested and direct (rather than indirect), and you spare the listener from phrases that sound accusatory or mind-reading such as "You did that because you. . . ."

HOW HIDDEN ANGER TAKES UP RESIDENCE

If you think passive-aggression is immature . . . well, yes, you are correct. To comprehend how people, even in adulthood, act this way and why it's challenging to change, we need to understand how children behave.

Children have a tough time recognizing another's point of view (what we call empathy). They're characteristically impatient, illogical, often selfish, impulsive, stubborn, sloppy, and sometimes rude. A parent's role is to guide and teach them throughout their youth so that they unlearn these traits and replace them with patience, logic, empathy, caring, flexibility, and so on. This takes years. If you're a parent, you know how trying this work is. Despite bumps in the path, most kids move from the terrible twos and turbulent teens to become outstanding individuals—if parents teach them how to be good.

The crucial word here is *if*.

When parents are unaware, permissive, self-absorbed, insensitive, or immature themselves, their children pay mightily. And we all pay a price when these kids reach the ranks of adulthood and become the troublemakers among us. Sometimes we'll see years of buildup that endured through many milestones as kids harbored hurts and cloaked true feelings with passive-aggression. In these families, children didn't grow beyond their hostility, so anger may still be emotionally on the run. The child, now an adult, has few to no skills for self-expression and has trouble holding it together except in specific settings, such as with friends or in comfortable relationships where there are few demands. That same child or adult may fall apart in an academic setting, at work, or with a close friend or sweetheart. He becomes a hot mess; you find yourself moving away from this person who seems difficult to be around.

Whatever seductive veneer attracted you and kept you around this person fades so that you see vindictive, mean intent in his motives. What worked so well for this anger concealer works no longer. But be assured—it once worked well, for to reap any gain, anger must serve a purpose—not always a good purpose, mind you, but a purpose, nonetheless. Here, we provide examples of where the cauldron of wrath started brewing in childhood because it served a specific vital function.

HIDDEN ANGER THAT PROTECTS

As a kid, Connie concealed her true thoughts and feelings because she grew up in her older brother's shadow. Nothing Connie attempted ever measured up. She kept quiet through college and, now married, Connie expects her husband George to read her mind. No surprise: they argue. Connie must tell George what she needs or expects, instead of hoping he'll guess correctly. Defenses that were designed to protect Connie in childhood have limited usefulness to her later in life. They need to be unlearned and replaced with communication skills. Passive-aggression was once thought to be an "immature defense" because it was indirect but also self-defeating.[3] Sometimes there are other reasons for defenses. Adults are supposed to do the protecting and defending. Sadly, when children feel emotionally unsafe, they resort to:

- Blaming ("He did it, not me!")
- Denial ("No, I didn't.")
- Projection ("I'm not bad, you're bad," when a child is appropriately disciplined.)
- Repression ("I don't want to talk about it.")

- Displacement ("Well, Nana said I could have it.")
- Rationalization ("I can't help it because . . .")
- Undoing ("You dipshit!" a kid provokes, only to soften with "Can't you take a joke?")
- Isolation of affect ("I didn't mind being beaten up. Really," a child says nonchalantly of trauma. He isolates himself from his emotions.)
- Reaction formation ("I do not like her," a boy claims though he sends her heart emoticons and romantic videos as if he does like her. His feelings seem odd to him also. His action masks one feeling and displays its opposite.)

Using defenses like these might merely help us navigate childhood. It's important to distinguish the difference between a child's developing expression skills and a child stuck in a negative rut.

When a child is overprotected, this poses other problems, as the teenager, then young adult, feels stuck. Parents who never allow wings to fly from the family nest foster ambivalence when their son or daughter wants to be independent. To these kids, safety equals dependence.

Take Sam, whose harsh mom and dad squashed his high school desire to become a photographer and study art. Most of Sam's opinions ran contrary to his parents' views, and when he tried to establish his own identity, their rejection stung enough to keep him in their grasp. In school, Sam's parents bantered SAT scores with other parents as if they were NASDAQ figures flashed across Times Square. Sam was tutored, coached, enriched, and prepped outside the home. Within the home, his parents hovered and smothered. Sam isolated himself from their diatribes when they told him he wasn't the child they imagined. After barely tolerating home life, Sam moved across the country to go to art school.

According to Scott Wetzler, PhD, one pattern that seems to appear with many secretly angry men is an overly close mother and a more distant father who relegated most of the parenting to mom.[4] This could apply to women as well, with implications later in life. If a woman who has had overpowering parents, for example, then encounters others in authority, she may see them as intrusive. All of us, in one way or another, tend to react to buttons installed back in childhood.

HIDDEN ANGER AS A REACTION

If a child faces unending criticism when attempting developmental tasks because a bar is set too high (or to perfection) or because the parents themselves are short on nurturance but long on impatience, the child learns to hold back. She might be the girl who doesn't raise her hand in class, never tries out for the lead in the school musical, and marries early, yearning for acceptance. Further, if this struggling family downloads its "bad side" onto her as it broadcasts the "good side" to the general public, this girl internalizes hurt and rejection. Who wouldn't want to escape the role of scapegoat? Yet with praise and encouragement, this young lady would take calculated risks—try for more, do more. Alternatively, if she learns that great is never good enough, or if much criticism clouds out few compliments, passive-aggression becomes a survival tool to keep family at arm's length.

When a child's home was not secure but was rather a place of physical, emotional, or sexual abuse—splenetic fury at its most forceful—a child's need to hide anger is the result of traumatic stress, which serves as protection but also as a reaction to such events. Children often learn to identify with a hostile parent or caregiver. They accept what comes their way and become convinced that if they do tell someone what's going on, more abuse will be heaped upon them. In the extreme, anger, disappointment, and shame culminate in deep depression and suicide. Not all kids who are criticized, scapegoated, or abused end up passive-aggressive. Troubled times hold some back, while others gather the strength to survive and thrive beyond such incidents.

Hidden anger might also grow from the challenge of living with a disability or something that makes a child feel different. Understandably, children who live with a learning disorder; speech, hearing, or visual impairment; developmental delay; or other problem may grow frustrated when learning is hard and when others can do things easily that they cannot. These kids begin to resent their lot in life (and sometimes the teasing that goes with it) unless they are taught how to cope and use their strengths. Teachers without proper perspective may chalk up a child's anger as just another behavior problem. Understanding the trigger is pivotal to improving the situation, for the child, the teacher, their classmates, even their parents.

"Disabilities prevent some students from attaining the developmental goals of each stage within the expected time frame. This is especially true for children with learning disabilities and emotional disorders whose disabilities are not apparent to others," write Nicholas J. Long and Jody E. Long in *Managing Passive-Aggressive Behavior of Children and Youth at School and Home.*[5] Anyone facing a disability goes through a normal grieving process similar to what the late Elisabeth Kubler-Ross chronicled in her pivotal book *On Death and Dying.*[6] The five stages she outlined for grieving are denial, anger, bargaining, depression, and acceptance. The process of acknowledging a disability is very similar. Larry B. Silver, MD, wrote in *The Misunderstood Child* that parents need to work through their own reactions to a learning disability, and that the three most prevalent emotions are denial (as in "No, it can't be true"), anger ("Why my child?"), and guilt ("It must be my fault").[7] Parents also go through stages of anger as school personnel try to help parents who aren't ready to accept their child's problem, or the reverse when parents advocate for accommodations or special education and meet resistance. The test of anyone's true mettle is their refusal to become their disability or to be defined by it; this is also true of parents and their refusal to define their children by their disabilities.

HIDDEN ANGER AS A STAGE

Given these behaviors—laziness, forgetfulness, procrastination, constant irritability—does a teenager come to mind? Physical growth during the adolescent years often catapults teens well beyond their emotional maturity. Not a child, yet unable to psychologically or financially provide for himself, a teen yearns for freedom, but appreciates limits. Most adolescents do just fine and are not a daily challenge to a parent's sanity, but all have their moments. One day they are independent; the next it's "can you take me to the mall?" Get to that mall and you'd better keep out of sight; it's so uncool to be with parents!

It's this push-pull between those two extremes that causes teenagers to test authority, give in to occasional peer pressure to conform, or become moody while undergoing a physical, psychological, social, not to mention neurological upheaval.

A certain amount of passive-aggressive behavior has always been a part of pushing the envelope into adulthood. When kids achieve independence, this silent rebellion usually ceases, and often they embrace previously resisted parental notions. Yes, they may well appreciate all you did by age thirty, or once they have children of their own. However, if you're concerned about continued opposition, blocking, simmering acrimony, or another troublesome behavior, it's always best to first check this out directly. Some kids will amaze you with their honesty when approached supportively.

HIDDEN ANGER SEARCHING FOR ATTACHMENT

Typically, babies and their caregivers form a secure attachment by the time the infant turns nine months old, but the writings of Mary Ainsworth, Mary Main, and Jude Cassidy distinguish three types of insecure attachments: babies who turn away or ignore their caregivers (avoidant attachment), angry, inconsolable children (resistant or ambivalent attachment), and confused infants not knowing what's happened with their caregivers (disorganized or disoriented attachment).[8] Troubled attachment could also result from a child's particular difficulties (autism spectrum disorder, adoption, etc.).

Numerous studies back the notion that the more secure the attachment, the more successful one's social interactions throughout life, as evidenced by increased empathy and trust, improved self-confidence, higher-quality relationships, plus fewer conflicts and behavioral problems. A securely attached parent meets the child's physical needs (when hungry, tired, hot, cold) as well as emotional needs (for guidance, encouragement, teaching). When the child attempts to communicate, albeit by whining, the secure parent encourages patience and teaches the child to say *please*. Yet if the insecure parent, caught up in her own problems, misses the child's attempts to communicate, over time the child ups the ante, becoming louder, more demanding. If the parent's exasperation effectively squashes rather than redirects and guides the child's communicative attempts, this child's need to communicate may shut off, go silent, or grow.

Thus, if the home is hostile or the child doesn't bond properly with his parents, the only way to retaliate may be through silence, sneaking anger out in small doses, sometimes unknowingly. Chronically depressed children, who have lost their zest for life, have developed a bleak worldview, feel that everything is out of their control, and often think, "Why bother?" Pay attention if a child sees the world as dark instead of at least half-full of hope and promise.

Let us be clear, however, that nurture isn't all of the equation. No matter how much they prepare or what experiences parents have had with their first child, their second, third, or subsequent child may be the same, better, or worse. This uncertainty is one of the proverbial challenges of parenting.

HIDDEN ANGER WHEN COPING WITH CHANGE

Changing family dynamics can cause hidden anger as well. How often do you find yourself slipping back into a role when you're with your extended family? If a younger sibling grows up and should become equal to her brothers and sisters, but the older ones try to restore their comfortable pecking order, they've got some problems. Why is it that some families can adjust amicably with one another through the life span and others cannot?

Theodore Millon, writing with Roger D. Davis, offered insight into such negative behavior. "Many negativists felt that they had been 'replaced' by a younger sibling and that their parents' affections were withdrawn and redirected to a newborn child," they wrote, acknowledging that there were typically strong feelings of jealousy and resentment.[9]

Perhaps some kids want so badly to be the "good children" that they can't risk being honest. No one asked them if they wanted a baby brother or sister who now steals all their thunder and gets presents while they get less attention and more chores. When mom or dad leaves the room, they may taunt their younger sibling. If caught, then what? Remembering that list of defenses, they'll cop a few, such as undoing ("I didn't mean to hit her") or rationalizing ("I couldn't help it, my toy just fell on him"). Millon and Davis suggest that displaced resentment might *not* be intended for the younger sibling but instead for the parents themselves.[10]

Once again, the risk of dealing with mom and dad directly is too great, and the younger sibling is an easier target for such anger. How parents address their older children regarding an impending birth in the family sets the foundation for sibling relationships.[11] "In better functioning families, parents initiate the development of sibling ties by involving their children throughout the pregnancy," writes John V. Caffaro, PhD, in *Sibling Abuse and Trauma*, advocating further that "parents can also help their older children understand their baby brother's or sister's development by discussing the baby as a little person with feelings and needs." When they discuss everyone's feelings and answer questions in developmentally appropriate ways, parents acknowledge an older child's continued importance in the family.[12]

HIDDEN ANGER AS A LEARNED BEHAVIOR

We're all products of our environment. Within the United States, regions differ in their attitudes and norms. Certain corporate cultures and the culture of southern hospitality give us messages of social grace—service with a smile. "My pleasure" became a Ritz Carlton motto, as employees learned to serve happily even if they were having a horrendous day. The client is always right, as the professional cliché goes. Or is he? If you're a service worker and you ingest a steady diet of whatever the public dishes out, you may find that it gives way to discontent on the job. Talk about being a product of a negative environment!

It's so important, however, not to assume that behavior is passive-aggressive until you've tested out other reasons for it. Certain cultures instill a sense of respect for one's elders that goes beyond Western cultural standards. In Asian culture, for instance, children are taught not to question their elders or to test authority because it's a sign of great disrespect if they do. Can you see how harmful an inaccurate assumption could be if you were a teacher with an unusually silent student and you assumed a problem? The child might feel frustrated by this learned cultural pattern of holding back while other kids raise their hands and offer debate.

Culture can cause anger in children when they leave an isolated community where they felt emotionally safe and understood. If they encounter prejudice against their culture, faith, or differences, they may choose to hide intrinsic aspects of themselves in order to fit in. At the same time, they may become ambivalent and later regret their choice to withhold who they really were and are.

Parents, of course, have the greatest influence over learned behavior. If a child never observes a parent work a problem through to resolution, but instead sees the parent storm off, sulk, smooth over difficulty, slam doors, or say "nothing's wrong" (through an angry smile), then that parent externally reinforces the message that anger is bad in favor of the slow burn. If a child continues indirect, inappropriate behavior long past its being a developmental stage, then the child lacks skills that could elicit positive attention. Chances are good that she's been reinforced in the wrong behaviors.

Sometimes parents hide their negative emotions by smoking, drinking, drug use, gambling, binging, or some other addictive means. While parents may think that their coping is well hidden, frankly most kids know what their parents are doing. If not immediately, they'll eventually figure out the family roots of anger, enabling, passivity, or addiction.

HIDDEN ANGER DUE TO OTHER FACTORS

Children who lack adequate opportunity to develop social skills are also at higher risk of concealing their anger. Isolated by geography, by the lack of same-age playmates, or by other circumstances, the child's play takes a solitary form rather than one with give and take, subtle cues, and growing empathy. Interpersonal play helps a child develop competent social skills.

Consistency between parents, teachers, and other caregivers is paramount. Think about trying to serve two different bosses. No one wins. The child who receives one message from mom, another from dad, maybe even a third from the nanny or childcare worker, legitimately feels confused and ambivalent. These kids must have their antennae up at all times because they might get opposite responses from different authorities. Just when they think they've done a job well, mom will come down hard on them. Whenever they expect a class sticker, they get a demerit, all because the teacher (or parent at home) is inconsistent. This inconsistency drives a child's frustration. Parents are supposed to help a child resolve feelings, not make matters more complicated.

TRANSFORMING AN ANGRY CHILDHOOD

If you grew up sloughing anger off as if it wasn't worthy of your energy or you expressed it in subtle, sugar-coated, even sarcastic ways, it's not too late to change your anger management. Keep reading for practical tips to strengthen your family, become less reactive, and express yourself openly.

As we close our discussion of childhood, remember Carlos—at twenty-nine years old, rarely decisive, often needy? Even his younger sister calls him passive-aggressive. Carlos says that's just the way he is. He likes Rosa's attention. Big deal. Do you think there might be a childhood root to Carlos's problems? Do you think that Rosa is picking on her husband?

Sometimes it's hard to tell. Beyond cultural or age-related expectations Carlos's seeking attention could stem from feeling replaced by his younger sister. Many older brothers or sisters feel robbed of their due. When a person complains of aches and pains, he might also return to that childlike state where a caregiver attended to every scrape or fall. Even with inconsistent parenting, mom or dad would usually rally around with a little comfort. The automatic thought for this passive-aggressive adult is: if saying I was hurt got me attention as a little boy, maybe it will work again.

CHILDLIKE NEEDS

Children often act out because of unmet needs or things they're afraid of, and if these conflicts aren't resolved by adulthood, fully grown people may appear immature, avoiding the same things based upon those age-old fears. They may keep searching, even without knowing they're doing it, for what they never achieved as children. In the table that follows, we list what you might commonly see and where it originates.

Needs	Fears/Avoids	What You See
To recreate earlier experience from childhood	Being loved conditionally	Wants to be cared for
To be seen as the "good boy" or "good girl"	Losing rank in family	Transfers issues to others
Independence yet feels dependent	Powerlessness	Seeks approval; unwilling to make decisions
To meet others' expectations	Never getting it right	Body aches and pains, whines, anxiety
Growing up and facing maturity	Responsibility	Ambivalence, waffling, resistance

Sometimes Carlos might like being dependent upon Rosa, allowing her to make decisions, but at other times he likes making them for himself. If this is a continued display, lasting a few years, then it might well look a bit immature to Rosa, who needs him to assume greater responsibility. Still, the situation is not beyond hope. In fact, understanding one's childhood and the troubles that may have stemmed from it can come as a tremendous relief to many people.

Where you've been doesn't define where you are going. No one escapes his or her youth without a few scars. Refuse to be held back by events beyond your control. If you've confused or walled off your emotions so that your own negative circumstances prevent you from connecting with your spouse or children, from empathizing with what it's like to walk in their shoes, then counseling could help.

PART 2

How and Why People
Act as They Do

four

Fractured Families and Friendships

Y OU KNOW THE OLD SAYING, YOU CAN CHOOSE YOUR FRIENDS BUT not your family? Well, problems tend to creep into both important bonds. No family or friendship is a perfect match of temperaments, personalities, and circumstances. Our weaknesses and strengths combine to give our groups their personality (for better or worse). While some families openly express anxieties or differences with one another, others hold thoughts and feelings inside.

In this chapter, we'll open a window into the family because relationship problems so often remind us of our very first relationships—those within our families of origin. This requires us to think differently.

THE FAMILY IS A SYSTEM

Most of us think of ourselves as individuals, but we don't live in isolation. We are part of a greater system—perhaps many systems or groups. A classroom is a system for children, whereas the office is one for adults. Any group of people comprises a system. The group that has the most profound impact upon us is the one we're born into—our family system.

Thinking Systems: Circular Causality

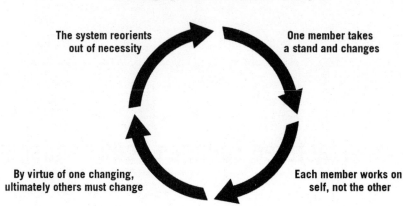

The system reorients
out of necessity

One member takes
a stand and changes

By virtue of one changing,
ultimately others must change

Each member works on
self, not the other

This is a circular, holistic way of thinking. Many researchers have contributed to the family systems movement. Systems thinkers feel that the family is more than its individual members, and how that family comes together—how their interactions play out—defines them.

One's family, for better or worse, has the single most important influence on one's psychological development. If something such as anger affects one member, it affects others within the family unit. Furthermore, when the process—how families function—goes underground, when members communicate indirectly rather than openly and honestly, and with a negative undertone, children absorb and most likely replicate this process. Many people look upon families as safe harbors, where everyone *should* get along, *ought* to understand each other, and *should* respect opinions and feelings. Right? News Flash: No perfect family exists. Anger plays a part in most families. Anxiety also plays a role, because it often accompanies coping with angry people and challenging situations. Make it your mission to maintain mutual respect. Now *that* is something to strive for, and when we fall short, it's best to see any anger mishap as an opportunity to learn.

As anger takes on a life of its own, it gets entrenched in a family's expression patterns. Sometimes we are too close to actually see the pattern unless we step back and really think about how we're behaving. It also helps to gain gentle feedback from trusted family members, friends, and professionals.

In the next chapter, you'll learn more about the Murphy/Oberlin framework for four types of families:

> Anger Is the Voice of Pain in the Troubled Family
> Anger Is the Voice of Stress in the Frantic Family
> Anger Is the Voice of Power in the Angry Family
> Anger is the Voice of Desire in the Indulged Family

Just as major film stars get called to reprise roles they once brought to everyone's attention, in families, it's often hard to break free from roles you got cast into and would like to jettison. Remember: if you identify one of our four types of families in yours, you can do something about it. Most families occasionally show a mixture of these four styles. It's only worrisome if a family remains stuck, and particularly if they have no awareness or take no responsibility.

FALLING BACK INTO A ROLE

Thanksgiving brought Albert and Martha, with their own families, to siblings Franny and Jim in Fort Lauderdale, Florida, with their eighty-four-year-old parents. Franny had relocated to provide more care. Jim, single and tired of being questioned about it, resided in Tennessee. Albert and Martha were on the West Coast.

After outward hugs and hellos, Albert whispered to Martha, "Tell me about Franny's stupid card proving points with dog humor."

"Dog paws with a caption 'I need a helping hand.'" Martha frowned. "Just another caustic comment. At least not a full-blown rant."

Soon Franny's taking charge of the turkey trumped conversation. They always ate at four o'clock sharp. Always. Thus, several people helped while some family watched the televised dog pageant.

"I'll give them best in show," Franny fumed at 3:15. "Martha, you changed the temp! This bird MUST be ready by four." Franny wagged her finger. "If you wanted to be a Martha Stewart, you should have been here last night."

"Franny, our plane only touched down at 9:46." Martha grabbed the oven mitts. "Use this meat thermometer. Undercooked poultry is nasty."

"You two sound nasty." Albert re-entered the kitchen. "What's that turkey hotline Mom used?"

"Butterball! Like you," Franny lobbed. "Here: chips. Low cal." She shoved a foil bag at his belly. "Give those regular ones to Slim Jim."

"Hey!" Albert chortled. "Remember how he howled when we called him Slim Jim."

"Jim asked you to stop with that." Martha shoved her casserole into the oven. "No wonder he doesn't bring any woman home."

As if on cue, Jim entered the fray. "I'm hungry. Need any help?"

"No! Fight over chips while I check on Mom and Dad." Franny left them perplexed.

"What's up with her?" Jim asked Martha. "She's impossible to please."

"Mad that the kids and I didn't pitch in last night," Martha said. "My helping now doesn't count."

"No one forced Franny to move here," Albert said. "I said I'd move Mom and Dad near us, but Franny wouldn't hear of it."

"Like a family traffic control tower," Jim said, midcrunch on a handful of chips. "One agent on duty. At all times."

At 4:30, they sat down to Franny's stern glares. The turkey turned out fine, but Martha's casserole needed a microwave fix. Martha swore she'd put it into a hot oven, but she took it out of a cold one.

And so it is with this family . . . and many others. The criticisms are unmistakable, innuendos a close runner up. Did you spot the sarcasm, name calling, gossip, triangles, rigid roles (and rules), plus unreasonable expectations? Coalitions exist between the oldest and youngest siblings. Several members are usually inside the circle and someone is in the outside position. Control and immaturity create communication that's cold, and well . . . how do you think the casserole got chilly, too?

Thanksgiving didn't start all this. Families who don't break dysfunctional cycles pick them up where they left off. Failure to fix old wounds in favor of holding grudges catapults you into unbalanced commotion where even a harmless comment erupts everyone into full-scale battle.

There are common roles in any family, including the hero/heroine, who on the outside seems responsible and rule-bound, but may seek approval, feel insecure, and hurt, while taking care of so many others. The protector may come across as uber-responsible, but also presents signs of being snarky, passive, annoyed, and actually may become physically sick and martyred in the effort to protect others. The victim may be the group member with an addiction—charming (but also manipulative) and blaming others while concealing his shame, guilt, and pain. The mascot, who clowns around to distract everyone, at first seems funny, but when you look deep enough, the immaturity reflects anxiety and insecurity. Most groups have someone who seems forgotten or lost—the person who is shy, spends much time alone, and may attach herself to things instead of people. Perhaps she does this because she feels rejected and her hurt masks much worry. Finally, a very common role is the scapegoat. Others see one person as the problem, and if only this problem person would be less defiant and go along with group norms (even poor ones), life would be fine. Ah, probably not because the scapegoat acts out the symptoms of *everyone* in the family or group. Inside, the scapegoat can grapple with jealousy, rejection, and deep hurt.

FAMILIES THAT ARE STUCK

Many families fall into one of the common roles. Which roles did our siblings play?

Indeed, this family tore each other apart. You had a full cast of characters—the impossible to please, the caretaker, the cynic, and the scapegoat. Stalled somewhere in their youth, Albert, Franny, Martha, and Jim needed to listen to one another. Truly listen.

Paying close attention captures content and emotion. It requires setting aside one's automatic thoughts. Each family member is entitled to feelings. When others react strongly, arguing the validity of another's feelings, it's a senseless waste of time. Feelings just are. Accept them. You need not agree, but acceptance builds bridges as opposed to barriers. But let's get back to the importance of communication.

How many times have you talked to someone and suspected that he spent more time in his brain formulating a counterargument to refute you than genuinely listening? How this plays out deserves attention.

Reflective listening is the ability to paraphrase what you heard and check out with that person if you missed anything. You'll find that it's fairly impossible to really ferret out precise meaning and hold all those antagonistic thoughts in mind. That's the point.

John Gottman, PhD, reports from his research on couples that criticism, contempt, defensiveness, and stonewalling undo just about any relationship.[1] Criticism and defensiveness abounded in our Thanksgiving Day example. People learn these communication techniques by sheer repetition if they see them modeled enough. Soon the style becomes a downward spiral.

"People who are hostile tend to be relentlessly critical when someone else fails to meet their expectations," writes W. Robert Nay, PhD, in *Overcoming Anger in Your Relationship*, where he also suggests that with unrealistic expectations people set themselves up for constant disappointment and frustration.[2]

FIGURING OUT YOUR FAMILY OR GROUP

Those That Foster Open Nurturance	Those That Harbor Hidden Hurts
Individuality and growth encouraged; opportunity to think, choose your own values	Expect groupthink: toeing the line; growth discouraged as it may threaten some in the group
Agree to disagree; open dialogue; respect (love, in families) freely granted	Discord, shame, verbal attacks; closed off; everything seems earned; nothing is unconditional
Comfortable freedom, flexible rules, few shoulds; new approaches embraced; feelings expressed	Tension, rigid rules, boatload of shoulds, musts and ought-to mandates; internal feelings masked
People first; responsibility and honesty embraced; few hassles exist; decisions made easily enough	Coalitions come first; secrets abound; numerous hassles and indecision about a lot of things
Communication contains "I messages"; facts and thought drive discussion; direct straight line between two people resolves differences	Lots of "you this/you that" accusations with interlocking triangles; emotion-driven discussion fueled by assumptions (thinking errors)

Body language relaxed and natural; what you see is what you get; people brighten in each other's presence	Crossed arms, heavy sighs, tight muscles and jaw line, rolled eyes, glares and stares; people tense around one another
People tackle challenges; feel energized as well as encouraged and cheerlead one another	People avoid challenges, complicate progress, feel fatigued and overwhelmed
Kids disciplined/taught with appropriate and immediate consequences	Kids punished by control and coercion doled out over time, leading to confusion/more of the same

© 2015 Loriann Oberlin, MS

HOW HIDDEN ANGER TAKES HOLD

The "Figuring Out Your Family or Group" table may help you sort through which process plays out in your interactions at home, work, school, or elsewhere. Anger in the second column may stem from a lack of differentiation, enmeshment, or fusion in one's family of origin, and/or characterological traits. If so, the hostility creeps into subsequent relationships if hard work doesn't take place to correct this.

A circular process and hidden anger can take hold within any system or group of people. One person starts by hiding anger, his genuine self, or the truth. The next person (second arrow in the graphic) may try to be honest,

Hidden Anger Taking Hold

Everyone learns that anger isn't tolerated. It gets pushed aside and hidden.

One person in group lies or hides the truth.

Others, wishing to please, take note.

This person is honest, but person #1 rebuffs and rejects any anger.

yet when the first group member rebuffs the second person's appropriately expressed frustrations (rejection), this sends a message to all others.

By the time any third, fourth, or subsequent person is affected by this hidden frustration pattern, the indirect/incongruent process starts to duplicate. It's a domino effect. Everyone learns by others' behavior not to show any form of anger, but to push it aside. Emotional contagion sets in. Until it all builds back up. Again.

During get-togethers or trips back home, family members might recycle old quarrels. Your parents may side with siblings, with whom you've never gotten along, and given these dynamics and stored resentments, it's unlikely you will get along unless each of you works on yourself (not the other).

In an extended family marked by covert hostility, people feel inferior or inadequate, yet gain power over others through passive-aggression. They succeed, unfortunately, because they discharge their concealed animosity; often control the outcome; and save face with sly, plausible excuses. The steps reinforce to them that the process works; thus, they repeat it.

Generational Ties

Many decades ago, families were a much closer unit, where older members who were able to reach out to the less stable young ones who were trying to find their way. The elders bolstered the family when life's storms blew through their lives. Youths and young adults found comfort and stability in knowing clear rules and expectations. Now people often have less support, and live by incoherent rules and unrealistic expectations.

There used to be a common Sunday tradition of visiting one's relatives; with frequent contact, family members cultivated the ability to work out difficulties and learned to cope through tough times. Pure geography has practically eliminated this tradition.

Technology Hinders

Some families are caught in cyclical problems that cell phones and e-mails do not mend. In fact, e-mails, with their immediacy and brevity, can make communication worse because they're not accompanied by nonverbal interaction to clarify your meaning. If you state something emphatically in person, your smile and pleasant demeanor carry part of the message. Emphatic e-mails are often misread.

The nuances of in-person nonverbal communication are missed with technology-driven communication. Emoticons do not make up the deficit. Consequently, misunderstandings occur and hurt feelings well up. Over time—as our hidden anger definition states—hostility and misinterpretations can erupt in anger. Instant messages, e-mails, and social media posts become Rorschach tests where the reader projects his own meaning onto them. Past or perceived resentments become toxic and eat away at his happiness. Whenever possible, use video chats to breach the distance.

Barbara LeBey writes in *Family Estrangements*, "Resentment escalates into grudges, then to rage and hatred, then to damaged and often completely ruined relationships."[3] She says that "knotted relationships" exist because of the need for control and the need for approval.[4] "Passive hatred" develops such that family members can't even revel in another member's happiness.[5] And it carries forth into subsequent generations—brothers, sisters, and cousins comparing notes on whose children won which awards or got accepted at what college. Instead of cheering on those who succeed, they feel jealous, withhold praise, and silently resent good fortune.

Covert Coalitions

Beyond geography and lack of traditional support, coalitions—a systems-theory term for subgroups—affect stability. These are situations where two or more people spend more time with each other than with others, agree with and often blindly back each other, and unfortunately resist confronting others of the group when there is a problem. Once established, coalitions endure. They can feed on faulty thinking and hidden anger. Not everyone lives in denial of what's honestly going on; it takes merely one to step in and call out poor choices. We saw this as Martha took a stand when siblings tried to lock Jim as the butt of an outdated family joke.

Negative humor, as we know, is a form of passive-aggression unless the person who is the main character in the old yarn laughs with you. People cop "I was just kidding!" as an excuse when they're caught scapegoating someone else. But beware! Just because someone laughs with you doesn't mean there's no hurt. Many people use self-laughter to survive around bullies.

Even celebratory moments can polarize because we're reminded of our differences—whether it's our cousin's alternative lifestyle, a break from our family's religious tradition, or opposing political views. In already angry or troubled families, members tend not to embrace diversity and do not appreciate everyone's potential for growth and change, but instead see things one way or another, as if there is a right or wrong side.

Certainly, coalitions surface in crisis, too, such as with a family member's failing health. Resentment sets in over who is (and isn't) on the scene and what decisions need to be made. At funerals memories of what was (or wasn't) stir strong emotional flashbacks to childhood. There's often also considerable strife over money and inheritance, displaying entitlement, greed, and obvious anger. When the family in crisis's core behavior pattern fits the indulging family type, things gets worse.

Some coalitions develop because members have inherent similarities or are close in age or have similar interests. When there's little familiarity or comfort with a specific person, it's harder to interact with such a coalition, and hidden anger flourishes. Subtle and not-so-subtle techniques put people through a trial by fire before being accepted. Remember movies like *Meet the Parents* or *My Big Fat Greek Wedding*? Any new daughter- or son-in-law surely understands trying to fit in, missing the context of situations, or traditions, and feeling distanced or pushed aside.

Occasionally, with very angry families, acceptance never occurs. When these types of coalitions become unyielding and underhanded, when people within them are charming yet cunning, they can destroy the overall family. New married couples related to these angry families are often challenged to make difficult choices. Do they merely continue to endure the pain? Those who grew up with the strife may have become inured to it; yet newcomers subjected to such drama may wish to flee and avoid. Furthermore, if each member of the couple caters to his or her family of origin rather than take a stand, which may work better for their new relationship, what then? And yet, if they circumvent crazy family events and opt to forge their own traditions, how long will they have to hear about it?

FRIENDS WHO SEEM LIKE FAMILY AND SOME WHO DON'T

Because passive-aggression abounds in all relationships, we see it in friendships. A friend, by definition, is someone we maintain a personal attachment to and with whom we are on good terms, is a supporter or person rendering assistance, or, these days, can be a contact we have made on a social media website.

Daily, people hide their frustrations in friendships. We don't have to air every grievance or divulge many of the thoughts that fleet through our minds. But when we silence these frustrations continually, the anger sneaks out passive-aggressively, and this can end up damaging or dissolving our friendships. In less close friendships, we usually aren't as stunned by problems that arise, but in solid, close ones—what some may call "best friends forever"—unleashed hidden anger can sever bonds. Here's a handy guide with eight types of difficult friendships:

Passive-Aggressive Frenemies	Fixing Your Role in the Frustration
Actor/Actress: pretends to be close but sends off mixed messages; you wonder when you're really friends and when you're not.	Pay attention to what you see, comparing it to what your friend says. Gently call out the discrepancies using "I messages." Ask person if there's something that doesn't feel right or seems off. Think about causes of disparities.
Competitor: strives to outdo, have more, be more superior, as if in a race for some prize; has not only an answer but the ONLY solution, often stemming from deep down insecurity.	Crowd-sourcing one's choices signals lack of complacency. Show and say how content you are with your own decisions while complimenting others' choices. Watch mirror-imaging others and accept what makes you unique. Limit social media.
Dominator: elevates self (his/her interests) to primary importance, rules the relationship, dictates the things that you do or time spent together.	When someone often exercises control, it's as if they do not notice you. Have you been a wallflower in the friendship? In a genuine one, your needs/wishes will matter, too.

continues —

— continued

Exploiter: mostly takes rather than gives and drains what works best for him/her with little concern over the effect it may have on others; also, may use knowledge about you as an emotional weapon; charms and flatters.	Tolerate vampires only at Halloween (not even then). If you tally the disproportion of giving versus taking, it may suggest where to place or remove your energy. Watch how much you share. Check motives and outcomes.
Faultfinder: finds fault with what and how you do things, points out your failures and blames you, often using the word "you" when lobbing remarks, including petty objections; will ask "You're wearing that?" rather than be direct and kind; sullen grumbling occurs; some crossover here with competitor.	Politely accept feedback while backing your choices: e.g., "I'm sorry you don't like __; it works really well for me." Don't instantly point the finger at his/her life, as that's niggling. Avoid sentences with "you" and "why"—both kick in defensiveness. Back away from the friendship with "When I feel criticized, I really don't enjoy our time together."
Hoodwinker: dupes you through disloyal, untruthful trickery; covers and hides genuine feelings; in worst cases, swindles you.	The origin of this word goes back to covering the eyes with a hood or blindfold. This friend keeps you in the dark. Solution: find out information yourself, double-check it, and be alert.
Intruder: welcomes oneself without permission or invitation; the friend who becomes overly involved in your life or feels she needs to solve all of your problems.	Establish better boundaries. Schedule times together. Watch out for your privacy, including what you share on social media. Assure this friend that "I'm on it" or "I've got it."
Juicer: squeezes and drains from you the energy you could put into your own life; overly dependent, sometimes out of neediness and other times because of poor motives.	Sometimes people need a helping hand, a shoulder to lean on, or someone to listen. Encourage this friend to seek help, work to become a strong self, but watch how much you do, as it can easily cross into enabling.

All eight types may fracture a relationship. The length of the relationship may add a protective factor, but if people (or you) have pushed problems aside, no party is immune. Hiding what really bothers you easily creates multiple layers that some minor incident may spark, then leads to an implosion (and subsequent explosion). If this should occur, work on the pivotal aftermath stage we discussed in Part 1.

TRIGGER POINTS

What are the most common triggers of extended-family discord?

- Irrational beliefs
- Strong, negative emotions
- The desire to control or jockey for position
- Triangles formed
- Sarcasm and cynicism
- Self-absorption

When new members are born into the family, being wounded by unleashed anger can at first be worked through, but research tells us that those wounds can lead to passive-aggressive behavior if the angst remains well into adulthood.[6]

Take your forty-five-year-old brother, who when invited to your daughter's fifth birthday, brings his photo album to show everyone his recent vacation, and offers to take *your* guests out for a spin in his new convertible. Look closely enough, and you might see a grown sibling still competing for attention or acceptance, certainly one who is jockeying for position and has a desire to control the situation (the child's party). Very likely there are strong, negative emotions and more than a few irrational beliefs.

HANDLING HOLIDAY HIDDEN ANGER

"My husband's brother was an angry child," wrote one of our readers. "Now, he's an angry adult exhibiting the same behaviors. It's gotten to where we must stay away because it casts a pall upon our holidays."

The holiday season frequently brings out the worst in families. We don't mean the stress of contending with the bustling crowds to find the right gift or the weekend you spent decorating. The real stressor during the holidays is gathering with family at a time when so many of us endure much excess—overtaxed schedules, unrealistic expectations, strained finances, and way too much food and drink—with people who we would not ordinarily choose to have lunch with, let alone something as symbolic as a holiday meal. We find ourselves stuck around the same table with old unfinished arguments, plus in-laws.

GIFT-WRAPPED ANTAGONISM

During the holidays, people conceal yet discharge anger through "forgetting" to send something, giving totally unsuitable gifts such as a bottle of rum to the known teetotaler, or flexing their muscles with their purchasing power. They let an inappropriate package push home points they're too hesitant to verbalize directly.

After a rather contentious divorce, one woman saw her daughter used as a pawn when the child's paternal uncle gave her a big-screen TV and video game system for her bedroom. Not only was this indulging, but it also smacked of anger when you understood the circumstances of the daughter's recently diagnosed learning and attention problems. The mom was having a hard time keeping the girl focused on school, and what's more, her ex-husband's extended family knew full well she had set in place a rule: no game systems and no TVs in the child's room.

Another man reported that his mother always used a stall tactic with his wife. She never committed to holiday invitations until the very last minute, causing them to have to delay their responses to invitations from other family members. Unable to ignore this burdensome habit and witnessing his mother's ambivalence about where to spend the holiday, the son asked his mother if she could please make a decision and inform them by a deadline. When she did not, he began to question whether she enjoyed the control that her silence granted her over the situation. Soon, his parents were the last to be invited to gatherings. The son and his wife felt relieved.

But what if the reason for the delay is not passive-aggression? Perhaps they have a hectic schedule or they are poor planners. Whatever the reason, when the rest of the family lets them know that they will not keep waiting, the delaying family member will get the message.

MANAGING YOUR EMOTIONS

For the holidays, assume that others will act the same but be ready to allow them to be different. And you? Act differently indeed. Analyze from where any strong feelings emanate. Are you trying to create the Norman Rockwell holiday portrait that never existed in your own childhood? If your own holidays lacked warmth, maybe you're striving to create perfection. Are you focused on competition? In some families, siblings compete to see who can set the most elegant table, cook the best gourmet meal, or impress people with outlandish gifts. Why not embrace and celebrate uniqueness?

Add in modern-day dynamics of stepfamilies, and you've got more holiday hot buttons. Children who reside elsewhere may feel like outsiders if there aren't enough beds, or they may miss simple conveniences such as their bikes to enjoy recreation with the other parent. It's important to make everyone feel a part of things, to talk about tensions before the holiday ever takes place, and to ease transitions for everyone. Some families wisely opt to do something entirely different, creating a new tradition, such as renting a cottage where they can all celebrate a holiday and also vacation together. In this neutral space no one can claim home-turf advantage. Here are some ways to avoid a merry meltdown:

- Discuss as a couple how you'll handle the push and pull from extended family. What is it that you like most (and least) about these gatherings? Try to support your spouse's wishes for closeness or distance with his or her own family, especially if you don't have a strong opinion yourself.
- Alternate holidays with different relatives or in-laws, relegate holiday trips to brief visits, or have a separate celebration that enables you to choose a time that's less hectic and stress-filled.
- Put your best behavior forward. Engage others. Ask what's new in their lives. Smile. Laugh when appropriate. Use empathy. Pay compliments. Offer to help with the meal or other tasks throughout the visit.
- Act differently. If your routine was to take a seat and watch TV, change that. This brings about new interactions and different dynamics may surface.
- Rein in your reactivity, because your anger escalated matters. Watch how you respond and what you convey through body language. If your sister pays you a backhanded compliment, don't get angry (old reaction). Keep your defenses in check, and learn how to ignore and walk away (new reactions). If you must say something, use "I" statements. If an altercation ensues, remember to work through the aftermath stage and clean up messes left behind.

- Never criticize someone in front of their children. This shows not only poor manners overall but can completely diminish that person in the eyes of a youngster.
- Determine to break out of any destructive coalitions. Listen when someone conveys heartfelt feelings that the age-old family joke really needs to be permanently sidelined. Likewise, don't participate in a triangle. If someone says, "Tell your brother . . .", calmly reply, "He's right over there for you to talk with."
- Be sensitive to those who are in transition from the death of a loved one, a separation or divorce, or the loss of a job, but also don't enable them to cast a pall upon the holidays either. Being kind does not mean that you must cater to someone's melancholy. Rethink traditions and become more sensitive to others' feelings.
- Bolster yourself, realizing that if people choose to be cross, their actions or words do not change you intrinsically. Such antics merely invoke the past; often those who are seething can't accept the present. Resist whatever role your family gave you if it's an uncomfortable one that pigeonholes you; the role is not you. Remind yourself that your feelings do exist, and yet their rudeness doesn't remove your responsibility for your reactions. Engage thought before impulse.
- If you are unable to be with your family or choose not to, do something helpful to take your mind off what you long for. Volunteer at a soup kitchen. Help out at a children's hospital or at a women's shelter. This will keep you busy, and you will also extend yourself to others, boosting your self-confidence and helping you feel gratitude for what you do have as opposed to longing for what you don't.

OVER-THE-TOP ANGER

When the attacks become purely personal or there's a persistent pattern of subtle torment, the passive-aggression becomes emotional or verbal abuse. However, there is no abuse meter that demarcates that boundary. It's usually attributed to being overwhelmed, frightened, or uncertain, and in many cases, ignorant of child development. Abusers struggle with unresolved anger problems and resentment. When that struggle becomes toxic, emotional abuse can last a lifetime. Too many people allow themselves to become the targets of someone's wrath until the pain becomes too intense and they start lashing out, too, in order to release it. Don't let that be you!

When we see a family member "dump" on another, the unloading person typically has little left to give. Her own emotional bank depleted, she has no patience, no unconditional love or acceptance, and no empathy. People who reach this point will push others away to avoid the possible pain of rejection or to avoid what memories the others conjure. If they're the self-absorbed type, they may steer family members into servitude to meet their own needs. On the receiving end, the message this angry person gives becomes: "You must comply to be accepted, included, or loved." At the core is the angry person's desire for love, but she fights against the very thing she needs.

No wonder relationships crack. Cruel words can range from sarcastic remarks to unkind appraisals ("You're such a ____") to vented regret ("I wish you'd never been born"). The same sentiment plays out in countless nonverbal ways as the absent or too-busy parent or the backstabbing sibling or friend. Emotionally abusive people have a knack for pointing out what's wrong, never focusing on what's right. Being without such balance leaves others with low self-esteem, trouble trusting or forming positive relationships, a negative worldview, poor social skills, body aches and pains, and too few good memories.

CONTROL WHAT YOU CAN, BUT MAP OUT A PLAN

In a best-case scenario, prominent family members will leverage their influence over the difficult, depressed, abusive, or addicted family member so that the person concealing his troubles becomes aware enough to seek solutions. In the worst case, you'll have to make your own choices about how you respond to the extremely difficult people. A few suggestions:

- What is in your control to change, and what is not? As the *Serenity Prayer* tells us, "God grant me the serenity to accept the things I cannot change, the courage to change the things I can, and the wisdom to know the difference."[7]
- Understand that unhealthy people project into others unsavory aspects of themselves that they later use to control others. We tend

to see in someone else the motives that we live by in our own lives (called projection), but we can also be made so blinded, so uncomfortable by our own flaws that we miss them in others.

- Be careful casting motives. Phrases such as "that's the way women (men) are" generalizes unfairly and relies upon all-or-nothing thinking.

- Recognize triangles as rarely productive. When the angry person uses others as messengers or dumping grounds, one more person becomes weighed down with the frustrations the angry person temporarily discharged. The angry person may breathe easier, but not for long! The closest distance between two points is a straight line. Speak directly to another person.

- As family members or siblings mature, reacquaint yourself with what's going on in their lives today. "Siblings often do not understand why a brother or sister acts the way he/she does, and that leads to ambiguity," reports Geoffrey Greif,[8] who wrote *Adult Sibling Relationships* with Michael Woolley. "In turn, a number of siblings we interviewed also felt misunderstood, isolated or excluded by family."[9] Get to know your family members' interests, values, struggles, and successes.

- Consider permanent cutoff with caution. Cutoff often fosters more anxiety than it solves. Yet don't lose your self-esteem to family members or coalitions that discharge anger onto you. If it's a long-term pattern (a decade plus), it's probably entrenched. You aren't going to change it so change what you do instead.

FALSE SOCIAL HEROES AMONG US

Some people grow into adulthood still sorting through suppressed anger in their demanding, self-absorbed families or friends. To a child there's nothing quite like discovering that a parent now does that which they took stands against before.

Yet some people play a vain role as false social heroes; that is, they need the appearance of good deeds in the community and/or an upstanding image to make up for inadequate performance, past misdeeds, or sometimes merely lost dreams.

False social heroes volunteer at the local soup kitchen, but they're too busy with their community work to go home and make a wholesome meal for their own families. You find them having physically lashed out at a family member when they were particularly riled up against the guy down the street who did the same. Or "Teacher of the Year" gets flashed in a local magazine, yet when students require clarification, that teacher has replied, "Don't waste my time with stupid questions."

False social heroes send a very mismatched message in which what they ascribe to publicly isn't what they practice personally. If you call them on it, they'll be contrite, apologize profusely, and yet tomorrow, they're back crafting an image.

FRACTURED FRIENDSHIPS

In text lingo, *BF* and *BFF* translate into "best friend" and "best friend forever." When tensions arise, it hurts the hardest in these relationships. Fractured friendships make us feel powerless, yet, if we work things out after misunderstandings, disagreement, or years of silent (or even not-so-silent) antagonism, we regain a personal sense of control, plus the bonds of a stronger devotion. Building a friendship requires a solid foundation, fortified block by block.

When tempted to drift away from a friend, challenge yourself to pursue and keep the relationship alive. Discuss any problems in a gentle, non-threatening, supportive ("I'm on your side") way. You may even leave a message or text that tells your friend "life is a little crazy right now . . . let's catch up in another month or two."

While some passive-aggressive friends may apologize when they feel contrition coming upon them, self-focused, passive-aggressive comrades will rarely apologize. On the other hand, chronically depressed and passive people will often express regret or say they are sorry much more than they need to.

Does your friend put herself in a place of honor while you're left feeling stupid or inadequate? Does she derive pleasure from your misfortune or misery? That is, if you tell her that you missed a great opportunity, lost your job, or just sat in traffic during the commute from hell, might she reply, "I could have told you so," or tell you she could have given you better directions in the first place? Does she lob remarks such as "How can you not know that?" to make you feel stupid and herself feel superior? What's more, if you try to talk, managing your own reactivity to truly communicate well, does her defensiveness kick in more criticism, stonewalling, or contempt?

Anyone can foul up or say something incredibly stupid once or twice, but if we hang around negative people who don't improve their demeanor, it can literally bring us down to their depths.

LETTING GO OR HANGING ON TO FALSE HOPES

When people change, circumstances shift, as does our proximity, and matters may solve themselves. But how can you end things civilly when you feel stuck with a frenemy?

With kindness . . . and caution.

"Defriending" on Facebook or Instagram takes on an energy of its own. Folks, they are merely websites. Indeed, not life itself. If you're this dejected upon being "defriended," ask yourself: What would you do differently the rest of today if your frenemy still counted you among hundreds of so-called friends? The answer: probably nothing different.

You may need to "defriend" your friend; consider it an informal break. If your friend asks why, it really is best to use tempered truthfulness: "I messages" about how you feel. If you're dealing with someone truly difficult, however, using the DEBUG mnemonic device is the way to go (this device is taught to children in many schools, but adults can benefit, too): Do ignore, Exit or move away, Be friendly, Use firm (assertive) language, and Get help if necessary.[10]

But getting help doesn't mean creating triangles by complaining to friends, making caustic remarks or backhanded statements intended for this other person to "accidentally" discover. In this era of social media, people may need coaching on how to step away politely. A little kindness goes a long way.

The *Journal of Personality and Social Psychology* ran a study regarding social rejection. It found that such public rejection made it more probable that the participants would behave in more offensive ways to people they did not know.[11]

Consumer magazines have run articles regarding sexting and revenge porn—acts perpetrated by jilted lovers or casual liaisons gone awry. High school and college girls have found themselves intimidated when they wouldn't agree to certain intimacies. Today, Photoshopped visual media seems to pick up where vicious rumors leave off.

Why does anyone who feels the brunt of a friend's negative feelings remain friends with that person? For the same reasons that people stay in unhealthy unions: they have core needs for attachment, they use the relationships as a means to assuage loneliness and self-doubt, or they have some internal rationalization that the other party solely caused the rift. When a person suddenly severs a relationship, it can feel like a death—something we avoid at all costs. In workplace friendships, people usually need to hold on to their jobs, so they often tolerate stinging remarks or harassment. Both women and men are harassed (sometimes sexually), and though it's illegal, often subtle intimidation is tolerated and goes unreported.

CYBERBULLYING: HOW TO RESPOND

A program at the 2009 American Counseling Association annual conference reported that more than 80 percent of adolescents owned media technology that allowed them to snap photos of their peers anytime and anyplace, even capturing them in school locker rooms and restrooms.[12]

Millions of children, teens, and adults have become the unfortunate victims of a cyberbully, a passive-aggressive tyrant who slyly sits at the top of her social stratum, even if only in her mind. Though you may not have encountered this—and we hope you haven't—read these tips to know how to ward off or counter such an attack:

- Limit your exposure to the cyberbully's mean posts. Not interacting keeps the bully from achieving any secondary gain (your anger). Cyberbullies are particularly skilled at provoking intense, immediate reactions in people, and because the platforms they lurk on often allow anonymity, they've possibly been at it for quite a while.

- Report abuse on social media or other sites. If you are threatened or the recipient of vulgar language or contrived, compromising images, inform law enforcement, and certainly reach out to online administrators. In many cases, they may close down a harasser's account. If the abuse happened to you and nothing is done about it, others remain at risk.
- Set up online alerts with your name and other keywords (especially for business purposes). This helps you to track abuse and act on it promptly.
- Remember that image-based platforms (ones cyberbullies often misuse) help people remain immature. Next time you're tempted to measure your worth through LIKES, TAGS, and HITS, consider the anxiety you can lessen by not engaging in it. Focus on the real world, where images don't force you to measure up to possibly unattainable ideals.
- Work through your feelings with a good therapist if the attacks result in you questioning your self-worth or if you have flashbacks to the experience. Some cyberabuse victims report symptoms consistent with posttraumatic stress disorder. These include runaway worry, panic, flashbacks, guilt, helplessness, and sometimes, depression.

five

Hostile Children and Teens

WYATT PLOPPED HIS TEN-YEAR-OLD BODY ONTO MS. OBERLIN'S couch, crossed his arms, and pronounced, "Why are they here? I want to do the talking!" The *they* he referred to were his mom and dad, who had initiated family therapy.

Days before, Wyatt's parents had come in alone to provide considerable background regarding four other siblings, repeatedly poor grades, and a home with more arguments than most courtrooms.

With Wyatt still complaining, Ms. Oberlin got a quick, in vivo snapshot of the antagonism in the family. "You're doing it all wrong," Wyatt grumbled before he stormed out to "chill" down the hall. Mom looked down, Dad sighed heavily, then they both confessed that threats, coercion, and giving in had not settled their son nor home. Very shortly, Wyatt returned, as if he couldn't stand his own choice of leaving.

"We can try something else," Dad promised, oblivious to his wife's glare as he had just undermined progress before any truly began. Again. Ambivalence and a lack of parental teamwork created a foundation for Wyatt to manipulate successfully and well beyond his years.

Ambivalence also played out when Dr. Murphy listened to teenage Chloé tearfully telling how her mom "forgot" to take her prom dress for alterations, suggested she pin it, then guilt-tripped her about how hard she had worked to pay for the dress. Self-conscious with every camera flash during prom, Chloé worried that her hasty seamstress skills would incite laughter and land her in the yearbook.

These parents remained clueless that their own avoidance, needs, and anger would put their children at greater risk for mismanaging their emotions. Wyatt was too young for him or his parents to see the long-term ramifications, but Chloé wouldn't trust her mother anytime soon. Passive-aggression complicates parent/child bonds.

TOP 10 REASONS WHY A CHILD USES PASSIVE-AGGRESSION

Reason	What the Child Gains
To manipulate	This child learns that asking directly doesn't work. He could manipulate a parent who says no when confronted into yes. The child responds when he wants to, but learns not to at other times. He learns that parents' requests hold no authority. Gradually, this kid teaches the parent as he redirects, like Jason, who positioned his earbuds to listen to music (not his mom) when reminded to do yard work. Dragging the rake just a few times would get her off his back and him out of even completing inside chores.
To punish	What this kid lacks in parental size he'll make up for with sly punishment. For instance, Tyrone figured out his forty-year-old father's sudden fascination with hair-care products and clothing: a girlfriend, one that made Mom spitting mad. Tyrone figures if he goes to the baseball game with a friend on Dad's time instead of Mom's, he'll make Dad squirm.
To control	Who needs classroom or parental rules anyway? No one asked kids! That's what kids think as they choose which rules to obey and which ones to disregard. Curfew? Just dawdle in order to stay out late. Pick up dry cleaning? Not if you whizz past the cleaner.
To retaliate	Different than punishment, retaliation directly responds to perceptions of fairness. At times, the recipient isn't even the cause but becomes the more convenient victim. Kids may also harbor resentments and wait for the right moment to strike, as in "You grounded me from skateboarding; see what it's like to miss an appointment when it takes you forever to find your car keys after I hide them."

To bully	Forget petty teasing, these ugly remarks cross the line into deroga- tion. Bullying is cruel, possibly sociopathic, and sometimes deadly. It doesn't even require that the passive-aggressor is angry at really anything specific; it's done to be mean, as when a teen boy tells a girl "give me sex or I'll say on social media that you did anyway," making the girl feel trapped with few choices.
To peck	Reinforcing the pecking order uses power to show who is smarter, faster, better, and stronger. "It's mine," or "I was first." This sibling rivalry goes underground a lot, so parents should remain vigilant. One brother changed the computer passcode so that he was the only family member who could gain any access. For him, it was all about playing games. For siblings, it complicated school and social connections.
To slack	Learned helplessness describes when a person shuts down when she can't avoid a painful situation or the work required to truly grow and succeed. Rather than teach her hope that comes through action, the family does things for her, locking her in as a victim. So if Maria's grades have spiraled downward and she resists her tutor, she might watch as adults try harder to improve her grades than she does. Her own passivity wins out over determination and hard work.
To fight parent goals	This child doesn't have a life; she has a parent's life. Mom or Dad live vicariously through this son. Who wouldn't rebel if the motive appears more to be about bragging rights? Mason overheard his parents compare him to other kids' achievements. So what if that kid trains for the Olympics? What's a Rhodes scholarship anyway? Reasoning with such unreasonable expectations hasn't worked in the past, but his mysterious ankle injury does keep him out of several soccer practices.
To seek attention	When adults get caught up in activities, issues, or within them- selves, children often gain their attention through negative, passive displays. Getting "talked to" means at least a morsel of attention, as when Liam wanted to help his mom bake for the cookie exchange. The perfectionist she was, Mom declined his primitive skills, but when Liam found the missing powdered sugar, she praised his detective abilities. Of course, hiding that essential ingredient sure made it easy for him to find.
To look confident	Lacking confidence and patience in her own abilities, a child or teen takes the "nothing ventured, nothing lost" approach, like Izzie, who took incompletes in half her classes rather than risk taking finals and failing. This stall tactic is born out of avoidance and the girl's need to be successful.

STARTING OUT YOUNG

Too bad childhood vaccinations don't immunize youngsters against the subtle meanness that kids who are learning social skills and forming friendships pick up at recess, on playdates, during after-school activities, or on sports teams. In May 2014, *The Wall Street Journal* ran "Very Little and Acting Mean: Children, Especially Girls, Withhold Friendship as a Weapon." Some schools now teach empathy in order to stem relational aggression. This form of passive-aggression manifests "using the threat of removing friendship as a tactical weapon," the article stated. Psychologists have witnessed where this manipulation has occurred as early as two and a half years of age.[1]

Relational aggression has long been prevalent. Teaching children about this phenomenon can occur through literature.[2] Choose kids' books where protagonists assert themselves and stand up to bullies. We can foster empathy by teaching kids to recognizing another's sad face, false smile, mad frown, or asking them "what's happening in this story?" and then generalizing the plot to the child's life as we begin a dialogue about social skills he or she can improve.

Sue Shellenbarger, columnist for *The Wall Street Journal* and author of "Wanted: A Best Friend," wrote that best friends buffer kids from stress, loneliness, teasing, and torment.[3] The majority of kids form their best friendships through school, sports, and extracurricular activities. Cell phones, texting, and social media keep them in touch, but also pose risks of overuse and unnecessary drama.

UCLA researchers studied being unplugged with eleven to thirteen year olds and found that the emotional distance of social media and online communication made it easier for kids to be unkind. Continually being plugged in and relating online do not promote healthy friendships and create residual effects that linger throughout life.[4]

THE FOUR STYLES OF ANGRY . . . EVEN ANXIOUS FAMILIES

A little earlier, we quickly highlighted families as having four different anger styles. Here, we'll go into greater detail, since each of these factors into children's behavior (and parents' too!). Anxiety also plays a part—anyone dealing with angry people becomes anxious trying to cope. Most families occasionally show a mix of these four styles rather than being all one or another. As you're reading, if any of these examples seems like it could be based on your family, remember: this recognition is the first step toward change.

Anger Is the Voice of Pain in the Troubled Family

Troubled families are overwhelmed by hurt that stems from marital strife or divorce, financial problems, substance abuse or addiction, mental illness, or trauma such as the death of a family member. Struggling parents might place their children smack in the middle of their conflict. We have both seen parents who dropped their child off in therapy, declining participation themselves, with the hopes that we could magically restore normalcy and "fix" their child. Thinking with a systems framework, people create change only in themselves, but reciprocally everything changes as a result of that individual's hard work. When first meeting with a family in counseling, each of us has asked, "How's your marriage?" If that question kicks in defenses, such as "What does our marriage have to do with our child?" we gain immediate insight that the parent's own difficulties trickle down to the child. A change in one member of a family creates changes in others.

When problems strike in a dysfunctional household, family members often are unavailable to each other, unaware of their emotions, or confused by multiple or conflicting emotions. Troubled families who hide their feelings must find solutions to the specific problems they face.

Sometimes we fool ourselves into thinking that adult issues have no direct bearing upon children and teens, yet indirectly, addictions, marital problems, finances, housing stress, and intimate partner violence definitely do.

Please understand that this does *not* mean that parents should communicate to kids as they would with adult peers. Family discussions require developmentally appropriate language that places more importance on the needs of the child than the needs of the adults.

The Trouble	Paths to Prevent Hidden Anger
Death and grieving	Read age-appropriate books (bibliotherapy) that help children understand loss. Children can keep a journal or attend grief counseling to ward off indirectly lashing out at or resenting those who have what the child has lost.
Addiction	It's tough to compete with powerful substances, alcohol, gambling, or any other habit. Make no mistake, the addicted person needs to get proper treatment, maintain sobriety, and prevent relapse. Without this, the addict remains committed to obtaining the next fix rather than the family. Children are not only aware, but in some cases, genetically vulnerable to repeating this poor coping strategy. Age-appropriate books, counseling, and Ala-Teen programs are good outlets for the pain, which will reoccur in their generation unless it's addressed.
Physical/Mental illness	Appropriate medical/psychological care comes first. Read our chapter about therapy and see our book recommendations to spark open, honest discussion rather than have information gleaned from less than reputable sources that contain inaccuracies. With severe mental illness, such as schizophrenia and bipolar disorder, individuals very often aren't even aware of their illness, which can frustrate relatives who try to get them to seek help.
Marital separation and divorce	So prevalent and complex, we devote a must-read chapter to it. School and private groups help children face the sudden loss of their intact family; outside counseling helps as well. Appropriate children's books (bibliotherapy) assure kids that they are not the only ones facing these topics.
Finances and housing	With economic fluctuations, unpredictable corporate changes, and individual career choices, most children and teens experience financial difficulties along with adults. Don't worry them unnecessarily, but assure that you'll take care of them. Reassure that steps are being taken to improve circumstances. Avoid false promises (for example, saying that you'll never move) and reframe negatives into positives as much as possible. False expectations regarding college prospects send mixed messages, so if particular schools are financially out of reach, be direct rather than dancing around this important issue.

Anger Is the Voice of Stress in the Frantic Family

Imagine a family where Dad, often gone on business, leaves sixteen-year-old Michael responsible for double the chores, and by default, Mom's companion when she cajoles him into using Dad's symphony ticket. Annoyed, Michael keeps his preference to play basketball to himself lest he have to listen to Mom dwell upon her loneliness. Michael's anger is the voice of stress.

The family might be stuck with Dad's travel, but the parents could realize the burden it creates for Michael. No teenage boy wants to become Mom's regular companion. She needs to call a female friend to use the extra ticket, and hire help or share in the extra chores.

The Frenzy	Paths to Prevent Hidden Anger
Activities	Nothing substitutes talking, problem solving, or sharing dreams, tears, and laughter. Yet, enrichment activities and overcommitted parents prevent outings, vacations, even walks through a park. Your budding gymnast won't lose status nor will your son jeopardize a scholarship if you create family time rather than designate every available moment to their achievements. Limit extracurriculars to two per semester and see the amazing results.
Mealtime rush	Though teens would much rather hang out with their friends, set sacrosanct time for meals and conversation. That the average soccer parent spends more time behind the wheel than at the kitchen table is sad. Mealtime offers an incredible opportunity to discuss daily issues. With discussion, most small problems don't fester into lingering resentments. Meals are not the venue to assign major jobs, chastise about messy rooms, or review report card troubles. Aid digestion, don't impede it. Connections form through calm sharing.
Disconnect	When conversation commences and ends by telephone, text, and e-mail, we miss 50 percent of the message or metacommunication (what words don't convey). The frantic family proclaims by word and action "We'll talk about it later," whereas the committed, expressive family finds time for "What's going on?" or "How was your day?" They touch base and meet eyes. If there's no way around geographic distance, use FaceTime, Skype, and other video programs to maintain some visual contact.

In 2000, researchers at the University of Michigan found only one in three US families dined together, whereas two in three did so in the 1970s. Those children who ate with family showed higher student achievement test scores in addition to better overall health.[5]

A frantic family only focuses when crisis looms; thus, solvable problems go untouched. The only remedy is to slow down. Make family time a priority. Schedule it. When you're together, tone down television, music, and cell phone noise. Take your teenager's headset off her ears and put down your iPad long enough to listen. Few things are more annoying or disrespectful than talking with someone who keeps checking their text messages and e-mails in the middle of that conversation.

Anger Is the Voice of Power in the Angry Family

When children are short-tempered, cynical, or controlling, anger can be very open, deliberate, or concealed, expressing a quest for power where no one ever really wins.

Austin is a typical teen whose main responsibility is to mow the lawn, for which Austin earns twenty dollars weekly. His father ran him through the routine a few times in mid-April. Six weeks later, "I forgot" has ceased to have any advantage.

"Austin, please finish your job," Mom said. "You know you're to sweep up."

"I mowed," Austin replied.

"Please finish the entire job, the way you're supposed to."

"Mom! I'm fixing my guitar. Get off my back."

Doubly frustrated from the disrespect, mom upped the ante. "If you don't go out there right now, young man, you can forget getting paid!"

"Slave wages; now, no wages!"

"Keep it up, Austin." Mom upped the ante even further. "You'll be grounded with no guitar, too."

Austin stormed past her to grab the push broom, yet later that evening, mom sat down in the driver's seat of her car. Grass clippings hugged her heels and the floor of her car.

Austin pushed buttons. While mom asked him nicely the first time or two, this episode led her to mete out discipline with multiple threats. When family members sense the situation is a power play, things can escalate and become counterproductive. Rather, teach kids that no payment will be rendered until the job is completed. Period. Calmly discuss higher wages later, not in the midst of an argument.

The Power	Paths to Prevent Hidden Anger
Barbs and sarcasm	Little barbs and sarcasm mock a person or situation through supposed humor in spiteful remarks, voice intonation, or hostile body language. A hurtful undercurrent frequently feeds upon itself, so listen carefully to your child's exchanges. If the recipient could feel discounted, overlooked, and isolated, pull your child aside or step in if you must to request a "do over" or the aftermath stage of anger. This cleans up angry messes.
Criticism	Talking in hyperbole with words such as "you always" and getting trapped in "why" questions spell criticism; for example, the youngest in the family sets the table and someone grumbles, "Why do you always forget the spoons?" Or, after a brother makes a homemade cake for his girlfriend's birthday, his sourpuss sister remarks, "Is that all the icing you're putting on it? Impressive!" Be specific when calling kids out on their harshness. Telling Sally her behavior was disrespectful is vague; instead say, "Sally, in this family, we don't put one another down. If you have helpful feedback, offer it nicely."
Personal putdowns and contempt	Derogation destroys trust. Putdowns are close cousins to criticism, cutting to a person's attributes, beliefs, character, and knowledge. Labels get lobbed, names called, and fingers literally and verbally pointed with "you did . . ." Putdowns usually derive their sting from an audience, yet sometimes people stash these for private use. Across cultures you see the left lip and face create a dimple. The deliberate attack can create a calamitous climb to counteraggression. Parental or sibling contempt seriously disturbs attachment and security. When parents/teachers spot it, redirect aggressors to express their own feelings/needs and point out the gross neglect of empathy and respect. Stunned parents may become immobilized, but if they fail to address contempt, it's carte blanche to continue.

continues —

— continued

The Power	Paths to Prevent Hidden Anger
Setups and withholding	Withholding info is a roguish tactic to wield power when the withholder can later ask, "Didn't you know?" This sets up a situation to their advantage in order to feel superior. Some consider withholding information right up there with outright dishonesty and lies of omission.
Intimidation	Blatant threats, innuendo, or ultimatums underhandedly exert control: "If you go to her house, we won't be friends." Nastiness disrupts equilibrium and kicks in a fight-or-flight response. Sometimes young people feel trapped, anxious, despondent, even suicidal. When you catch intimidation, you must step in lest others, or your household, be held captive. Reiterate that friends/siblings do not treat each other this way; educate adolescents about coercion and intimidations in friendships and dating relationships.
Hostile body language	Often it's not the content but the hostile sigh or grumble, void of compassion or praise, that sends the bigger message. Habitual kinesthetic hostility eventually becomes insidious, and gets passed down through the generations. Recipients guess what they did or didn't do and why the person is in a huff. Call out body language as teachable moments. While audio/video of oneself is hard to see replayed, viewing oneself motivates behavior change. Only use audio/video playback when you've given fair warning.

Regardless of the power play, it's vital that children and teens learn to express their needs, wants, losses, embarrassments, challenges, and more. Caregivers and teachers can model how to put their own feelings out into the open so that these negatives don't seep back into behavior.

Instead of the critical "I can't believe you forgot the silverware," an older sibling could say, "Thanks for setting the table, but I'm not finding spoons. Could you bring some over please?" It's factually correct, better delivered, and teaches rather than insults.

Other things are better left unsaid, like criticizing someone's best effort. So what if you could make a better pie? If you let someone else enjoy the experience of baking one and serving it to you, celebrate their success (or their attempt). If you have greater skill or knowledge that could come in handy, wouldn't you rather be praised for helping and sharing those talents? Otherwise criticism or copping superiority makes others feel uncomfortable. Sadly, some people do not care how they come across.

Anger Is the Voice of Desire in the Indulged Family

That cell phone, given in elementary school, could save time and make mom or dad available whenever they are needed. That tablet keeps your child busy on car trips or when waiting for older siblings at soccer practice.

Just because you didn't have the benefit of freshly laundered clothes as a kid, what's wrong with doing your young adult's laundry? You're just making life convenient, right? But indulgence is a covert culprit that doesn't help in the long term.

When parents give in to a child's desires or society's pressure, they too often respond out of temporary emotion such as guilt for not being around or sadness that they grew up in poverty. When your child needles you and you relent to such requests, you may set him up for a life of limited coping and zero tolerance for the words *no*, *wait*, or *not right now*. Where anger is hidden by indulgence, there's no demarcated boundary. Parental

The Indulgence	Paths to Prevent Hidden Anger
Not saying "no"	"If only" the young child in the grocery store checkout could have that candy bar. "That's not where I wanted to go on vacation," one boy demands. "Most in the senior class apply to out-of-state schools. Don't you want me to have a quality education and get a job?" your daughter might cajole. And then there's "I have better things to do than make my lunch. Just give me money for Burger King across from school."
Techno overwhelm	Phones, laptops, tablet computers, music devices, watches that do it all, video game components, elaborate surround sound systems, and the largest flat screen have become battlegrounds. "Other kids have TV's in their bedrooms," your daughter mumbles, and another parent's son bargains for more pixels and laptop megabytes—not for graphic arts, but for goofy YouTube videos or to conquer the world in the latest video games.

continues —

— continued

Too much, too fast	Decades ago, teen driving was indeed a right of passage, but owning a car? Wi-Fi is a convenience until children are left with gadgets and unrestricted Internet access. Children come to counseling when parents suspect they've been exposed to questionable material, were propositioned on-line, or are sexually active because of risqué selfies found on their phones. These same parents might haplessly turn over an open device to a youngster rather than a kids' book when the child has idle moments to spare. If this seems like you, develop limits and parental controls, and stick to them.
	Kids who work a part-time job, save their money, and show respect for someone else's possessions (the family vehicle) learn adult responsibilities. When children hone the social skills of getting along, interacting well while playing a board game, or carrying on a conversation, they may be ready for a telephone to check in after school. We do not recommend cell phones in elementary school. If there's an extraordinary need for communication, then provide only a simple device that dials calls and does nothing else.

indulgence often takes on one of three forms—surrender, confusion, or spoiling.

Parents too often surrender to keep the peace or maintain a connection they so desperately want with their child. They might act confused, as if leaving a child's request unfulfilled is somehow harmful or unhealthy. Spoiling equates to lavish gifts and permissiveness. Those parents who have overindulged should make a concerted effort to change their parenting style and distinguish their own conflicts from the child's true needs.

HOW MODERN CULTURE BREEDS HIDDEN ANGER

As a new generation enters child-rearing age, some news outlets have bemoaned a culture of digitally native parents, trophy-saturated kids, abundantly Facebook-friended moms and dads who have fallen into crowd-sourcing for advice. Parents don't wait any longer to send out that hospital-generated first photo; they post it on Instagram seconds after the child's birth. Out with helicopter parenting, in with drone-style attitudes—that is, one-third hovering with two-thirds following everyone else's lead, including their child's. What's wrong with this picture?

You have one opportunity—only one—to influence your child, so don't squander it comparing your path to anyone else's progress. Live your values, and value the lives you have!

In *Overloaded and Underprepared*, the authors recommend free play (even for teens) and for parents and teachers to emphasize face-to-face interaction rather than social media. They suggest parents remove all social media devices from bedrooms at night and to keep this activity in monitored rooms at all times.[6]

In *Beyond Measure: Rescuing an Overscheduled, Overtested, Underestimated Generation*, Vicki Abels reports that American teens get at least two hours less sleep nightly than what is recommended: one-third of high schoolers sleep five or six hours on an average school night.[7] Published findings from the American Academy of Pediatrics and the National Sleep Foundation support this, some naming homework, extracurriculars, and social networking as culprits of a healthy night's rest.[8]

Stanford researchers recently found that too much homework is associated with greater stress, health consequences (headaches, exhaustion, sleep deprivation, weight loss, stomach problems), and less time for family, friends, and extracurriculars.[9] This empirical evidence showed how many young people feel obligated to choose hours of homework,[10] which prior research has suggested plateaus at about two hours per night,[11] over developing other talents, skills, or fun pursuits.

And while this point may prove unpopular with most kids, we know that children who help out at home succeed better in life. A 2008 University of Maryland study found that kids six to twelve years of age spent only twenty-four minutes a day helping around the house, a 25 percent decline from 1981.[12] Dr. Marilynn "Marty" Rossman at the University of Minnesota concluded in a 2002 study that young adults who began chores at ages three and four were more likely to have good relationships, achieve academic and early career success, and become more self-sufficient, compared to those who delayed having chores until their teens.[13] Compare this to a Braun Research survey, cited in *The Wall Street Journal*, that 82 percent of adults reportedly did regular chores in their youth, but only 28 percent require their own kids to do them.[14]

How is it that so many parents and school systems believe that yet one more AP class or a higher SAT score will spawn success, when these and other studies have shown this isn't the case? Yes, we should nurture achievements that contribute to a child's growth and goal attainment, but we need to do it in ways that teach them how to be flexible and self-assured.

PARENTS WHO GIVE MIXED MESSAGES = KIDS WHO DO SO ALSO

Erika had just finished her last college semester. Move-out day was bittersweet, but finishing her degree early after she studied abroad one summer, she upheld her bargain. Moving back home, Erika would find a job and save up for her master's degree.

As she said a tearful goodbye to her roommate, mom Juliette smiled before saying, "I just couldn't convince her to stay. It's not like she didn't have money available from her grandmother's estate."

Erika had no idea that extra funds might make grad school an immediate option. She had gotten the impression that her mom didn't recognize the need for higher credentials; today she felt embarrassed and confused. Did Mom resent Erika for going to college when she admitted she hadn't been able to herself?

Since we're proponents of the "do over," let's explore this situation's options:

1. If Juliette had mixed emotions about her daughter eclipsing her with education, Juliette could have smiled as if she was proud but lied through her pearly white teeth.

    NOT a good option! Lies of omission build. Chronic lying gets established in one's youth when a child grows up with an authoritarian parenting style steeped in punitive, callous communication and caretakers who dismiss emotion with hardhearted words or actions. Not wishing to face further wrath, a child continues this deceitful pattern to escape severe judgment, to feel less inferior, and to create stories where she'll be appreciated. By adulthood, this attention-seeking habit reinforces itself such that little lies get shrugged off as seemingly harmless. This predisposition toward telling untruths invades other pivotal relationships.

2. Juliette could have been up-front about how bittersweet it was to watch her daughter get ahead, by saying "Erika, I'm so proud of you. I'd always dreamed of going to college. I'm glad you could." Of course, this takes self-awareness and the ability to be vulnerable.

3. Juliette could prepare to find fulfillment during these empty-nest times or see a therapist if it truly caused an inner struggle. When a parent embarrasses her child due to her own jealousy, it may be worth exploring the extent to which they are enmeshed.

Erika's developmental task as a young adult is to differentiate herself from her family of origin—find herself, determine her values, and learn to express all of this in thoughtful, nonreactive ways. Erika would be wise to tell her mother "I felt blindsided by your revelation of grandmother's funds. If I could have used those for my master's, I feel you should have told me sooner."

Note the "I messages" and attempts to clean up any hurt feelings. Yet proper, calm assertiveness is no guarantee that Juliette would accept the message well. If Juliette further guilted her daughter with "I missed you so much and was afraid you wouldn't come home," she's lobbing her own emotional struggles onto Erika. Were Juliette to suggest that they figure out a plan, this could work (sidestepping enmeshment) so long as proper boundaries and differentiation occured. Finally, if Mom mocked or mimicked Erika by saying "Stop with how you feel . . ." or completely disregarded her daughter by declaring "I don't care what you want . . ." these exchanges signify deeper communication and psychological deficits to address.

six

Sabotaged Romance and Relationships

O NE DAY AT WORK, TOM GOT A CALL FROM HIS WIFE, SARAH.

"It's been a tough day. What do you say we go out to dinner to-night?" Sarah asked.

"I'm not sure when I'm going to get home," Tom said. "You go on with-out me."

"But I usually dine alone. Can't we do something together?"

"Look," Tom said. "I'm in the middle of something and you interrupted me again. I have to go. I'll see you later." And at that, Tom hung up.

Sarah called back right away. At the implication that her calling was a regular habit (which it was not), she was now even more annoyed, but Tom just let the call go straight to voicemail.

In this chapter, we'll reveal negative undercurrents in relationships like Sarah and Tom's.

SURPRISING BENEFITS OF DOMESTIC BLISS

According to sociologist Linda J. Waite and researcher Maggie Gallagher in *The Case for Marriage*, "The evidence from four decades of research is surprisingly clear: A good marriage is the best bet for living a long and healthy life."[1] Many scientific studies record the links between marital status and one's well-being.[2]

But findings presented at the annual meeting of the American Psychological Association in 2004 revealed that a lousy marriage can make you feel . . . well, sick. Negative spousal behaviors such as excessive demands or criticism seem to increase the likelihood of developing ongoing health problems.[3] So while there are plenty of positive effects to be gained from marriage, being in one that's troubled can do more harm than good.

Carried resentment, buried emotion, and unresolved issues cost a hefty price, bankrupting our spirits, our loved one's disposition, maybe even our bank accounts. When people get caught in the cycle of rejection, resentment, and revenge, sometimes their anger wells up to the point where they experience visceral reactions—noticeable anxiety such as a fight-or-flight response, a rapid heartbeat, or other somatic symptoms—when they must deal with a manipulative or self-absorbed spouse or significant other. When the behavior escalates, this becomes emotional abuse.

Researchers have also studied how our genetic makeup influences the quality of our relationships and how both will affect us. This "gene by environment interaction" means that our DNA makes us genetically predisposed to certain things. Let's say you inherit an anger trait, but if you grow up in a loving, emotionally open home, that trait never gets activated. Surrounded by irritability and yelling, however, this same trait runs on overdrive. People in happier marriages were also healthier, yet in a rather revealing finding called the "orchid effect" (because ideal conditions are required to thrive), genetics contributed to overall health at the highest and lowest levels of marital satisfaction.[4]

HOW TO SPOT WHEN YOU'RE OUT OF SYNC

If you're still a little unsure of where you stand in your relationship—that is, if your style conflicts with that of your partner—answer these questions:

1. Do you criticize that which first attracted you to your partner?
2. Does it feel as if competition or rivalry has set in?

3. Do you have trouble committing your angry feelings to not-so-angry words?
4. Do you know what emotional buttons you shouldn't push on your spouse, but sometimes do anyway?
5. Have you felt that your needs regularly take a back seat to your partner's?
6. Do you ever feel as if your spouse had a blow or revelation coming; therefore, you don't quite wince when incidents occur, as you mentally think he or she deserved to be uncomfortable, even knowing how hurt he or she must feel?
7. Are there fewer meaningful conversations and is there little room left for laughter?
8. Have simple courtesies seemingly vanished?
9. Does much less affection fill the space between you?
10. Has a sense of dread taken over where once anticipation filled any time spent apart?

The more times you answered "yes," the more concerned you should be. Let this raise your awareness of the importance of building communication skills and strategies when coping with frustrating emotions.

WHERE IS THE LOVE?

Wouldn't it be wonderful during the courting stage to see in skywriting such as "Speed bumps with mother issues!" or "Dangerous curve: disengaged partner!"

We project into the future what we hope the relationship will be, but if we don't accept the other person as he is, adapt to new information we gain about him, and nurture his growth, our hopes will be dashed. Albert Einstein is credited with the insight that "men marry women with the hope they will never change, and women marry men with the hope they will change. Invariably both are disappointed." How true! It's simply unwise to view a significant other as "a project."

Premarital counseling can be very useful as you identify issues that incite arguments and learn about a partner's background. This is one of the most important emotional commitments you will make. Don't be afraid to do it right. People spend tens of thousands of dollars on a wedding—one day in their lives—while amazingly little, if any, investment goes toward premarital counseling, education, or relationship skills. If you spot an opportunity, through your house of worship or in a private practice or seminar, sign up. View it as a wise investment in your relationship, even after you've marched back up the aisle.

A lack of education about and poor preparation for marriage are certainly factors in hidden relationship anger and divorces today. In the excitement of new love, optimism that runs wild, and feel-good hormones, people become blinded. Even when a paramour has one foot in, one foot out of the relationship, we may gloss over ambivalence we don't wish to see. Hidden anger also takes root on account of unrealistic expectations, hopes of changing the other person, or altering a regretful relationship history.

HOW HIDDEN ANGER SURFACES

Tracy and Joe, in their late twenties, have been married a year. They knew each other pretty well, but as time went by, the individual way they each processed daily annoyances crept between them. Wisely, they decided upon counseling.

Tracy shared how they were not on the same page. While they both had established the goal of saving for a house down payment, Joe disparaged her for living frugally. He mocked her in front of his parents, like a little boy tattling to mom. When it was his turn to speak, Joe dubbed Tracy as too sensitive and questioned why she wanted to reinvent holiday traditions when his family's traditions worked just fine. Tracy added the point that she had silently tolerated these traditions, but that the holidays they shared never really bore their joint identity.

Tracy may not have recognized it, but she described a lack of differentiation, a therapy concept where one is too emotionally drawn to his/her original family at the expense of the new union created. Undifferentiated individuals (less emotionally mature) absorb a lot of stress from their more emotional relatives. Marriages and partnerships suffer if one or both people are more enmeshed or fused because they borrow trouble from extended family members when they likely have enough of their own. Anger concealers such as Joe refuse to cut the apron strings at the expense of adult independence, and here it is at the cost of a warm, connected marriage.

As minor as this couple's complaints may sound, these incidents add up, provoke ire, and further incite resentment when they are trivialized with brush-off phrases such as "she's too sensitive" or rigidity with "we've always done it this way." Left unchecked, Joe and Tracy will get stuck and live a rather dishonest relationship.

When you get right down to it, many couples quarrel about little things that aren't worth the argument. Yet when bigger problems occur (unpaid bills, fender benders), they haven't developed a skill set for forgiveness and working together.

FAMILY INFLUENCES US

Murray Bowen, MD, worked with families at the Menninger Clinic in Kansas and at the National Institute of Mental Health in the 1950s, and continued his research with families at Georgetown University. Bowen embraced a radically different view of emotional functioning, seeing the family as the pivotal influence, with behaviors passing down through the generations. All families, he found, traveled along a continuum with emotional fusion (more closeness than normal) on one end of the spectrum and differentiation (independence) at the other end.

Most of us leave our families at a time (late adolescence) in which we're gaining the outward appearance of independence and learning to exist emotionally on our own. Young adults transform their parental relationships. Too often it is not a *fait accompli* by the time they pack their bags and set up their first apartment. An undifferentiated person hasn't accomplished all of this independence. Consequently, when situations arise, he responds with more emotion and less self-control, especially around issues that raise anxiety. Quite simply, our original family installs our emotional buttons, and if we don't free ourselves of that intense influence, they remain in possession of the remote control. As adults, we may react with the same level of adolescent petulance we did when we were teens if they or others push our buttons. This fits with the research that says that passive-aggression is an immature reaction.[5] Even grown, well-established people can react this way.

continues —

— continued

Bowen posited that people tend to choose mates who are similarly undifferentiated or emotionally reactive. When we talk about keeping hidden anger at bay, this means that if two people who have not gained a fair degree of emotional independence marry, there may be problems, or at least some work, transforming important relationships. Roberta M. Gilbert, MD, writes in *Extraordinary Relationships* that people at lower levels of differentiation have greater difficulty making decisions because they choose more out of emotion than out of thoughtfulness. This stems from an inordinate concern over being loved and accepted, and when people are worried more about what people think of them and less about what they truly want, relationships are more difficult.[6]

FINDING THE LOVE AND SUPPORT YOU NEED

What if Joe had some valid points as they continued counseling? To Joe, Tracy appeared to be bossy. Whether she was or wasn't, appearance is everything. If Tracy came from a family lacking in warmth, she might have had high hopes for the new start she established. Joe certainly shouldn't embarrass his wife, but instead should smooth the way for her with his family. This would reveal how important Tracy is to him. Their marriage would also be stronger if he could look at Tracy's intent and see what comes across to him as negative (her wanting them to adopt new traditions) as positive.

Tracy might be a very direct and linear person, with a plan in mind to get from one point to another, evident in the way she thinks as well as in her conversations. Joe's process might be more indirect, as seen by his making wisecracks rather than directly communicating a point. Tracy may need to lighten up a bit, or it could be that Joe makes jokes to avoid discussing certain topics or to steer clear of anything unpleasant. The problem is that marriage and partnership require a bit of surrender, each person allowing him- or herself to become more vulnerable to the other person. Their styles are clashing here, and that's gotten Joe and Tracy stuck.

In *Getting the Love You Want*, Harville Hendrix, PhD, explores the theory that while you might think that men and women would look for the opposite of what they had in an unhappy childhood, most people are attracted to mates with a mixture of their caretakers' positive *and* negative traits.[7] Of course, the negative ones grab our attention far more readily. As Hendrix found, there is a close correlation between the traits in one's partners and the traits in one's parents. We gravitate toward the old order or conditions similar to those of our upbringing so that we have a second chance to make things right.

Anger can set in when one partner places undue expectations for getting it "right" or believes that a spouse will satisfy all emotional needs. That's simply setting the bar too high. One person's expectations are left unfulfilled. This is also the case when partners can't admit the error of using passive-aggressive behavior because it appears to be a more "civil" way of dealing with one another, however misguided this is. Remember, passive-aggressive people vacillate between wanting to be dependent and wanting to be independent. During those dependent times, partners surely don't want to risk "offending" a spouse. So, they conceal their feelings.

KEEPING HIDDEN ANGER OUT OF YOUR MARRIAGE

John Gottman, PhD, founder of The Gottman Institute, is also a noted author and relationship researcher. Through years of analyzing the interactions of married couples, Gottman has applied hard science to the understanding of loving relationships. He and his colleagues have developed a mathematical model that predicts a couple's potential for divorce. While couples discussed money or annoying habits, he recorded data such as heart rate and perspiration, and observed their language, mannerisms, and responses. Within minutes, Gottman's team found that if the ratio of positive to negative behavior and communication stayed at five to one, the couple was likely to have a happy future. They called this "positive sentiment override." Displays of contempt, defensiveness, criticism, withdrawal, or the use of diminishing language or behavior predicted shorter longevity of the union.[8] Gottman has also identified "Four Horsemen of the Apocalypse," four negative communication styles that when they appear, must be addressed. Gottman's research reveals that the chronic presence of these four factors—criticism, contempt, defensiveness, and stonewalling—may often predict, with approximately 94 percent accuracy, which couples will eventually divorce.[9]

Gottman does not believe in the term *constructive criticism*. While it's healthy to discuss disagreements candidly, attacking character and personality are off limits. "You're so selfish" could be communicated much more effectively with "I really feel that comment was one-sided." Expressing one's feelings in "I messages" and directing comments toward a behavior are gold standards of communication.

Contempt, more complex than criticism, involves tearing another person down and taking a superior attitude. It is quintessential passive-aggressive behavior that manifests in sarcasm, name-calling, mockery, eye rolling, or other angry body language. It's the greatest predictor of relationship failure, according to Gottman. The antidote to contempt is respect and appreciation. Defensiveness stems from righteous indignation or playing the victim.[10] To overcome this, one must accept one's own responsibility for all or a portion of the conflict. Finally, the first three horsemen contribute to stonewalling, the last one, where a partner withdraws rather than works through to overcome conflict. Instead of pulling out of the relationship in this way, Gottman suggests taking a short break, calming down, and then continuing a discussion.

Recall the Murphy/Oberlin Four Types of Families that create anger; the same types lead to unhappiness in a couple. Whether troubled, frantic, angry, or indulging, the prescription for steering your relationship to happier interaction rests in a few frequently forgotten tips. Happy couples:

- Appreciate opportunities to communicate. They don't shy away from conflict, stuff emotions, or hide matters, hoping these will mysteriously vanish.
- Listen without comment, avoiding knee-jerk reactions made out of a defensive posture. They quell the desire to interrupt, realizing they'll each get a turn.
- Express appreciation for a spouse's honesty and willingness to share. When partners reflect what the other has said, they demonstrate true understanding—that they "got it."
- Show interest in the other's feelings and consider new opinions, especially their partner's. No black-and-white, all-or-nothing thinking here. To solve a problem, happy couples see shades of gray

and develop a middle ground. They accept differences for what they are — differences in thought, not attacks upon the person.

- Express empathy through words, body language, and behavior.
- Hold foolish words and surly behavior in check. They express matters openly using "I" statements, engaging the other party, not withdrawing or isolating or venting frustration to show displeasure (e.g., by slamming doors or using sarcasm).
- Respect individual boundaries, physical as well as emotional.
- Watch out for unresolved issues. Red flags: When your partner becomes silent, harsh, or defensive in response to a fairly benign remark. Give-up lines like "It's no use talking to you" or "Oh, never mind" are also tip-offs.
- Convey pride for each other's achievements and concern for hardships. Honor boundaries such as knowing when to gently tease and when teasing is hurtful.
- Find time for one another, including unscheduled moments to read the Sunday paper, enjoy recreation, or take care of household errands or chores together.
- Share their lives but don't rely upon a spouse to be one's life or only fulfillment. Each finds satisfaction independent of the marriage.

Obviously, a relationship under job stress, illness, the strain of lingering issues, or during the parenting years has less stamina to endure frustration. The words *over time* from our description of hidden anger can remind couples to live genuinely in *every* moment so that positive behavior prevails.

IRRATIONAL BELIEFS ABOUT CONFLICT

As we have unveiled, people who hide their anger often fear and avoid conflict. In a successful marriage, conflict indeed has its place.

In a 1989 study published in the *Journal of Consulting and Clinical Psychology,* John Gottman and Lowell Krokoff found that disagreement over the long term of a relationship is not harmful. Quite the contrary, it's a withdrawal from conflict as well as continued defensiveness and inflexibility that lead to the demise of many marriages.[11]

continues —

— continued

Expressing one's heartfelt feelings may be uncomfortable, maybe even painful, but if they are honestly expressed (or at least not expressed inappropriately) so that the partner can tolerate them, this adds to the strength and health of the marriage. Research conducted by Donald H. Baucom at the University of North Carolina, Norman Epstein at the University of Maryland, and their colleagues found that when both partners avoided contact, they may have protected each other directly, but the act of avoidance had other negative effects upon their intimacy and marital satisfaction.[12]

ANGRY COUPLE DYNAMICS AND RESOLUTIONS

Conflict happens. If one partner shies away from it while the other faces situations head-on, you can see the inherent struggle. Too often it leaves real indecision, loneliness, jealousy, or other uncomfortable feelings. Powerful emotions leak out, without our even knowing it, causing tremendous hurt in those we love and care for.

EMOTIONAL DISTANCE AND PURSUIT

When one partner craves closeness and more conversation while the other needs substantial alone time, therein may lie misunderstanding. Historically, women desire closeness, men more distance. While we refrain from stereotypes, we recognize that men's and women's brains are wired differently. Women often include more emotional input in their thinking. They have, at times, an innate ability to access many more words, far faster, than most men retrieve. Men's thinking is more targeted and linear, goal directed on specific accomplishments and the data needed to get there. When pushed to discuss problems that they haven't fully thought through, men may shut down, back away, or wait it out until they're ready to deal with the request or demand.

Women are more comfortable with their emotional data while men may want to offer the logical solution and move on. She says, "I just want you to listen to me." He interrupts with, "Here's what you need to do" as a truly caring offer, yet she gets upset that he interrupted. He's frustrated because she keeps talking about her feelings and isn't fixing her dilemma. Each is right; each is frustrated. Each may even think that the other acted this way to make misery. Hence, they stop and walk away from one another.

This can look passive-aggressive when it's really a matter of timing, process, and maybe even neurology. Give the same man time to gather his thoughts, and he may become a far better communicator next time around. Give her time to see that his solutions to her problem show that he cares about her, and she just might find real value in his offer. Time can breech the chasm of distance.

Here too, women should explore their unrealistic expectations of men. Women validate each other through conversation, sharing an interest in similar subjects, browsing, shopping, or exchanging kind gestures. Men swap stories of experiences, actions, conflicts, and accomplishments. So often when a man and woman are caught in some sort of pursuer–distancer dynamic, a woman thinks if she keeps after him, he'll get the message. Instead, he might grab his fishing pole and tackle and head to the river!

FANTASY VERSUS REALITY

Realizing her need for companionship, a woman is better off showing her husband that she has a fulfilling life and rewarding work. Better yet, she could go off with a good novel or on a weekend getaway with gal pals, for this sends a stronger message and allows him to ultimately approach her instead of her requesting closeness. Ladies: make him think togetherness is *his* idea! Men: give her some time together in exchange for time to do things with your friends. Will this paradoxical tactic always work? Of course not. Nothing is foolproof, but this does work with some couples.

Too often partners erroneously think that a mate completes them when in fact two strong, solid selves accompany each other to and through relationship success. Fantasy is the thought that you can change a partner; in reality you realize you can only change yourself.

THE TOO CONTENT AND THE NEVER SATISFIED

Nagging or distancing could reflect a profound passive-aggressive tussle. True intimacy requires a degree of vulnerability and sharing as well as the ability to receive 100 percent of a loved one's true self. That means the rose-colored images as well as the murkier ones. When people grapple with their own self-concepts, their relationships seem less stable. That's why we cannot stress enough the concept of working on yourself (as opposed to trying to fix another person).

THE DOERS AND THE DEPENDENTS

Marriage or any intimate relationship often equates to the final surrender for a person harboring hidden anger. In psychology, there is the phenomenon of overfunctioning and underfunctioning, a type of reciprocity where one person in a union does quite well, often happily in contrast to the struggle and melancholy of the other. As Roberta Gilbert outlines in *Extraordinary Relationships*, "One is the teller, the other the listener; one the preacher, one the congregation." She points out that usually both parties agree that one of them does well, and that the dysfunction rests with the other, yet few couples know readily how to break the patterns.[13]

Overfunctioners must lessen advice giving, worrying about the other, having goals for others that they don't have for themselves, and ultimately feeling responsible and knowing what's best. By contrast, underfunctioners need to up the game for themselves, follow through on goals, gain skills, become mentally and physically healthier, treat addictions, plus think more independently. Each partner remains caught in this process, Gilbert notes, reminding us what family systems theory tells us about differentiation and emotional maturity. The unhealthy habits of overfunctioners show up, however, when their responsibilities for two (or more) lives turn to burnout or stress.[14]

Scott Wetzler and Leslie Morey expressed their views of this dynamic: "The passive-aggressive individual is caught between dependency, which they resent, and autonomy, which they fear. They want others to think that they are not dependent, but such people bind themselves closer to others than they care to admit. They foster dependency and then struggle against it because they feel controlled and vulnerable, feeling trapped when they are expected to express intimate feelings."[15]

In their 1996 book, the late Theodore Millon and Roger Davis wrote that being unpredictable and discontented—another form of distancing—produces certain secondary gains. "A negativistic man, who is unwilling or unable to decide whether to 'grow up' or remain a 'child,' explodes emotionally whenever his wife expects 'too much' of him. Afterward, he expresses guilt, becomes contrite, and pleads forbearance on her part."[16] If you see this type of behavior, it's manipulative because it essentially halts any additional requests (seen as demands) and affects the ultimate need as the outcome—to be left alone.

To be fair to both genders, women can also contribute to these unpleasant and passive-aggressive dynamics. Once some men show their softer, more emotional sides, some women resent them for no longer being the alpha males that protect and defend them. A woman may have set up a scenario, resenting the man for a situation she helped place him in, with the attitude of "If you can't stand up to me, how will you protect me in the big, bad world?" The man, who dared to become vulnerable and surrender a bit of himself, now doubts his ability to get the role quite right—the one she expected him to play. Though typically more verbal, women can also show their disdain quite indirectly through the hostile sigh or nonverbal cue that leaves men chagrined.

Remember Joe and Tracy? Less caught up pleasing their families of origin, they should discern their own values (not someone else's), cherish what the two of them did together, and back each other.

THE FINANCIALLY STRESSED

Money, the way it validates us and influences our daily decisions, affects couples. Quite simply, it often equates to power, and therein lies the proverbial battle. When secretly annoyed, money becomes a weapon to wage war upon partners, to "one up" or prove a point.

One partner may accrue much shopping-spree debt unbeknownst to their spouse. When the bills come and the credit-card collectors start calling, the spender feigns ignorance, not understanding how things got so bad.

Money can even become the sword that never directly touches one's hands. Take the couple who remodeled their kitchen. They thought they had selected all the cabinet components and colors, but when the wife changed the countertop and backsplash selections (without consulting her husband), she held him captive in a color and design scheme with his least favorite choices. Every morning, he poured his coffee surrounded by constant reminders that his wife had her way over his. In order to fix it, he'd have to cough up another $6,000.

Couples must establish mutual goals early and routinely discuss where they are financially and what may have changed due to career changes, job layoffs, taking time off to raise the children, or some other unexpected scenario.

IRRITABILITY IN MEN AND WOMEN

Jed Diamond, author of *Male Menopause* and *The Irritable Male Syndrome*, surveyed nearly ten thousand males between the ages of ten and seventy-five, finding irritability in various forms. In three of the seven types he identified, a passive-aggressive style was present with primary behaviors such as impatience, blame, frustration, hypersensitivity, moodiness, and just plain being grumpy. "These males often have a lot of anger and rage but are trying to hold it back," Diamond says. "The result is that it comes out in indirect ways . . . They can also be quite explosive, seemingly over small slights." Additionally, these men face consequences in the form of high blood pressure, diabetes, obesity, and erectile dysfunction. Diamond believes that men need to recognize this emotional pain and anger instead of blaming them on others in order to regain control of their own lives and feelings.[17]

THOSE IN CRISES

When spouses shut each other out emotionally, they're ill-equipped to handle urgent situations that demand their attention, whether it's a sudden job loss, a family member's illness, a child who gets into trouble, or merely a child who needs more of their collective attention because of social, educational, or health-related concerns. Having a sickly baby significantly increases the chance that a father will walk out, according to a report published in *Demography* in 2004, where Nancy Reichman and her colleagues at Robert Wood Johnson Medical School in New Jersey described their study of the families of three thousand newborns.[18] Four to five years later, two other studies tracked families where parents with children who had been diagnosed with autism spectrum disorder or ADHD broke up, with divorce rates 10 percent and twice as high with these situations, respectively.[19]

Similar relationship fractures occur when a child is diagnosed with disabilities after birth. For whatever reasons, women typically endure the strain. Men might feel that they have failed somehow, deny what's really happening, and resist being supportive based out of that denial. So, too, we've seen couples come together with previously unknown emotional and spiritual strength under the same circumstances.

Children with disabilities often consume much of the couple's energy, finances, and free time. Parents of children with autism spectrum disorder reveal how heartbreaking it is to forgo vacations or an evening out because no one among family or friends wants to take on the responsibility that special-needs children require. Some must make difficult choices, opting for residential placement to save themselves from overwhelming stress. For some, a child's issues make them talk more and focus on things that bring them closer rather than those that divide.

In already troubled marriages, crisis unearths further problems that have been stuffed into the closet and never resolved. Lacking problem-solving and communication skills, new burdens have the power to seize any remaining energy the couple has left, so that they further attack one another rather than rally around a common cause.

Mental illness is another such crisis. Research from the University of Colorado at Boulder revealed that when one spouse endures depression, both spouses report an unsatisfying, unhappy marriage.[20] The more intractable the condition, the more the relationship suffered. If this sounds like you, seek help from a qualified professional to counsel you individually or as part of couple's therapy. If one partner feels coerced, awareness probably won't result, and worse yet, he or she may prolong therapy to frustrate a spouse, run up debt, or receive attention with no real motivation toward change. Some less-than-willing patients may select the least competent therapist or agency, further stall progress, and/or avoid realities they'd rather keep concealed.

THE JEALOUS OR UNFAITHFUL

Where hidden anger lurks in a marriage and communication has broken down, jealousy and entitlement set in. Even in what we look upon as good unions, as the late Shirley Glass, PhD, noted, marriages become vulnerable to affairs. Glass, who with Jean Coppock Shaeheli wrote Not "Just Friends," discussed how infidelity can sometimes reflect an ensuing power struggle. Certainly there are many reasons behind straying from one's vows, including power, neglect, or giving up on the commitment, but when there is an ensuing power struggle, the affair is attempted, however foolishly, to correct the perceived imbalance. Whereas the spouse with more financial wherewithal, personality, or the better job feels entitled to indulge him or herself, the less powerful partner, Glass writes, may also attempt to even the score.[21]

When this happens, expect that the unfaithful spouse will be filled with negative self-talk, rationalize actions, project blame, and often feel more entitled. Not a lot of introspection takes place at this stage. We would call this a truly troubled family/couple. Not surprisingly, work on the true problem ceases; concealing the affair or other acting-out behavior often becomes the priority.

Infidelity is often less about sexual satisfaction and much more a barometer of other emotions, including hidden anger built upon unrealistic expectations, beliefs, or fears. In What Makes Love Last? John Gottman points to research suggesting that the vast majority of affairs are not caused by lust. "If the relationship is satisfying both partners' emotional needs, they build a wide fence around these lustful thoughts," he writes. If the trust metric is low, however, he advises couples to talk about brief attractions to others. This doesn't have to be done in a callous way. Gottman advises honest and productive statements, such as "I do sometimes notice other women. I think it's because we haven't been talking or having sex much, and it's starting to get to me. I miss you. I miss us."[22]

Infidelity can also arise from one's depressive or impulsive symptoms. Being intimate with someone else puts distance between the betrayer and the spouse, and the truly promiscuous partner, afraid of revealing too much in a committed relationship, has significant trust and vulnerability issues. Infidelity can also be fueled by one or both partners' inability to admit a failed and totally mismatched relationship. Rather than solve their conflicts or separate, they remain bound in their joint misery. They may stay together, as miserable as they are, because they cannot stand to be alone. They see the hurt they endure (and often ignore) from each other as preferable to loneliness. And they are tempted into a whole host of behaviors that hide the hurt.

As one partner spends time in Internet chat rooms or views pornography in a compulsive way, that partner tunes out of the relationship, looking away from rather than to the relationship, not honestly attempting to salvage it. Two partners who view erotic material together to rejuvenate their intimate life are working positively to change their relationship. One partner who uses erotic material as a distraction from a failing relationship is displaying destructive, compulsive behavior. If the intent is to "get back" at your spouse because you carry a grudge, clearly it's wrong. John Gottman's research points out that overuse of porn creates distance, diminishes intimacy, and makes negative comparisons. Oxytocin and vasopressin, male hormones that fuel emotional connection, then bond more to images, thus lowering the erotic value of one's real-life partner. Viewing porn serves as a ladder toward actual straying.[23] Rather than put energy into one's marriage, this person saps energy from it through such undermining.

Discuss your needs, expectations, turn-ons, and turn-offs. Together. Don't have the conversation with yourself! Passive-aggressive partners want to be both in and out of the relationship. They depend upon their partner, yet feel entitled to their own way as well.

When any type of unfaithful, discreet behavior becomes the epicenter of punitive actions, the anger will only flourish when the truth is revealed, even becoming much more overt (e.g., in outbursts), at least for a period of time.

Expect more strain when trust has been broken, because it needs to be earned back. For reconciliation to work, both parties must work to strengthen their relationship and overcome their own problems. In other words, if a spouse discovers evidence of a cyberaffair, he now becomes more reactive, distrustful, and vigilant (with good reason, given what's been lost). This, in turn, annoys the passive-aggressive partner, who further pulls away because this now "proves" the irrational beliefs at the core of her mind-set. Negative self-talk takes over, and it becomes self-perpetuating until the cycle is broken. Playing victim is always easier than becoming the mender or problem solver.

OTHER ESCAPES

When frustration festers, spouses act out of character. Sometimes, if there is awareness and an open attitude, one party might only need to say, "That's not like you. What's really going on?" Other times, that suppressed anger could spiral and self-destruct with addictive behavior, alcoholism, or substance abuse, as well as produce avoidant conduct (e.g., Internet addiction with or without cyberaffairs) and workaholism, where the person finds more meaning at the office than at home.

While affairs are obvious examples of extramarital triangles, disenfranchised spouses often triangle in other substitutes: hobbies, workaholism, food, possessions, second businesses, for instance. Sometimes the mere act of letting go of one's self-control and body image is a passive-aggressive, distancing act. The person who can't honestly communicate that she wants out of a relationship might not take care of herself, gaining significant weight and becoming less desirous of any sexual advances. It's a roundabout, indirect way of saying "Not tonight. I have a headache" when there really is none. It's a silent withdrawal that leaves her partner confused, still searching for explanations.

When self-destructive behavior sets in—manifesting in drug or alcohol use, gambling, pornography, or leading a double life—dysfunctional patterns are clearly more entrenched, and it will take much more than a self-help book to overcome them. If there isn't anger driving the behavior in some way, it will be there in the clean-up stage as guilt or self-blame sets in, though you shouldn't avoid this aftermath phase. The real issues that triggered such conduct need to be addressed. Sometimes these preoccupations stem from an inability to love and/or be loved.

Finally, anger-concealing partners use silent escapes to cope with ordinary life transitions. When baby makes three, some wives use the child to keep their husbands away (and then complain that he's not a family man), or the demands of parenthood overwhelm a husband so that he feels he's competing with his own child for his wife's attention. According to Scott Wetzler, these conflicts about being a parent, at least to some degree, can mirror a man's conflict with his own father.[24]

HEALING AN ANGRY MARRIAGE

When spouses are unhappy, they're more likely to attribute the difficulty to some negative trait, attaching the label of "lazy," "irresponsible," or "selfish" to whatever bothers them. Each spouse gradually projects the blame elsewhere. Instead of admitting with any awareness that they contribute to the problem, they enhance it. This stymies meaningful change and their chances of growing closer. One of the cruelest passive-aggressive actions is to just stop trying. Without effort things continue to slouch into mediocrity. Little things that attracted you to one another turn into big annoyances. Emotional aggravation feeds the self-fulfilling prophecy of "it's not worth the effort."

Any relationship worth having is worth the effort of not being so angry. Healing bitter feelings and resentments takes forgiveness, learning to fight fairly (even for the fight-phobic), commitment to change . . . and just plain commitment. Where compromise is a true art form, commitment helps you to resolve difficulties rather than run from or ignore them. Remember that there's an ebb and flow in most any relationship. Reread this chapter, this book, periodically. If you learn and practice what we've shared, you might just see your relationship dreams become a reality.

seven

Underhanded Battlegrounds in Divorce

T HE DYSFUNCTIONAL DANCE DIVORCING PARTIES ENGAGE IN CONTINU-
ally confounds people. Why can't two people just do right by their
children, many wonder? The parents themselves choose the path of
different homes, with kids shuffling between them, while one or both parents moves on with subsequent relationships, lifestyles, or the self-reflection
of finding him- or herself.

In a divorce, hidden anger—a mainstay in a couple's marriage—incu-
bates in two separate homes, a petri dish that can compromise the lives
of multiple players. This includes each parent, their children, significant
others and/or future spouses, as well as their children, grandparents, and
friends.

Family court is not always the autoclave you might think that rids all
contaminants. It can become a pressure chamber filled with hot, angry
words and paperwork that drowns everyone in discontent.

This chapter outlines the mistakes to avoid and how to deal with partners hell-bent on making your life (and unwittingly their own) more miserable. To provide hope, it features an example of a healthy divorce process;

yes, people *can* separate without exacting unnecessary damage upon those they once loved.

THE BUILDUP: PASSIVE-AGGRESSION THAT CRIPPLES COUPLES

Colette and Henri met during their senior year at a northeastern university. Colette had immediately liked Henri, who had moved to the area from Quebec, with his French name. Like hers. Only his got whispered about for its foreign spelling. She paid no attention to rumors that he was a loner who spent more time in town than on campus. Their common need to fit in attracted them both, and they married.

When baby made three, Colette insisted they move close to her Lake Erie family so that they could babysit when she entered a physical therapy program. Henri quietly conceded. Laundering onesies wasn't his thing, nor was hearing Colette's sighs when he didn't.

Henri used his public health degree to become director of a health clinic. But soon, Henri had trouble convincing physicians to negotiate lower fees, part of his job description. He hid his failures and sadly got hooked on painkillers, a few legally obtained with his feigned limp; others he smuggled out of clinic drawers.

Colette and her family stepped in. The grandparents funded a quality daycare for the now toddler, and believed Henri's plausible points: he was "stressed out," "winters were rough," and, after all, "the move was Colette's idea." When Colette brought in the day's mail, she recognized a casino return address, the same name as she found on their credit card statement that Henri tried to dismiss as a networking outing for work. Colette's stomach churned as she realized how Henri's resentment played out professionally and now personally.

PROCESSING NEW PERSPECTIVES

It looks as if Colette and Henri made an important life commitment when their endorphins were raging and obscuring troublesome traits they would only recognize later. Their desire to assimilate and Colette's rigid insistence to live near family may smack of enmeshment. Add quiet adherence to others' expectations, the proverbial mixed message so prevalent in passive-aggressive dynamics. Addictions and triangles also played pivotal roles.

During (and after) any separation and divorce, we hope that two parties can set aside their grievances to act as maturely as possible. Colette and Henri do have options—many good, some not.

From a systems perspective, we hope that they can tolerate one another's presence in a room or by telephone long enough to banter about schedules, educational plans, and medical treatment; find the strength of mind to problem solve limited budgets and parcel out funds for future lunch money, sports equipment, uniforms, and class trips; and wish one another well as each gets on with life amid career advancement, vacations, and holiday plans. Talk about a tall order!

We've witnessed angry people create divorce realities that often turn into nightmares. During this tense passage, society hopes that people have the skills that they simply did not have months prior, in the marriage. We've seen how if both parties have some wits still about them, they can work out the dissolution of their union through mediation or by using a collaborative legal process (explained later). Yet we've also seen how hidden anger hoodwinks parties into fight mode to exact revenge.

And so the work begins. Divorce is indeed better than remaining mired in mutual (or sometimes one-sided) misery. Collaborative, sometimes legal efforts commence, and in time, healing occurs. Other books detail healthier conflict resolution, such as mediation and collaborative divorce. Here, we advocate for the healthy emotional divorce, obtained with work on the self, not on fixing the other. Striving for this is the best way to hold on to one's sanity, physical health, and finances far longer than those who continue to bury or percolate anger. When ingrained reactivity, poor communication, hidden agendas, and problematic personality traits impede progress, manipulation, control, self-absorption, and childlike behaviors tend to rise.

SPARKS TO SEPARATE LIVES

If you've read sequentially, you have learned concepts to understand the four horsemen that met their final apocalypse, faulty relationship dynamics that grew onerous, and the families where people did not clean up their livid messes. These days, not all parents have legalized their unions, and yet their breakups are no less heartbreaking, especially to the children.

DIVORCE ANGER RUN AMOK

Though plenty of separated or divorced people claim, "I'm not angry," neither of us has encountered anyone unscathed by this process. Life stress scales routinely cast this personal crisis as second highest, just beneath death of a spouse. Unless the union and all you did with this person meant absolutely nothing to you, the upset is there, only it is often hidden.

If you've contributed somehow to your own or your children's disappointment, then you have a greater capacity to remedy it. This is nowhere more important than in divorced families. When you don't do this important growth work—encouraging your children to move beyond silenced anger also—that's when we see kids caught in the middle of a subtly antagonistic war between their parents.

PASSIVE-AGGRESSIVE PARTNERS

Negative, anger-concealing people tend to re-create disappointing relationship experiences that parallel previously dissatisfying ones, according to Theodore Millon and Roger Davis.[1] Current relationship patterns may be traced back to failed parent/child relationships or intimate relationships, and this re-creation, in turn, helps to form their pessimistic worldview. If the patterns continue, you'll see a host of fractured relationships on the horizon. On the other hand, let's look at the woman who marries the exact opposite of an ex to avoid re-creating what she just left. If she engaged in any introspection to understand what *she* had contributed to the breakup, it may indeed be wise to marry the opposite personality. But where it's a knee-jerk response born of frustration or blinded fantasy, it may re-create misery. Admittedly, it's counterintuitive that people would shy away from similar experiences, going with dissimilar, on account of their disillusionment. But it happens all the time.

Despite feeling negative or ambivalent about life, passive-aggressive people also feel that a new relationship will be different for all the shallow reasons you read earlier. These folks fully embrace their relationship fantasies. The past doesn't impact their predictions; thus, they think that this time they'll capture what they're after. When the passive-aggressive person realizes the next relationship requires just as much effort, problems seem like shackles, and answers once again get sought through another escape. Happiness must lie elsewhere.

FOUR ANGRY EMOTIONS IN DIVORCE MODE

Nowhere are the Murphy/Oberlin Four Types of Families more evident than in those experiencing separation or divorce, in single-parent homes, or in stepfamilies where anger is often the voice of all four emotions—pain, stress, power, and desire—that we outlined earlier. These days, a single dad may be as overwhelmed as a single mom, wanting to grab a beer with buddies and watch a basketball game. Only he's afraid to leave his teenage son, who might opt for that same beverage and an impromptu party while Dad's not home.

In stepfamilies, where children never asked for any shift in the family makeup, hurt, confusion, and uncertainty trigger anger that goes underground. In the context of all of this strife, being a parent, the first and foremost responsibility of the adults, can easily be forgotten.

Any relationship requires nurturance. Even a one-parent, one-child family is still a family unit. When two families merge, birth order often shifts, and step- and half-siblings often complicate the family portrait. This can all be quite positive, once sorted out and after everyone settles in. No matter what your family shape, setting aside time just to be together sends a potent nonverbal message akin to "You're worth my time" or, in a new stepfamily, "I want to know you better."

While you, the parent, are often doing the best you can, realize the strain you're under and how that may cloud your vision. We have had parents tell us that their son or daughter was fine with their divorce, sometimes with their new homes or new companions. In 99.9 percent of the cases, that just hasn't been so. The child may not show any immediate, visible signs, but there is always deep emotion, even if it's extremely well-hidden. While divorce may signal a new start and gain for a parent, any way you cut it, it's a loss for a child.

In the Troubled Family, Anger Is the Voice of Pain

Remember Deepak and Sunita with their four children? We'll show the exact pain that anger is the voice of, as we offer various scenarios. For instance, if Deepak tells the children that their mother "is divorcing all of us," and swears he won't give Sunita a dime, he's creating emotional turmoil and prolonged legal complications, which (again) cause financial hardship. For him as well as his departing wife.

If Sunita allows her anger to flourish as she ruminates and plots revenge over Deepak's dalliances, she may move her mildly anxious and depressed mood to what clinically could be seen as obsessed and disordered traits. What's worse, if she acts out by stalking, she might land herself in legal trouble of another kind, and any trouble or pain she experiences impacts their kids.

Infamous passive-aggressive ploys in divorce include lowering one's income and trumping up false charges. If Deepak made false allegations of child abuse against Sunita, she might be placed on leave as a nurse. Guess what? He now has a bigger financial burden to support his children. And if either party purposely makes their income more paltry, they compound their own financial misery and look foolish (possibly manipulative) to colleagues and future employers. This is not the reputation they want to spread at the next networking luncheon!

Divorcing parents who complicate their lives through passive-aggressive behavior often need to take years to dig out from underneath the rubble, and if you think the residual pain won't last long, guess again. The children the passive-aggressors clamor for at present (because they can) may be the same ones who avoid their parents out of embarrassment or fear of a fracas at high-stakes events such as graduations, engagement parties, and weddings. Kids become adults who later make choices from their memories. Will those be positive recollections? You decide.

In the Frantic Family, Anger Is the Voice of Stress

The children in Deepak and Sunita's family already had academic stress with too many advanced classes and extracurricular activities. The harsh reality for single-parent families is that there is less time, fewer hands, and more tasks. This frenzy, often seen in single-parent families, is the reason most children and adults act out in distress. Most custody orders give that other parent first right of refusal when the one with custody can't be with the children (when that parent needs help or a favor). Thus, it makes sense not to antagonize your child's other parent.

In the Indulging Family, Anger Is the Voice of Desire

Both Deepak and Sunita had education and jobs and maintained a solid upper-middle-class lifestyle that by Western standards is predicated on how much you have to show for that schooling and success. If Sunita showers the kids with gifts to ease her exit from a fit-filled marriage, then she indulges the children for the wrong reasons. This gives them a pseudo sense of security, especially when she later skimps on school lunches.

Bad motives bring about even worse outcomes. Their children will continue to expect more, and when, as adults, they realize the world doesn't work this way, there will be additional, delayed fallout from this nasty divorce. A single parent could rationalize "Just this once, I'll [do my child's chore, buy that toy], because I hardly ever see my kids," but one time becomes two, three, and ten times, leading to an indulging pattern.

In the Angry Family, Anger Is the Voice of Power

If Deepak accused Sunita of having a boyfriend, after a history of two affairs himself, he would project onto his wife traits he could not own within himself. Blame and projection are two of the most commonly used defense mechanisms when passive-aggressors try to cast off the unpleasant light that shines on their own behavior.

The letters from Sunita's family guilted Sunita into further enmeshment by making her focus on duty to her family first and responsibility to herself (and the family she created) second. While subtle, there is unmistakable power in such exchanges. Sometimes grandparents (and other family members) need to stop their dysfunctional dance and become better models for their grandchildren, especially if they know divorce drama surrounds the children. In very high conflict cases, counseling might even assist extended family members who become frequent caregivers for the children involved. Sometimes counseling is useful for extended family members merely to help them stay centered themselves during the divorce.

KIDS CAUGHT WHEN MOM/DAD PROVE POINTS

Kailee, a nine-year-old girl, nails the uneven parallel bars and finds focus on the mats while at gymnastics. At home, however, Kailee's emotions catapult her as if she's still on the trampoline.

Her mom, Jae Sung, has taken yet another job as a project manager. Her income is important for their family, but Kailee overheard Huynh, her dad, muttering audible sarcasm while he prepared dinner. Is Mom staying away on purpose? Maybe that mean girl at school is right: Kailee's a "castoff." Not one girl likes her. Not even her own mom.

This child is privy to the silent standoff her parents call a marriage—a convenient arrangement (for them) that most other adults would see as a separation, but since it's a rather informal one, Kailee isn't aware of that concept. Children do not need all the messy details. But a child-sized explanation is necessary, or they may well internalize their own often misinformed theory.

Kailee prays at night that Mom will return. At breakfast, Huynh says, "You don't mind if I invite a friend over, do you?" Kailee agrees sheepishly, thinking what's the harm, but when he adds, "*She'd* like to go to the pool," Kailee is now trapped by her initial yes, given without proper information. A tough spot for any child!

Some couples separate formally but place their egos front and center as they prove points, parading around their new "arm candy" relationship, hoping their ex will discover it (often through the children). Think about the intent and motive here. Both are bad.

Are we out of touch or old-fashioned? No, we understand adult needs. Yet when one relationship blossoms prematurely on the heels of another's collapse, we know that most parents are making decisions out of the drug-like high their surging endorphins create. This situation can also fuel a child's imagination as to why parents are not together. Trust us when we say none of this is truly good.

CUED ELSEWHERE, OFF-STAGE

Kids in situations like Kailee's never really understand why parents split. If they hear sarcastic phrases such as "boy toy" or "home-wrecker," what good possibly comes from that? Being told "it's not your fault" rarely assuages a child's belief that somehow they weren't good enough. These kids spend inordinate amounts of time at a parent's house with the door closed, headphones firmly planted, turning away from their parent (who is often distracted by his/her own frustrations). They get dragged by one of their parents to counseling—which is great if it leads to healing, but not so good if the child later returns to homes where neither parent works on redefining themselves and what created their troubled family in the first place. This is the epitome of being wedged between two equally incomprehensible predicaments.

True also is that sometimes one parent is more invested in helping the child than the other; both should be fully invested. In some divorced households, the child's needs get overlooked. Walk-off parents, who function only in front of extended family or when there's something to gain or take credit for, aren't participating in their child's life at all. Some pull down six-figure incomes that their educational path obtained for them yet summarily refuse to pony up a dime to further their child's education. When asked to do so, they proffer passive-aggressive excuses such as (a) the law says I'm not obligated to help, (b) I can't afford it (as they hold the latest smartphone), (c) your mom/dad took all my money (a frequent exaggeration or flat-out lie), and (d) you can take a loan (creating inconvenience, debt, and obstacles for their child as he or she begins adulthood).

GLIMPSES INTO FAMILY COURT

See if you recognize the passive-aggressive traps and enabling that occur below:

"Your honor, my client contends that he couldn't make it to the pharmacy to get the child's medication and inhaler," Attorney Aldridge stated in court one afternoon. "Not enough time."

"This was at eight o'clock that evening, correct?" asked the family court judge.

"That's correct."

"What time does the pharmacy close, and how far is it from Mr. Smith's home?"

"Nine o'clock, your honor, and I believe the pharmacy is forty minutes away."

The judge hastily scrawled notes at the bench. As his chin rose, it signaled opposing counsel to summarize the plaintiff's testimony.

"The child's mother would state that this pharmacy in question is twenty minutes at most from her husband's apartment, and that there is an even closer one, your honor. Here is the route printed from MapQuest. Returning Alyssa in the midst of an asthma attack instead of caring for her needs directly posed a potentially dangerous situation in that . . ."

"I object, your honor."

"Overruled."

"It posed a danger because it delayed treatment for a chronic medical condition and caused Mrs. Smith to miss work the next day caring for the child, seriously jeopardizing her job. And the hospital bill could have been avoided with reasonable conduct. Furthermore, Mr. Smith has refused on numerous occasions to follow the court order by paying for such expenses, and he's withheld insurance cards for their three children though we've asked repeatedly for them."

"How many times have you asked for this information, counselor?"

"Three times within six months, by telephone, via e-mail, and surface mail to Attorney Aldridge."

"Excuse me, your honor, Mr. Smith never remembers receiving any correspondence nor speaking with Mrs. Smith, and I can't recall that request."

"Can't recall?" the judge replied, peering over his glasses.

"Well . . . I'm not sure."

The judge sighed. "I'll take this testimony under advisement and have a decision for you shortly." With that he got up from his leather chair and headed for his chambers.

Twenty-five minutes later, he sent a member of his tipstaff out to hand the court order to the attorneys. Crossed out of the motion were the words "finds in contempt," "counsel fees," and "extraordinary medical expenses."

In big bold letters, as if written with a Sharpie marker, was the word "DE-NIED," then "defendant should make reasonable efforts to have necessary medications on hand and provide Mrs. Smith with medical insurance cards within thirty days."

What minefields do you see in this scenario? How about manipulating the facts, inconveniencing others, and withholding information, for starters. Furthermore, lack of cooperation and jeopardizing child safety/welfare. As this stems from a custody battle over which parent is more fit, spot the huge disparity in what Mr. Smith purports to want and what his actions actually show.

Parenting is inconvenient and is not solely about you. It's about the children, who in divorce often become pawns knocked aside in a parent's quest for checkmate. These kids won't look back on affectionate times; their memories will be rife with turmoil.

In our example, not only did Attorney Aldridge enable and protect his client from consequences, but the judge was the ultimate enabler, believing this man's excuses. Opposing counsel had begun to show a pattern of difficult behavior. When the judge expects compliance from a person who has a history of withholding, obstructing, or causing inconvenience, and does not mete out a consequence for such difficult behavior, it will only encourage him to be *more* difficult. When hired attorneys or court personnel grant free passes to (enable) passive-aggressors on a *frequent* basis, behaviors they would rather eradicate become reinforced.

There's little reason for the passive-aggressor to behave better or to cooperate. His resistance—and everyone's ignorance of this process—keeps him locked, and the free pass given by his enablers allows him to rehearse (once again) any misguided justifications he has for his actions, or more accurately, lack of actions.

We don't intend here to sound harsh, but in far too many cases, burnout occurs with lawyers, judges, court personnel, therapists, and physicians who handle this type of behavior routinely. If you are a professional working in a family court, always remember that you cannot fix or change another, but by you changing what you do (adding a consequence for passive-aggressive actions), you increase the odds of righting the wrong dynamic.

SHOULD YOU LET YOUR EX OFF THE HOOK?

Once court action commences, and if venom starts spewing, it becomes difficult to turn around the process—especially with retainers paid and nasty legal letters rushed off and received. That's why thinking ten times before you start down this path is critical.

You can stop unnecessary litigation and settle at any time, as long as you don't feel manipulated or pressured. Divorcing a passive-aggressive spouse gets exhausting, and some people who get caught in the drama stop fighting their cases merely to have them over with. Indeed, this might be what the other side strategized for, so be careful. Seek legal advice first.

Eventually, your case will wind down, outgrow the need for a retained lawyer, and you can ask counsel to withdraw his/her appearance. Representing yourself in court on minor matters is not that difficult, and plenty of pro se legal programs give limited advice. If part of the vindictive modus operandi has been to run up legal bills, this may cease when it backfires.

Just because a party may have a legal "right" under state law, it doesn't mean you can't ask for frivolous matters to be thrown out for lack of merit. Keep careful records and safeguard them away from your home in a secure location. The more evidence, dates, and details you have, the better your chances of showing these attempts to be purely repetitive, harassing, or an abuse of the system. Prepare yourself and recognize that proving intractable behavior will take potentially months or even years. You must decide: Are the stakes worth the time and effort, and does dropping the matter enable poor behavior?

Finally, should former partners ever help each other or is that enabling also? *Infrequently,* in extenuating circumstances, stepping in, offering a hand, may be the best (and most cooperative) solution. However, when you lose track of the times you've bailed out your ex, mitigated the consequences, or become stressed with too many responsibilities yourself, *this is NOT helpful.* The requests will occur again; unfortunately, you may have invited them.

BATTLE SCARS

Divorce does not always completely unravel children. But high-conflict divorce frequently does. The unnecessary custody battle is the most prevalent passive-aggressive tactic in the process, but also frequent is day-to-day warfare that plays out in the following ways:

- Withholding information (homework, school or insurance information, possessions)
- Refusal to cooperate or lend an answer
- Resistance toward authority figures (treatment plans, doctor or teacher recommendations)
- Double scheduling or accepting invitations on access time that's not yours
- Obstruction (blocking a move, holding up a property or vehicle sale)
- Foot-dragging (delaying a child's bike or eyeglasses repair, forgetting to sign permission slips)
- Interfering with the child's love and concern for the other parent (open criticism, denying the opportunity to buy a gift, belittling their praise for the other parent, mocking new partners)
- Hanging up the telephone when the other parent calls the child or needs an answer from you

When you hate the other parent more than you love your child, expect big problems. This teaches the child that it's okay to hate, and remember, you're a parent, too. You might be next!

Some passive-aggressive parents have intercepted letters at the mailbox so that their child wouldn't hear from their other parent; they've refused to do something required for the child's health (e.g., refusing to obtain medicine because they resent the extra expense beyond child support), or they've undermined their child's future success by complicating their collegiate path. We

> When hired attorneys or court personnel grant free passes to (enable) passive-aggressors on a frequent basis, behaviors they would rather eradicate become reinforced.

have seen children pulled from therapy whenever the reactive parent cannot accept feedback. If the therapist dares to disagree or offers even the gentlest correction, this parent may jump to the automatic thought that the therapist is "siding" against them, which is rarely the case.

Other passive-aggressors deliberately alienate the other parent, often because they feel betrayed or abandoned (even if they were the party to leave or damage the union). They fail to act civilly in the company of their child's other parent, or withhold ordinarily kind gestures (saying hello and thank you) out of their staunchly entrenched spite. They send kids empty-handed when an inexpensive or homemade greeting card would be an appreciated token on Mother's or Father's Day.

When a passive-aggressive parent also has self-absorbed personality traits, you'll see a lot of "in your face" flaunting (parading around a new partner), "saving face" maneuvers (postdating a check to look like the payment isn't late, promising indulgences to the kids), and when the hidden anger mixes with immaturity, you'll see childish behavior (caustic, jealous comments or petulance).

Chances are the problems existed long before the marriage ended, and they often remain far past the divorce decree. Kids become ambivalent, not knowing how to react to the passive-aggressive parent (it depends upon the day, the mood). They shift loyalties to survive emotionally between their antagonistic parents with their differing expectations. There's little certainty in these children's lives, and as we stated before, the child's anger becomes the voice of unremitting pain, stress, power, and desire.

When a passive-aggressive parent limits access to the resources available for the child's divorce recovery—access to grandparents, therapists, doctors, or best-interest attorneys—they remove the remaining, trusted lifelines their child could rely upon. How is that for poor motive and unfortunate outcome?

ADJUSTMENTS: WHEN NO ONE SEEMS TO UNDERSTAND

Domestic-relations officers, special masters, and judges see so much anger that everyone is impugned by poor behavior. You're considered angry until proven happy, and sometimes you are treated accordingly. On any given day, court personnel expect to see manipulation and nastiness.

Where does this leave the honest person who tries to convey accurate information? Research published in the journal *Family Relations* revealed that while high-conflict cases in post-divorce are often assumed to be a shared interaction between two hostile former partners, it's not uncommon to find one enraged or defiant partner and the opposite party who no longer harbors anger and attempts to solve problems for everyone's sake, but to no avail.[2]

What do you do if that defines you? When dealing with a passive-aggressor becomes interminable, enlist the help of mental health professionals or a parenting coordinator, who can size up the interactions, and in some states, report to the court. Only do this as a reasonable means to extricate yourself from the dysfunction. If your ex has violated other rights, broken into your home, or stolen property, escalate the matter to the authorities. Seek legal advice for harassment or stalking.

Sometimes, you must live as best you can with the circumstances you are dealt. Retrying court battles keeps two parties locked. It allows one or both of the parents to avoid the real emotional work at hand. So when you've tried your best but are stuck with a less than ideal custody schedule or support calculation, try to live with the ruling for at least a year. Otherwise you come across as litigious and difficult yourself.

NEW PASSAGE, NEW YOU

Whether you recognize in yourself any tendencies to hide anger or you're dealing with a passive-aggressive ex, do your best to move on with your life. What have you put off because you never found time for it? Use the time that your child is with their other parent to explore interests, perhaps obtain more education, volunteer, broaden your circle of acquaintances, and as we've said countless times, focus on your self-growth.

To the average onlooker, it may appear that your ex, who has possibly recoupled, remarried, or had more children, has moved on more than you. Of course, none of this equates to the emotional divorce that's necessary for complete recovery. It's harder to obtain, we realize, when there's entrenched behavior at play. For every few steps forward, expect to falter back a few times as you figure out a new rhythm rather than responding from your old reactive self.

Know that with self-absorbed, passive-aggressive spouses everything is supposed to work for them, to flow their way—not yours. With that in mind, you may never have closure on what anger issue truly lurked in your marriage. The passive-aggressive person might never fully grasp that anger either. This can be terribly confusing. Attend to *your* life. Operate within *your* values, recognizing that no one "makes" you do or say anything. Your behavior is your choice.

THE UNCONTESTED, COOPERATIVE DIVORCE

The July 2015 issue of *Time* featured an opinion piece titled "The Rise of the Good Divorce," in which its author made the point that raising children post-divorce is indeed a dicey proposition. "The patience and compassion needed to navigate a money crisis, a child's illness or a new partner can be the very traits that disappear first under stress," wrote Susanna Schrobsdorff.[3]

Mediation and collaborative divorce provide healthy and powerful alternatives to expensive, exhaustive litigation where a significant amount of communication and control rests in the lawyer's hands. In court, the determination rests entirely with a judge who first meets you on that day. A mediator facilitates discussions and agreements on custody and property settlements between the couple that are then run past their individual attorneys, hopefully avoiding litigation.

In a collaborative divorce process, professionals (lawyers, parent coaches, child experts, and a financial consultant) play a more supportive role in order to keep the control and determination with the divorcing clients.[4] All parties agree to open and honest disclosure and to keep the matter out of court, and know that if their collaborative process breaks down and a court path results, the couple must start over with completely different professionals. This provides an incentive to make the process work.

Yet when one party determines to mete out misery, if there's violence or secret-keeping, the case may be rendered inappropriate for such alternative dispute resolution tactics.

Imagine the bank balances for our fictitious parents if, instead of retainers for depositions and motions, Deepak and Sunita literally retained the funds for vacations, college expenses, and a rainy day account. Mr. Smith might feel a sense of pride when he successfully managed his child's medical emergency, and his child would feel a sense of security, remembering how dad took care of him.

If anger keeps you shackled, expose yourself to the alternatives of empathy and cooperation—perhaps with a bowl of popcorn and the movie *Stepmom*, where a pivotal moment bore witness to two adversarial women who later shared vulnerabilities over raising the dying Jackie's daughter.

"Look down the road to her wedding," Isabel says. "I'm in a room alone with her . . . telling her no woman has ever looked so beautiful. And my fear is she'll be thinking, 'I wish my mom was here.'"

"And mine is . . . she won't," Jackie solemnly offers.[5]

There's true power and surrender for these characters . . . and we hope for the same potential in everyone's divorce and future path.

eight

Seething Through the Work and School Day

WORKING WITH PASSIVE-AGGRESSIVE PEOPLE INCREASES YOUR ANXiety and drains your energy whether you're the employee to the mixed-message boss, the coworker hearing another sad-sack tale, or the one inheriting the work left behind by the last shift's dereliction of duty. Leaders with staff who undermine the organization's mission know how this thwarts success.

SLACKERS IN THE WORKPLACE

Destiny managed an urgent care clinic where the office and medical staff's long hours resembled barely organized chaos. A flu epidemic or post-holiday week could put it off the charts. Literally. The clinic only slept six hours (at best) before it dawned a new day.

At 6:45 a.m., Destiny spotted last night's patient notes that hadn't been logged into the computer. "'Tis the season," she mumbled. Last week, lab techs had written so sloppily on specimen labels that a half dozen patients had to be handed a plastic cup again or stuck twice to get a usable blood draw. This incident had Tara and Malik, the clinic's malcontents, written all over it.

If there was an hour to breathe, those two sat back until Destiny asked them to pitch in. Tara once mumbled that she "didn't get paid to do extra," but Destiny often caught them playing online solitaire at their desks. Two days ago, they claimed the docs created a hostile work environment for not chatting . . . about football. Never mind there were sick patients in exam rooms waiting to be seen!

Complaint letters came in, and of course, morale suffered. So did salaries. The Web surfing continued, but if they were fired, Tara and Malik would likely file grievances and drown the clinic director in even more paperwork. What could Destiny do?

WHOSE PROBLEM IS IT?

Destiny, like many caught in the grip of angry employees, has to dig to the bottom of the problem. Along the way she must ask herself: Is it me? My style? Problems I'm not privy to? Difficulties at home? Plain laziness? Uncontrolled stress here that takes its toll?

Let's face it: many people spend easily eight to twelve hours a day, often more, at work or in school. If you must deal with an irascible boss, a disagreeable student, or a backstabbing coworker, the encounter stays with you and you might often relish a fast exit out the door. However, you need the income or the education in order to create a better life, so you must cope with these personalities while you work to keep your own demeanor positive.

At any time, there's going to be someone on staff at your work or in your classroom who is dealing with a large life problem that impacts their performance—deep financial difficulties, child care or elder care, a relationship breakup, a tragic accident, a death. Some deal effectively with such stress, others struggle, and a few fall apart. These issues are best handled with compassion and guidance.

If coworkers don't share that compassion and instead resent those who struggle, everyone ends up with a problem. Again, think systems theory: a change in one creates reciprocal changes. Ask yourself the role *you* want to play in making things better or worse.

QUIZ: WHAT'S YOUR PERFORMANCE STYLE?

Take this quiz to become more aware of your own on-the-job or in-the-class-room style, using the key below:

1	not like me	3	somewhat like me
2	only slightly like me	4	very much like me

1. _____ It bothers me when requests are made of me at work or school.
2. _____ I prefer to work my own way to get the job accomplished, even if it takes longer.
3. _____ I'd rather keep my feelings to myself.
4. _____ I'm comfortable with my job duties and don't look to increase them.
5. _____ Most people seem to tolerate conflict better than I do.
6. _____ Criticism bothers me.
7. _____ When asked to do things I dislike, it's not a big deal because the request may be forgotten.
8. _____ Appearing successful is all that counts.
9. _____ I wish I could change things but can live with the way things are.
10. _____ I shouldn't make my frustration or anger obvious.
11. _____ Talking things over creates more problems than solutions.
12. _____ I'm skeptical of new assignments and plans unless I had a hand in creating them.
13. _____ I've felt the same concerns/disappointments before in similar situations.
14. _____ If I know I'll be getting feedback I might not like, I'd rather be absent that day.
15. _____ I can do the job better if I'm allowed to do it by myself.
16. _____ People at work/school are not to be trusted.
17. _____ I feel pretty good knowing things others don't and having an advantage over them.
18. _____ When I disagree, sarcasm works better than being direct.
19. _____ I wish I felt more confident about my skills, my talents, and myself.
20. _____ It's tough to tell others about my decisions most of the time.
21. _____ When something requires quick action, I feel uneasy and pressured.
22. _____ When new supervisors/teachers are hired, I feel extra cautious.
23. _____ If someone isn't doing his job right, I'll keep quiet; let them find out the hard way.
24. _____ If I make a mistake, I definitely do not want to discuss it with my supervisor/teacher.
25. _____ I'm uncomfortable when someone talks to me about how to do my job better.

Tally the total number of points and compare with the key below.

A score of 25–33: Your style is fairly direct and open to self-expression, adaptability, and new challenges. It's unlikely that you hide much and you aren't afraid to deal productively with problems.

A score of 34–62: Your style is somewhat direct, but in certain cases, you might shy away from or feel uncomfortable with confrontation. Be aware of this, because remaining open and willing to adapt yields great things.

A score of 63–81: Your style is fairly indirect. Confrontation makes you uneasy. If this sounds like you, it might be wise to talk this over with someone you trust, who can offer you honest feedback.

A score of 82–100: Your style is on the indirect side of the pendulum. While it may work for you, it's likely that you've hidden some frustrations because you sidestep people, situations, even challenges that might actually benefit you. Be open to assistance to boost your assertiveness and self-confidence.

These scores merely give you insight into your motives or behavior. Don't read the results as a psychological test score that's written in stone, but rather as something to improve. If you've taken a new job where you feel things are better, or you changed to a new school, then answer these questions based upon how you behaved in the former position and compare scores to the answers in your current job. The comparison may uncover patterns for how you operate at work or in school.

WHAT GOT US SO ANGRY?

Today, rather than having a lifetime-guaranteed job, the typical worker will change positions possibly a dozen or more times. And when someone asks impressionable youth what they want to be when they grow up, they rarely say a stressed-out doctor, disgruntled employee, laid-off dot-comer, or cynical civil servant. Mix and match. Add other positions. Every career has its stressors.

In professional services, millions of people start each day fearful of grievances and angry lawsuits. Much-needed physicians stop delivering babies or retire early from their practices because they can't afford the steep malpractice premiums. Do you think these professionals, accustomed to giving care, don't react with a little anger, in need of care themselves? And, according to the American Psychological Association, in the academic setting, there's been a dramatic increase in college students with mental health concerns in recent decades.[1] While anxiety, depression, and sexual assault made up this picture, so did stress and anger.

Following 9/11, the anxiety of working in a high-rise office complex as well as fears about a cyclical economy predisposed many workers to job insecurity and aggravation. Beyond threatening health, safety, and finances, office gossip and poorly trained workers annoy us. Additionally, management might institute ill-conceived changes, and later, when productivity or morale suffers, dodge any responsibility for their ruinous decisions. Many people live paycheck to paycheck to cover bills and childcare expenses—stressors that spark some to unleash frustrations wherever they can.

In 2012, National Public Radio encouraged people to merely listen to the verbal exchanges around them—rude phrases, commanding verbs, shortened courtesies: for example, "I'm good" instead of "thank you" or "sure" rather than "you're welcome." Retail workers eyeball their gadgetry rather than the customer and delivery drivers pay more attention to a cell phone.

Enjoying your work, feeling self-assured and safe that you make a difference and have input, yields a tremendous emotional lift. Ditto for those who feel they work with a respectful, above-board group of people. Employees with adequate work–life balance also show higher rates of self-esteem and overall satisfaction. Unfortunately, potential employees these days often state up front: "I don't live to work, but I work to live, so what are you going to offer so that I feel personally fulfilled each day?"

One twenty-five-year-old male worker quit his office job on day two, tearfully complaining that looking up data was harder than he expected. Another young man showed up for a job interview with his mother. Needless to say, he didn't get the job. Some workers undermine teamwork and morale with immature self-focus that should have been left behind in high school.

Wise employers know it's their responsibility to run an organized and respectful workplace. That said, they may declare their own version of: "In this office we work hard to inspire creativity, make great products, and sell them, but if your top priority is pursuing your inner development, this may not be the place for you." When the boss does hire self-absorbed employees, the investment put into training them evaporates when they leave. If she hires the sullen, resentful type, everyone will take part in a miserable passive-aggressive dance.

In *The Nurses*, Alexandra Robbins cites one nurse's first day reporting to a physician's assistant (PA). The nurse worked closely with this PA for hours yet was mostly ignored. When the nurse went to the computer, she found the PA's indirect question: "Labs drawn??" The nurse couldn't remember receiving a direct request. Further, she didn't know which patients were set for discharge and who would be admitted. She was at a loss to provide information to her patients.[2]

Robbins revealed research from Boston Medical Center that found nurse bullying is responsible for 60 percent of new nurses leaving their first job within six months of hiring, and 20 percent leaving the profession entirely within three years.[3] Some of the most frequent forms of this lateral aggression included nonverbal innuendos (eye rolls, faces made), verbal affronts (overt or covert snide remarks, abrupt replies), undermining (making oneself unavailable), withholding information, and deliberate sabotage and setups.

In *Beating the Workplace Bully*, Lynne Curry, who reveals that she was once a victim to the trend, shares statistics that in 2014, 37 million workers reported abusive conduct during the average workday and that 28.7 million witnessed such abuse, according to a workplace bullying survey.[4] Curry sheds light on how some workers or students may signal that they are an easy target by showcasing sensitivities or vulnerabilities that the bully picks up on and uses for his sly gain. This can hurt any size of business and its customers, clients, or patients with wide-reaching ripple effects far beyond the passive-aggressive act.

DOLLARS AND SENSE OF ON-THE-JOB STRESS

Workers in the United States who have, at some point in their lives, been diagnosed with depression are absent from work an estimated sixty-eight million more days each year than those peers who haven't faced this. Thus, depression costs US workplaces $23 billion in absenteeism each year.[5]

Workplace stress is responsible for up to $190 billion in annual healthcare costs in America.[6] In many high-pressure work climates, stress-related medical conditions such as migraine headaches, gastrointestinal ailments, anxiety and depression, panic disorder, obesity, high blood pressure, and heart disease caused health insurance premiums to jump 30 to 40 percent from previous years. Absenteeism is costly.

Not surprisingly, when employers recognize the effects of unrealistic demands and undue stress placed upon their workers, morale improves, productivity climbs, healthcare costs decrease, and employee retention rates increase. Researchers at University of Colorado Health found that when specially trained healthcare providers offered "enhanced" treatment (antidepressant medication and/or counseling) for depression, depressed workers were more productive and missed fewer workdays than those who had standard treatment. That additional productivity added up to an estimated value of an additional $2,601 for each depressed, full-time employee.[7]

Sometimes stress is unavoidable. Honest and straight talk with employees can motivate them to keep their hopes high, but when worry builds, you've got a problem. Creative solutions can be found.

When people face losing their jobs and income, fear spreads like wildfire.

Bob Chapman, author of *Everybody Matters*,[8] didn't want to lay off employees for his business to survive. He took the problem to the employees. Rolling furloughs rather than layoffs resulted. When the recession lifted, they all thrived.[9]

JOB-RELATED STRESS BROUGHT ON YOURSELF

We call addiction to a job *workaholism;* often it's caused by perfectionistic (anxious) thoughts that no performance level is good enough (therefore, there's constant work to be done), or it's imposed upon workers by an organizational culture that demands more than most can bear. Regardless, it makes workers seethe inside. When difficult personalities enter the picture, burnout sets in. Job anxiety or stress = burnout = increased risk of anger and negativity.

Even medical interns and residents saw their weekly hours capped in 2003 and the issue emerged again in 2011, after growing concerns surfaced regarding sleep deprivation and the dangers posed to patient care.[10]

ARE YOU A WORKAHOLIC?

1. Do you feel married to your job and are you at work early in the morning, during the lunch break, late into the night, and on weekends when you could be relaxing?
2. Are you highly competitive? Are you prone to anger if you can't assume your driven schedule?
3. Does work always come before important relationships, parenting, or household responsibilities?
4. Do you drive yourself so hard with so many projects that you feel disorganized? Are you unable to accomplish your work in the time allotted?
5. Are you the type that can't utter the word "no" when presented with more work?
6. Do you thrive on the constant pressure of deadlines? Or use the escape that work affords to create distance from other areas of your life?
7. Do you read only work-related literature?
8. Beyond income, are you obsessed with getting in good with the boss, boosting your own sense of self-worth, or the ability to brag about how many hours you put in at the office? (Mind you, *obsession* is the key word here.)

Working occasional overtime due to a personnel shortage, seasonal work (e.g., a CPA at tax time), or new, unexpected demands is understandable, but over time, the stress of working too many hours without a way to balance your life adds up. It also signals to others their relative lack of importance, comparatively speaking.

BURNOUT, COMPASSION FATIGUE, AND THE ANTIDOTES

At one time or another, most of us have felt burned out. Burnout equates to physical and/or emotional exhaustion after long work. Staffing considerations or scarce resources may be among the culprits. Compassion fatigue, which we'll detail, is caused by stress related to those for whom one works to help.

Viktor Frankl, a neurologist, psychiatrist, and Holocaust survivor, once said, "What is to give light must endure burning." Those in helping professions—physicians, nurses, social workers, therapists, dentists, veterinarians, teachers, clergy, police, firefighters, and others—constantly give, and over time the demands take a toll if there are no built-in buffers. Compassion fatigue, sometimes called secondary traumatic stress disorder, is caused by the strain of repeated giving to one's patients, one's parishioners, or others one renders assistance to.

The typical case of student or worker burnout consists of exhaustion, overextending of one's efforts, and having to expend more energy to achieve what was prior output, and it culminates in cynicism and hopeless negativity. Time away from work, even if just over a lunch hour, a work break, or stopping intense study to spend a short time having fun assuages most episodes of burnout.

Sometimes the attempts to relieve the stress actually make things worse. One in five lawyers report drinking problems that reached the "hazardous, harmful and potentially alcohol dependent" level, and 30 percent have symptoms of depression, compared with about 12 percent among a highly educated workforce that doesn't include lawyers.[11] Nearly half of the attorneys surveyed self-reported depressive symptoms over their career. Such findings should sound an alarm to reduce workplace stress and provide access to effective counseling. When addiction and substance abuse spikes, it's characteristically accompanied by other strains and tensions among coworkers. Even when people overtly claim there's no problem, there often is.

Employers can mandate time off, allow the carryover of earned leave, close businesses on holidays for employees to celebrate and enjoy family, and respect boundaries by allowing workers to unplug gadgetry so as not to have e-mails or questions to answer after hours. Above all, they can assure that employee access to counseling support services is easy.

Frankl shared further wisdom in a classic existential tome. "When we are no longer able to change a situation, we are challenged to change ourselves," he wrote in *Man's Search for Meaning*. He reminds us that self-care is essential. We cannot give to others without caring for ourselves first, much like the flight attendant instructs in case of an in-flight emergency.

You will be of little use to your child or others who depend upon you if you cannot breathe yourself.[12]

Whether you identify with working too much or you give repeatedly of yourself in a job that depletes you, here are some suggestions to de-stress:

- Become aware of your workaholism. Pick up on "hints" dropped by family, friends, or even your coworkers.
- Let your body (fatigue, hunger, heart rate, gastrointestinal symptoms) and mind (moodiness, worries) inform you of compassion fatigue when you feel depleted. Improve your self-care regimen by planning time for aspects of life that replenish you and from which you derive enjoyment. Hobbies, travel, therapeutic massage, exercise, people with whom to talk to about your life are all valuable assets.
- Make daily goals and to-do lists. Completed tasks provide a sense of accomplishment. Focus on these accomplishments and not just the climb before you.
- Watch your diet. Avoid refined sugars, flours, and fats (found in vending machines). Snack on fruits and vegetables. Sip water to stay hydrated. High-protein lunches keep you energized. Those other foods may add to your stress level, if not immediately, then later.
- Cut back on caffeine. Some coffee can perk you up; too much, and you're ready for a fatigue-fall. The same applies to caffeinated soft drinks and tea.
- Exercise at least twenty to thirty minutes each day, more if you can. Schedule workout time. Walking during lunch or your commute burns off stress and calories. Grabbing sunshine lightens your mood as well.
- Don't work right up until bedtime. Sleep at least eight hours each night or determine the right amount of sleep for you. Too little shut-eye gives way to irritability, anger, and, you guessed it, acting on that anger.
- Take a daily respite from cell phones, digital devices, pagers, e-mail, and other devices, especially during meals and family times.
- Take regular vacations from routine demands. Feel a sense of accomplishment doing something out of the ordinary. Schedule the

time and stick to it. Use your driven nature on the job to be as perfect at home with your family. Recharge your batteries.
- Find what positive-psychology guru Martin Seligman, PhD, calls your *signature strength*, or what you do well that sets you apart. Your current job should play to those strengths.

IMPROVING WORKPLACE CULTURE AND MORALE

Historically, workers have been let go in corporate downsizing, during recessions, and in a loss of American manufacturing jobs, yet the workload has been delegated to a dwindling group of employees. According to the National Institute for Occupational Safety and Health, which was directed by Congress to study the psychological aspects of job safety and health, stressful work conditions include: heavy workload; infrequent breaks; long hours; routine tasks; underutilization of workers' skills; lack of participation in decision making; few family-friendly policies; lack of support; conflicting or uncertain job expectations; too much responsibility; job insecurity; lack of advancement, growth, and opportunity; rapid changes for which workers are unprepared; and unpleasant or dangerous conditions.[13]

You build a pleasant workplace based upon a desire to do well, take pride in your work, support each other, and share in successes. Employers can create an atmosphere where the stressors that feed hidden anger decline if they:

- Involve employees. Honor their experience. Enlist them in decisions whenever possible, especially if they will be the ones to implement changes you decide upon or inherit the new technology you acquire for on-the-job use.
- Listen and pay active attention. Ego and entitlement wall off good ideas. Managers who are poor listeners often feel their own opinions haven't mattered. So they repeat patterns modeled in their own careers. Stop and listen. Very often employees have great ideas on how to do things better, especially in workplace safety.
- Provide trainings, if necessary, to address e-mail etiquette, perfectionism, and procrastination. *Scientific American Mind* ran "I'll Do It Tomorrow," pointing out that "15 to 20 percent of adults routinely put off activities that would be better off accomplished right away," and that the financial loss

continues ——

— continued

to procrastination can become severe.[14] Procrastinators are stressed. Perfectionists have much anxiety. Those who use e-mail poorly often lack communication skills.

- Choose problem solving over power-oriented conflict resolution. Brainstorm for ideas, evaluate your options, think through any obstacles, and make your decisions accordingly.
- Offer outlets and ideas before problems percolate into frustration—from the suggestion box to teaching employees how to communicate more effectively, assert themselves, and make better decisions.

EIGHT ANGER TYPES AT WORK OR IN SCHOOL

Scott Adams outlines workplace anxieties through *Dilbert*, making us laugh. No one aims to become comic-strip fodder, but indeed you meet all personalities at work. We outline here our own list of eight passive-aggressive personalities you'll face at work: backstabbers, avengers, controllers, cynics, Eeyores, blamers, mutes, and stars. You may encounter people who fit into more than one category.

THE BACKSTABBER

How This Type Behaves	How You Should Respond
Betrays (trust, company secrets, collegial relationships)	Remember, this person craves attention and needs a bully pulpit; don't provide one on your time, but pull them aside and let this person feel heard.
Takes credit for your work	Hand deliver your work to the boss to lessen the chance of the backstabber taking credit for it; leave a paper trail; document, document, and document more.
Breaks confidences	Deal directly but gently with the offender; use empathy to prevent repeat offenses and be prepared with facts. Keep information (especially personal news) to yourself.

How This Type Behaves	How You Should Respond
Plays up to those in authority, treats subordinates poorly	Approach them with kindness and keep to yourself; smile—so they'll have nothing to use against you.
Sabotages others' work directly or through gossip	Don't gossip. Refuse to listen to it, and do not spread it. Understanding how triangulation works will help you to think about this and realize that triangles are rarely useful.

The barber who sells his business to another barber, agrees to a noncompete clause, takes the money, but whispers to customers that his scissors are ready again six miles up the street is a backstabber. Forget being grateful that he found a buyer, this guy bites the hand that feeds him. The fact that he's in violation of a restrictive covenant means nothing to him; he feels entitled to customers that should legally convey to the new owner. The backstabber often resembles the avenger, who is described next, but the distinction is motive—with the backstabber it's his own promotion, whereas the avenger is motivated by revenge.

THE AVENGER

How This Type Behaves	How You Should Respond
Acts on anger when provoked and feeling hopeless, so lashes out from a lack of options	Since revenge is often about views of injustice, resist attacking the person. If you sense they feel stuck, help them (if you can) to see that a range of other choices could address the injustice. It's a win-win situation for all.
Obstructs goals, violates norms and promises, withholds	Ask what seems fair and unfair. Promote honest communication without the anger.
Sabotages, pulls the wool over people's eyes, embarrasses	Hold the person accountable for her actions but without your own anger.
Assails power or status, "disses" or criticizes, uses covert and overt actions	Be respectful of others and don't fall into the trap of gossip.
Rationalizes own behavior as self-defense	Don't allow someone else to blame you for what is not your fault.

With sights set on vengeance, workers operate from an "I don't get mad, I get even" approach, for example, cutting a customer's hair too short because her tips aren't lucrative, waiting until a team meeting to disclose embarrassing information, or purposely excluding someone from an important event to cause intentional humiliation.

Let's say a person receives an agreement (contract, syllabus): for example, a policy statement signed at the orthodontist's office. Months later, a mother misses her child's appointment, but rather than pay the no-show fee that was disclosed through the policy document she signed, she makes a stink, demands a waiver, or threatens to seek services elsewhere. A parent the day before faced a similar charge but apologized and willingly paid up. What's the difference between these two people?

One seeks revenge while the other takes ownership. No one relishes extra charges, but the second person understood there was loss in income for the office, lost opportunity for the care someone else needed, and most of all, an agreement she willingly entered into.

Perceptions play a huge role in angry minds. Some people become provoked when they perceive others to have authority over them. If they've resisted authority before, their thinking may well get jammed with motives to obstruct, fight back, or break promises—indirect attempts to undermine or derogate status or power. The vengeful person rationalizes reacting to the perceived injustice as self-defense based upon irrational beliefs rather than factual evidence.

Sadly, many of these people operate with the motto "anything not for me is against me," and they are too ready to attack. Psychologist Steven Stosny outlines how resentment can make us *reactaholics*: when others "push your buttons, you're a powerless reactor rather than a powerful actor."[15] And in a school or a work setting, often one person's upset becomes contagious; payback ideas begin to buzz as others catch on to the avenger's tactics.

THE CONTROLLER

How This Type Behaves	How You Should Respond
Manipulates for control	Resist sharing heartfelt thoughts even when they turn on the charm because this sharing could be used in a self-serving way to manipulate you in the future.
Demands his/her way, threatens and wields power	Document facts, keep communication lines open between workers, and listen for honest complaints. Be suspicious of any attempts to control the flow of information from key personnel. Have a check and balance system.
Wrestles with anxiety, may be overwhelmed by demanding organizational culture or job	Find common ground; agree with the person occasionally.
Vents frustrations, lacks confidence when not in charge	Get the person to back your idea by pointing out how it serves his/her interest.

A professional organization's outgoing executive director hired a close friend to take over. Whenever staff insinuated that their new boss got the job because of connections versus substantive knowledge, this new director began to question their abilities and loyalty. She prevented them from attending conferences and excluded them from listservs, even from the organization's own social media. When confronted about this blocking, the director blamed technical glitches. Effectively, those who aspired to other duties were now seen as out of touch and told they lacked leadership potential. Members resigned, dues/income plummeted, yet it took years to understand the root of problem—this executive director. As is typical with sabotage, her replacement and staff had to rebuild the membership all because of her motive to control rather than lead the organization.

When the supervisor selects the Friday after Thanksgiving for a mandatory, noncrisis meeting, knowing it will pull countless people away from their long holiday weekend, we see a controller. Causing such inconvenience and doing something that deliberately annoys others indirectly discharges frustrations, placing this exasperation on others.

THE CYNIC

How This Type Behaves	How You Should Respond
Acts suspicious and paranoid, especially of authority.	Use humor to distract them; smile (genuinely).
Uses sarcasm	Steer clear when at low ebb so as not to fall under the person's influence.
Sees things negatively	Work hard to stay positive; be polite. Seek out positive people at work.
Criticizes	Arm yourself with stats, quotes, and facts to counter their cynicism. Refrain from taking on your colleague and their prickly personality. Stick to what's really the problem.
Rationalizes away criticisms as just and appropriate	Question your own sense of dread; is it their suspicion, rather than yours?
Uses cynicism as a superficial pseudo-intellectual to seem as if they are knowledgeable; act as if further analysis isn't worthy of their time	Don't play the same game of sarcasm and cynicism.

If anyone championing a particular cause aims for 100 percent goal attainment and accepts nothing less, she sets herself up for a letdown. It spills onto others in any workplace.

Producing medication, manufacturing precision equipment, or filing tax returns requires a 100 percent quality-control goal. You want the carpenter building your house or the auto mechanic fixing your car to do these things right.

When a student engages in learning, however, aiming for flawlessness might be more appropriately reserved for a senior seminar or doctoral dissertation. Learning means skill acquisition; thus, it means one does one's best, stays respectful, and sets realistic expectations.

A businessperson who allows her critical commentary to multiply enters the office with not only a briefcase dangling from her shoulder but also a large chip of cynicism as she undermines others' attempts to succeed. Some cynics hide behind the label of whistleblower, trumping up charges of safety violations when really items may have been improperly positioned and the problem easily and immediately corrected. Phony whistleblowers abuse legal protection to create or inflate problems as they watch for minor issues and then magnify them (e.g., the two malcontents in our clinic scenario).

Unable to adapt, cynical people feel unnecessary competition or suspicion when newcomers join the team. They feel spied upon and vulnerable—what if they don't make a good impression or someone sees them as incompetent? They may avoid, lob sarcastic comments, and push people away with other behavior before these others reject them. Think about the substitute teacher. Yes, anyone new experiences the desire to normalize, but there's a line between a little pushback and a lot.

THE EEYORE

How This Type Behaves	How You Should Respond
Plays victim, whimpers, moans; exhibits mute traits also	Ignore because you don't want to positively reinforce whining. Fulfill your own job description.
Sees things as "glass half-empty" rather than "half-full"	Remind the person she's got a chance to leave and direct her own destiny. Forget hiring her for the front-desk position; first impressions aren't likely this person's strong suit.
Feels sorry for him/herself; self-sabotages	Refuse to do work that isn't yours.
Passive and pessimistic; complains; often underemployed; may have chronic low moods or addictions	Offer assertiveness training if you're the supervisor.

"I'm really trying," Eeyore, the popular character in *Winnie the Pooh*, might say, as does the sad-sack worker in your office. This person greets you with a long face and offers a host of excuses for why things don't get accomplished. There's a bit of the blamer in him because he is a perpetual victim—a martyr to his own cause.

"You don't understand," complains the worker who has let the tragic loss of a loved one define even her failures at work. Her boss has seen this inertia and incomplete work before. No amount of compassion budges the worker from her victim status. The boss has had enough.

"You're right. I've never lost someone so close. But after six years, you need to move forward, and you can't reasonably blame your performance on that loss. We have an employee assistance program to help you." He hands her the information. "I really don't wish to make this a mandated referral, so I urge you to take this resource seriously."

At her desk, victim mentality sets back in as she tells coworkers, "Would you believe what a tyrant he is? He threatened me and said I have issues. Do you think that's right? He's so insensitive."

Now she has split the staff, embarrassed the boss, and created an undercurrent of gossip. She remains the injured party, perhaps not truly wanting to move forward. Her excuse of "You don't understand" remains at the ready, and she continues to derive secondary gain out of sadness. What will happen if she undergoes counseling? Therapists are trained to see two sides to every story, but this woman can cast the company as a callous institution. Though employee assistance program sessions remain confidential, mandated referrals raise flags that the person's behavior interfered with work.

What might happen if the woman in our example gave up her sadness? Well, she might falsely equate healing to not having loved the departed enough, as odd as that may sound. Some people become Eeyores when they don't get what they want, and potentially have tantrums or emotional meltdowns. Accustomed to much admiration from K-12 peers, the most popular girl or the jock may face more competition and less admiration beyond high school. That's life.

This wake-up call happens among the best of the best. Navy SEALs are famous for their courage in combat and endure weeks of extremely physical and emotional challenge in early qualifying tests. Many are all-star athletes who find themselves facing failure for the first time as they go through sleep-deprived rigors. Some make it, but some are emotionally defeated by a sense of failure. Nonetheless, they have to start the next day at 110 percent, since another's life will literally depend upon them.

Remember that the passive-aggressive person sometimes needs attention, love, and admiration, but at the same time exhibits behavior that literally pushes others away. Ambivalence results. A half-empty world concept leads to hypersensitivity, addictions, and self-medicating hurt with alcohol or substance abuse, overeating, gambling, acting out sexually— anything that numbs emptiness.

If you spot procrastination, intentional inefficiency, or a victim mentality, the reason may be lagging self-esteem, underlying (sometimes crippling) anxiety, or depressed mood, classic signs of the Eeyore. As Scott Wetzler and Leslie Morey pointed out, "They doubt they can win, and should they win they expect success to make them even more vulnerable. . . . Consequently, they inhibit their competitive drive and ambition (tying their own hands), making the competition covert."[16]

CHANGE HAPPENS: HOW TO BOUNCE BACK

Disappointment reverberates while pursuing education or building a career. A dream dies. A loss occurs. Something long sought after isn't within one's grasp. Holding on to the pessimism can start in youth when you don't make the team or the cheerleading squad, or don't get accepted by your first choice of college.

How is it that some people can be let down by a lack of acceptance, sports medal, opportunity, or even political election and rise the next day, erasing the loss until they brim with pride and success? Others awake with a negative attitude that, left unchecked, leads to hidden hostility, and possibly depression. Some people fail because of trying circumstances, others survive despite it, and still others become stronger over the long run.

If you failed a course or got fired from a job, how would you cope? Forgo the degree? Stay unemployed? Never really correct the personal pitfalls that caused it? Or, without obsessing, learn from what went wrong, hone your skills, build a better outlook, and land an even better position?

We can shape some adversities into success and happiness. Having control over our own thoughts grants us the chance to change a situation and see it in a new light. In all too many cases, the crisis isn't truly the problem; the problem is your response if you let negativity and regret shake your moorings.

THE BLAMER

How This Type Behaves	How You Should Respond
Can't argue fairly	Point out a clear grasp of the facts. Keep calm (do not cry or blame back) and watch how you defend yourself. Ask for a subsequent meeting that will be less heated.
Avoids responsibility	Don't do his/her job or work. State that their insight comes as a surprise. Ask for concrete examples, agree to think about any feedback. Possibly reconvene to discuss.
Dumps on everyone else	Limit time for his/her dumping; walk away if you can (harder to do if person has more power than you do).
Minimizes or exaggerates	Argue fairly yourself. Though you may not agree, look for elements in this person's appraisal where you may be able to learn.
Rationalizes	Avoid emotional, knee-jerk reactions. Should emotions get the better of you, apologize, and hopefully later on you can gain specifics and solutions to problems.

In a healthcare setting, it's not uncommon to see the noncompliant patient who shirks responsibility for getting better. These help-rejecting complainers are angry for being afflicted or in pain. Of course, there's a certain amount of justifiable frustration; no one wishes to be unhealthy. But patients who point the finger at others (filing unnecessary malpractice suits) or self-sabotage recovery by eschewing advice and treatment have a secondary gain they hope to obtain.

Though Helen has some back pain, it presents far worse than doctors might expect from the X-rays taken. A physician has referred Helen, a perpetual complainer, to see a counselor and a psychiatrist to consider antidepressant or anxiety medication, and sparks fly from Helen's hidden anger. It's reasonable for a doctor to screen for depression and require such consultations; there is an increased co-occurrence of depression, stress, and back pain.

"This doctor can't fix me. He thinks it's all in my head," Helen says. She twists the truth to avoid a mind/body connection and blames her doctor. Helen might be a bit self-centered, because calling attention to her ailments does gain her attention. By projecting negativity, she receives sympathy. This easily becomes a self-perpetuating, circular pattern. It keeps the doctor on edge such that he may refer Helen to another provider, where she may then complain about being "abandoned." Or, doctor shopping (and abandoning her own care) may provide Helen a steady stream of sympathy from new healthcare providers. They likely don't possess a miracle cure either, but they also don't have a history with Helen. This keeps Helen in control, yet this sympathy cycle drives her family and friends absolutely nuts.

In a business setting, you may have sent a colleague spreadsheets and attached files multiple times. He's done nothing except ask "Can you send those again?" right before your deadline. One more delay. You feel like screaming, "Lack of planning on your part does not warrant an emergency on mine!"

When this colleague honestly has a legitimate excuse, you may be rightly skeptical. Open communication would clear away misunderstandings. Remember though: if your colleague is a blamer and this is about secondary gain, any compassion and support will feed the problem.

THE MUTE

How This Type Behaves	How You Should Respond
Ignores, avoids, denies	Don't feel invalidated.
Uses silence	Maintain your self-esteem.
Swallows everything	Expect them to deny problems.
Has no follow-through	Offer warmth to their icy demeanor.
Procrastinates, is indecisive	Refuse to match their mute behavior.
Purposely excludes you from information or meetings	Be very clear in your communications.
When the going gets tough, gets quiet	Clarify your expectations of their behavior.
Gives little to no answers, even when pressed for one.	Don't assume that silence means agreement (or disagreement).

Imagine the unhappy child whose parents enroll her in a private school, only once she's in uniform, she skips classes, silently voicing her displeasure. This girl misses the bus one day, has a migraine the next, and claims the teacher picks on her another. When her continued excuses disguise her true intent (to drop out of school), she manipulates everyone and most likely self-sabotages her future.

Adults misuse silence as well. Suppose a bad storm has inflicted property damage on an office complex where you house your start-up enterprise. The building owner, worried he may lose rent, fails to inform you of the remediation company's repair list, sharing only 30 percent of the recommendations. He hires cheap labor to perform quick fixes, and months later, as the paint blisters and the ceiling tiles crumble, you face massive business interruption because of his silence.

Or take Bart, who did casework for a county agency. When his boss asked him if he needed help, he said he had everything under control—until people called saying they had not heard from Bart in weeks. When questioned, Bart claimed the clients were high maintenance or he was waiting for information from them. Yet as Bart abruptly left one day without even two weeks' notice, the staff found seventy cases in his drawer where no action had been taken or no return calls made. Bart is a classic mute.

THE STAR

How This Type Behaves	How You Should Respond
Concerned with their own agenda, preoccupied with self	Realize that you may feel positive about them, but over time, recognize the problems.
Ingratiates self successfully and forms numerous triangles since they cannot be direct	Realize that they reject mentoring, for there's nothing to learn when they know it all.
Think they are superstars; legends in their own minds; often showcase own achievements beyond customary sales-minded sensibility	Use their strengths; help the person to feel that their ideas are vital.

How This Type Behaves	How You Should Respond
Requires special treatment but displays little or no empathy for others; snubs others and lives/works above the rules; in fact, rewrites the rules with a different set for everyone else	Ignore their know-it-all nature.
Sees you as the competition; may engage in bullying and likely argues for the sport of it and/or for attention	Don't argue over who is right; these people think that they are always right. Document carefully. Engage human resources and other authorities, if necessary, to address collateral damage and halt bullying or cyberstalking.

We saved the star for last, as it frequently coexists with other passive-aggressive styles. In any career, you will run up against those who believe that they are stars. This behavior overlaps with self-absorbed or bullying traits that we discuss elsewhere.

Stars think that they deserve higher status than others. They are indeed self-crafted legends, adept at stealing credit (or clients), grabbing publicity, or gaining notoriety as they insert themselves into opportune moments. The typical star pushes his agenda, not yours, such as a lawyer you hire to represent the educational interests of your special-needs child. He touts his abilities so that you buy into his ball-of-fire image, yet once his retainer is deposited, he disregards your input (or anyone else's). Countless mistakes crop up. On documents, he doesn't even get the child's name, school, or disability straight. He bills you for revisions but becomes indignant when you ask for a credit for his mistakes. How could you be so darn ungrateful when he tells you he's one of the best?

Do the Perks Outweigh the Path?

Channeled constructively, many stars can use their ego for constructive outcomes. It takes a little chutzpah to get up in front of a crowd to speak, act in a play, or take on leadership. According to Nina Brown, EdD, who wrote *Working with the Self-Absorbed*, healthy adult narcissism means having

> Plenty of government or military officials, actors and actresses, athletes, and business leaders have achieved superstar status. Many have a right to be proud. They've earned their perks. True class, of course, means never stepping over or on anyone to get your way, achieve, or maintain your status.

empathy, creativity, and the ability to delay gratification while accepting personal responsibility and others' personal space and boundaries.[17] It also encompasses the ability to laugh (even at oneself) and form satisfying relationships. Plenty of government or military officials, actors and actresses, athletes, and business leaders have achieved superstar status. Many have a right to be proud. They've earned their perks. True class, of course, means never stepping over or on anyone to get your way, achieve, or maintain your status.

When the Star Becomes a Problem

Although star qualities can be used for productivity and strategic vision, too much narcissism becomes pathological, controlling, harmful, and sometimes explosive. Stars send mixed messages to disguise their words and actions to project a good image. They morph into false social heroes impressing others with their great deeds. Often, they need to impress themselves. While they project self-esteem, it's often inaccurate and inflated, not a healthy self-concept. They fear rejection and embarrassment, and never—ever—want to admit that they contribute to their own problems. This explains their sloughing off guilt and self-blame at all costs, and why they frequently launch verbal attacks.

In certain fields, you must talk a good game. Here's the catch: then you need to deliver. If your motives are genuine and your communication is congruent, you generally do. If the home contractor puts out mixed messages, he'll also hammer you with added hassles and costs. Your three-week kitchen replacement might take six months and ten grand extra if done by the star!

These people become the brightest in their own constellations. At school, the student who announces he'll make his first million in the five years following graduation comes across just as off-putting as his mother did when she bragged to her spinning class how her kid was Harvard or Yale material. Meanwhile, he got accepted at an excellent but less esteemed school, where he perpetuated his intergalactic status.

The star's indirect style can also suddenly shift, with him becoming obsequious or contrite, but still not truly humble.

Stubborn stars form triangles, take issues to third parties (to make others look bad, themselves powerful), or cite others' opinions. They never got the geometric concept that the shortest distance between two points is a straight line. Forming such triangles perpetuates everyone's anger. Triangulation is troublesome when a person bypasses you and takes the problem to the next level (your boss) without first attempting to solve it with you. This spreads the problem three ways.

However, if there's an impasse, if the matter is timely and the clock's ticking, or when your problem is so specialized that it requires a supervisor's insights, taking a matter above and beyond you and the star (triangulating it) may be the best solution. But otherwise, triangles rarely solve the original problem between two parties, and they usually provoke anger and/or hard feelings.

What can you do with all this shining light? When your boss is the star, you won't feel you can have a life beyond the office, but you must. Otherwise, stress may show up in somatic complaints such as tension headaches or stomach ailments. When working with the star, remember, it's not about you. Don't take her clipped conversations as personal put-offs and don't internalize the attitudes and criticisms. Don't hitch your wagon to this boss's cart, either, as mentoring you probably isn't top priority; her career matters most. You are there only to serve. If there are too many stars in your organization, and they prevent your own qualities from shining, you may need to consider a new job. Document hard work that solves problems and eschew office gossip.

When the star is your coworker, his stair-stepping ingratiation becomes the whatever-it-takes approach. "This is the individual who likes to sit in the boss's chair after everyone has left for the day, just to try it out for size," write Alan A. Cavaiola, PhD, and Neil J. Lavender, PhD, in *Toxic Coworkers*.[18]

You won't change this; only much awareness and effort on their part can do so. Arguing will tend to get you nowhere, so pick your battles cautiously. Keep your concerns with true out-of-the-office confidantes, not on your sleeve. Empathy will be hard to find around a star. Sharing only renders you more vulnerable to this self-absorbed person, who may use your heart-felt concerns to manipulate you and break any boundary of confidence.

When employees are stars, expect ambivalent loyalty with charm on the surface and subterfuge everywhere else as they simultaneously work to take you down. The star's distorted thinking has convinced her that rules meant for the staff at large don't apply to her. Anticipate her poor personal boundaries (barges into your office, interrupts a lot, invades your personal space) and failures to follow the chain of command (goes around authority). She will ignore cues to redirect her to what's reasonable and what many would consider right. Since arrogance makes a very poor first impression, this isn't your ideal front-desk candidate. If you think this person can be mentored into humility, we suggest you forget that notion. You may have the most well-intended feedback but the guilt trip this person sends you on will make you wish you kept it to yourself (as a momentary mute!). Sometimes it's best to play to this person's need to be superior. Reinforce what you wish to see more of with phrases we offer here:

> "I'd like for you to achieve more because everyone *admires* your drive and determination to close a deal. Let's set a new, *great* goal with that in mind."
>
> "You're simply the *best* at figuring these things out. Do you think you could create another *win* by close of the day tomorrow?"
>
> "I'm looking for an *outstanding* person to take this on. I need just the right employee."
>
> "You've got such *superior* strengths in this one area, Jane. That's why we're taking you off of this other project so that you can focus on this for us."

Once your star is onboard with a project or request, provide ample opportunity for her to hear others' feedback, because this shifts the star, even momentarily, off the pedestal with enough redirection to be productive. Maximize team efforts in order to downplay harmful competitive instincts and help everyone toward a common mission of excellence.

TOXIC MENTORS AND PROFESSIONAL JEALOUSY

Like Wade, Crystal, and Shannon, the law school classmates we discussed earlier who set out affably but once they worked together grew resentful, many offices experience professional jealousy.

Is there enough opportunity for success that all can celebrate collegial achievements? We sure hope so, but frankly folks, we have seen unkind assumptions rendered too often.

A group of professionals with their own business identities leased an office suite but shared the waiting room, each contributing to the look and feel that would make first impressions. They agreed that one gentleman could display books he had penned for his customers. But over time, this man's hard work disappeared from the shelf and got hidden underneath the coffee table. Maybe once, possibly twice, a person might actually have set them back in the wrong spot. But if this becomes the norm, it's highly suspect. Constant removal rats out one of these officemates as incongruent (at the very least), jealous, or resentful (at worst).

Even in academia, where good souls share their knowledge to make the world a better place, there's strife, and a saying that goes something like this: "Those who can, do. Those who cannot, often opt to teach instead." We add to this cliché that those who cannot do a job well do a disservice to learners if they lack empathy and fail to cheerlead achievements.

With tenure often used as a shield, a passive-aggressive educator can make your learning stressful and your career path potentially complicated. Just as a job seeker examines the company's profile and products, it's wise for the student to ask others about their experience in a particular class or with a professor. If the person's grade was low, watch how much blame this individual places upon herself or others, but also listen up if she says the professor was abrupt, belittling with feedback, and unnecessarily exacting with an unattainably high bar. Few people learn well by surprise attack either. That's exactly what it feels like when a stealth educator withholds the intensity of assignments until after the drop/add period, thereby rendering students captive to a professor's power to extend value or exact misery.

Choose instructors who have actually worked or continue to work in the field you intend to join once you finish school. These professionals bring an understanding that can't be matched by theory and ivory towers alone. You'll weed out those who may resent their own failed opportunities or those who feel jealous because their students sign on to exciting new jobs with entire futures ahead of them.

Jealousy is a common human emotion and often at the root of hidden anger. If you feel envious of another person, acknowledge it to yourself, and maybe even to the other person if you have an open, honest relationship there. Recognize the potential for positive reciprocity that lies ahead. You may not realize it now, but any celebratory good wishes that you extend do two compelling things. Immediately, your goodwill shows you to be kind and supportive as opposed to standoffish. People like to be around the former and steer clear of the latter. Second, whatever their contributions, someone else's achievement may help your learning and career growth. While your evolution may not seem parallel, the two of you may land in similar circles in this vast but surprisingly small world of ours.

DEALING WITH HIDDEN ANGER AT WORK AND SCHOOL

We hope you take from this chapter new awareness about how to cope better, work harder, and avoid becoming like any of our eight angry types. Remember that many passive-aggressors do well with a nine-to-five schedule. Don't fight against their natural proclivities.

In a family business, know that you're dealing with two systems—a professional one and a family system. Any hidden anger, tendency to step in for another, manipulation, or even addiction will have twice the impact. Systems theory applies well to organizational psychology. We urge you to read this book in its entirety, as many aspects we discuss may apply to your situation.

No matter what predicament you're in, refuse to own a colleague's or superior's anger. Misery might enjoy company, but you get to choose how you feel and how you act on those feelings. If you're asked how you feel and you think that what you feel might be offensive to the asker, you can likely find something to say that's true but not impassioned in order to navigate the situation successfully.

When you sense passive-aggression or any hidden agenda at work, document problem behaviors in performance appraisals whether you're the supervisor/teacher or the employee. Exposing a superior's hidden anger is tough to do, but it may help if you keep private notes securely at home. And of course, document your own progress and performance in case any doubts about those arise in the future.

Take account of your mood outside of work, as researchers have found that coworker incivility has been associated with increased anxiety, depressed mood, and work-to-family conflicts. If the stress has spilled over onto partners, children, or friends, consider it a red flag that you need to take action on changing your career situation.[19]

Finally, distance yourself, if necessary. The worst-case scenario may call for a change in work environment, a switch into another class or academic major, or careful analysis of who brings out the best in you . . . and the worst. If you are able to wait it out or circumstances evolve, those concealing (and projecting) anger may quit or retire. And then, you can work in peace.

PART 3

Healing from Hidden Anger

nine

Deeply Seated Anger

ADELE AND TIFFANY VENTURED TO COLORADO TO VISIT COLLEGE PALS. Tiffany talked Adele into staying longer, but when they rebooked, their airfare cost a hideous sum. Instead, they agreed to split the cost of a rental car over a long weekend. Tiffany said she wanted to see Dallas en route back to New Orleans. Upon return, Adele e-mailed a funny photo to Tiffany and a reminder of what she owed toward the bill for their car.

Her eyes widened at Tiffany's response: "I was shocked to see you so obsessed with money, Adele. What would Emily Post say? That 'fun' time was blasting hot, and I had to hear all about *your* work. I have a life, too! You hardly asked about *me*. Manners, Adele! I only mean to help you. Others agree. I think we are done. Love and hugs, Tiffany."

Outrage churned in Adele's stomach. Tiffany had just twisted reality into something ugly. Adele hadn't *needed* to ask Tiffany about her life, for she talked about it through New Mexico and half of Texas. Adele had politely (she thought) kept quiet.

She drew in a cleansing breath, removed her hands from the keyboard, and shut down her computer. But the insults from a fifteen-year friend stung as if a beehive had descended upon her. It was as if Tiffany had morphed into someone else entirely . . . but why?

When hidden anger manifests way beyond what is normal, set your radar to the possibility of a more complex concern (e.g., attention issues, depression, oppositional defiant disorder) or something more toxic (e.g., characterological issues).

Where you might think a person is being passive-aggressive, it can cross over to something that runs deeper and requires treatment. We'll show you what can and cannot be handled alone. If any of the following portray you, first rule out other things, then obtain a solid diagnosis and find treatment for your intense anger.

ANGER OVER THE TOP AND INFRINGING ON OTHERS

We've unraveled the signs and symptoms of passive-aggressive behavior but we have not yet delved into extremes. The following pages give a cursory overview of deeper disorders and just enough psychopathology for you to understand when to keep your antennae active. Quite often, your sixth sense picks up on a deeply entrenched problem.

An important caveat: while this is a self-help book designed to offer comfort, if you're on the receiving end of difficult behavior or struggle with anger yourself, this will not give you a diagnosis. Only qualified mental health professionals can do that, and we urge you to recognize the limits of this or any other resource.

On the other hand, if reading this book helps you to put behavior into a better context, to be more empathic toward a person or problem, that's positive and useful. But don't confuse empathy with enabling: identifying a deeper-rooted problem is not a "get-off-without-taking-responsibility" ticket. Indeed, although some people see a bona fide disorder as a lock, others see it as a key. With that key, they can unlock a passage to change and happiness.

MIRROR, MIRROR ON THE WALL

Let's go back to Adele and Tiffany for a moment. Have you ever been angered by an arrogant person who seems to feel entitled to take cheap shots, taints shared memories with an abrupt 180 twist, lacks empathy to the point of exploitation, and bolsters himself on a pedestal that no one else puts him on?

Welcome to the world of vanity. Because vain people soak up any attention or praise they can, they often evoke intense reactions in those who stand back, not in awe or admiration, as these conceited people may believe, but in shock at how insensitive and outrageous the vain ones act toward others. As we've seen, there is a crossover between passive-aggressive tendencies and self-absorbed traits. Both involve a sly element because the inflated person must be seen in the best light. No mirror ever seems large enough to hold this person's self-image of success, brilliance, beauty, and power.

Tiffany surely had those qualities. Her trip with Adele to see college pals may not have started out all about her, but in private, alone with only one other person, it definitely ended that way. This is venomous narcissism. In front of a greater audience, the person usually behaves, though not always. Men tend to end up identified with these traits more often than women do, but vanity has no gender boundaries.

Speaking of boundaries, there are none. Notice how Tiffany talked Adele into staying (manipulated her) with little consideration as to the consequences. Tiffany managed to finagle a side trip based on her agenda, and when Adele chatted with her during their tedious drive, Tiffany conveniently reframed it (sheer projection). The fact that she ducked out of their verbal agreement to share costs and then lobbed both famous ("Emily Post") and anonymous ("others") ammo Adele's way is another self-absorbed hallmark. They reinvent rules for themselves, struggle with self-image and self-doubt, and thus form triangles to justify hideous actions. They'll use anyone. Signing off with love and hugs may have been unconscious and automatic or completely sarcastic (and was definitely incongruent).

For people like Tiffany, doing anything for someone else comes purely as an afterthought and only if it's easy. Should you hold back, even briefly, any admiration and praise, you'll pay a substantial relational price by their sullen pouting or caustic, dismissive comments about you, report W. Brad Johnson, PhD, and the late Kelly Murray, PhD, in *Crazy Love*. Such problems aren't the sole domain of intimate relationships. If you are, however, in a romantic union with a vain partner, these authors suggest that "failure to accommodate the narcissist's entitlement will certainly result in some form of relational punishment or conflict."[1]

And so the anger dominoes. What happens if this isn't a friendship or intimate relationship but happens in your home and/or is the model you grew up with? Children of the self-absorbed parent aren't usually viewed as separate and developing beings, but merely as extensions of the self.

Covert narcissistic families look fine to outsiders, and actually they don't look too bad from the inside either. But Stephanie Donaldson-Pressman, MSW, and Robert M. Pressman, PhD, the authors of *The Narcissistic Family* write, "If the children are expected to meet parental needs, then they are not getting their own needs met, or learning how to express their needs and feelings appropriately."[2] What they do learn is how to mask their feelings, pretend to feel things they don't, and keep their real feelings under wraps.

Family members wall off emotions, often forgetting them until something else occurs later and the emotion floods back in an unhealthy, destructive way. Reactivity sparks, and concealed anger resurfaces. What's more, maybe the narcissistic parents have been emotionally absent, and the children are just plain tired of putting their parent's needs before their own. There's no magic answer to turning this around. If this is you, and you can find little emotional support from your family, try to:

- Reconcile your past. Perhaps you grew up with many mirrors and not much light reflected onto your needs. Work to heal your frustrations, learn from them, and create healthier relationships.
- Acknowledge your visceral reactions (headaches, gastrointestinal symptoms, tight muscles, a lump in the throat, or anxiety). Be aware that emotions arise on autopilot.
- Set appropriate boundaries and fortify existing ones. Otherwise, you risk "catching" the self-absorbed person's faulty feelings (including bitterness).
- Hold family members accountable for their actions and what they should do for themselves. Don't do their work for them. Refuse to become codependent.
- Work on yourself, not others. The needy, dependent personality is the only style that can coexist for any great length of time with someone who is narcissistic. It's a trap waiting to lure you in.

LABELS AND CODES DEMYSTIFIED

Consumers need knowledge and to be a little wary when too much emphasis is placed upon testing or labels derived from it. Formal testing is only part of a diagnostic picture. Proper assessment, administered by a qualified, licensed mental health professional, creates awareness and often presents increased options for effective treatment (see Chapter 12).

Throughout these pages, we have outlined certain behaviors, such as control, manipulation, self-absorption, and childlike or immature conduct, in our charts. Here's another chart focused on depression. While it may resemble the Eeyore type, this details what we know as clinical depression.

DEPRESSION

Depressed people exhibit the traits below based upon core needs, which often haven't been met, as well as what they fear or avoid.

Needs	Fears/Avoids	What You See
Hope, support, security; social interactions and enjoyable activities; energy	Loneliness, failure, rejection	Glass-half-empty mentality; low self-esteem; sense of feeling lost or helpless; isolation
Optimism, positives	Living or working without support	Low mood (especially chronic); little or no life direction; negative outlook and/or irritability (especially in males)
Self-worth; sense of agency over one's life; improved habits with sleep/diet	Unhappiness, difficulty	Addictions (self-medicating behavior); often passive in nature; sleep/appetite disturbance

The World Health Organization estimates that 350 million people deal with depression, making it the leading cause of disability worldwide. At its worst, depression can lead to suicide.[3] In 2013, the Centers for Disease Control and Prevention put the number of American adults suffering from a depressive illness at 18.8 million, with merely 29 percent having contacted a mental health provider that past year. Surprisingly, only 39 percent of the severely depressed did so. Persons diagnosed with a chronic medical illness double their risk for depression, and when untreated, depression worsens overall health and can double treatment costs.[4]

We also know that many people suffer in silence, thus making actual instances of depression much higher than official reports. The condition does not discriminate, but we do know that adolescents and young adults face higher rates and that postpartum depression strikes approximately six hundred thousand women in the United States annually. Some cases end tragically for both baby and mother.[5] Men dealing with depression tend to be more reluctant to step forward. Often when they seek treatment it's at the behest of others. Irritability is a frequent symptom for men. To address this, the National Institute of Mental Health provides a website link featuring men's personal stories about depression in order to erase stigma and encourage them to seek treatment.[6]

Regardless of gender, passive-aggressive or negative people frequently experience anxiety and depressive symptoms because, according to the late Theodore Millon and his colleagues, they feel their ambivalence through moodiness, being out of sorts, and worry. Verbal venting or covert behavior temporarily discharge pent-up anger, tension, and conflicted feelings. According to Millon and colleagues, these personalities aren't beyond using anxiety to escape others' demands. [7] Phobias provide innocent cover.

A short overview of depressive disorders appears here, including a new condition that stemmed from concerns that too many children were being diagnosed with bipolar disorder.

ANGER, SYMPTOMS, AND TREATMENT

Clinical depression is far from merely a bad mood, is much more serious, and frequently thoughts of death emerge with it. These range from "I wish

Depression Type	Anger Component/Symptoms	Treatment/Remedies
Adjustment disorder occurs during external stress or transitions (grief or loss, separation, divorce, job loss, miscarriage, even good events) with social, home, or work impairment.	People feel overwhelmed, anxious, sad, and frustrated. Stuck thinking, abrupt or poor communication, pressures, low-level frustration, and irritability often signal adjustment difficulty.	Solution-focused therapy, cognitive-behavioral therapy (CBT), or family systems therapy are best. The person with adjustment disorder should up his exercise and coping skills. Mindfulness reduces anxiety and promotes better sleep. Prescribed medication also works. When genetic tendencies or biochemistry breaks down, major depression or persistent depressive disorder can set in.
Seasonal affective disorder (SAD), otherwise known as the "winter blues," has been determined by research to be very real. A lesser constellation of symptoms suggests **seasonal affective syndrome**. Mood and productivity plummet alongside short days and lack of sunlight. Lethargy, large amounts of sleep, carbohydrate cravings, and isolation often occur.	Irritability may be the most common manifestation of anger in the sufferer. Often those living in the midst of SAD become frustrated and resentful and lose patience with the one who frequently hibernates and/ or isolates. Thus, it tends to affect family and social life, sometimes also having financial consequences or academic fallout.	Adding light therapy outdoors in the winter months and/ or with indoor therapeutic lights (10,000 lux) restores the body's circadian rhythms (body clock). Low dose antidepressants mitigate the symptoms. Self-help measures should always be tried, regardless. Talk therapy promotes behavioral strategies and assists patients in thinking about topics in more productive ways.
Postpartum depression is more complex than mere "baby blues" after childbirth. All new mothers suffer with fatigue. This is more profound. A sense of hopelessness and guilt accompanies other markers and does not lift easily. **Postpartum psychosis** means delusions and paranoia that put both mother and child at risk.	The sadness, crying, irritability, and lack of enthusiasm take hold along with repetitive, negative thoughts that intrude upon the mother in such a way that it alarms her or others witnessing her struggle. Having turbulent relations with the baby's father and little outside support make the mom more vulnerable and contribute to a reoccurrence, as will a history of anxiety and depression.	Moms find it difficult to admit that they feel sad during what others consider to be a celebratory time. Counseling helps, especially for nursing moms. Not the first course of treatment, medication must be considered if symptoms don't remit. In cases of postpartum psychosis, emergency treatment with one's physician, therapist, and/or hospital emergency department is paramount.

continues —

—— continued

Depression Type	Anger Component/Symptoms	Treatment/Remedies
Major depression is a deeper disorder where the person's struggles slip into greater despair, hopelessness, and anhedonia (losing pleasure in things they once enjoyed). Impaired judgment can lead to greater risk of suicide if the person does not seek treatment or stay on medication.	Persistent anger shows when the person has low frustration tolerance, blames, broods, and reacts irritably. There may be guilt and restlessness coupled with impaired decisions such that irrational thoughts take hold more easily, and with low energy, the person doesn't do much to check out the validity of his/her feelings.	Medication is standard in cases of major depression. Once antidepressants reach therapeutic levels, the patient may get more value from CBT, but therapy should be started at the outset to form a good working relationship in counseling and learn better coping. Monitor diet, weight, exercise, and medication compliance.
Persistent depressive disorder (used to be called *dysthymia*) is chronic, lasting at least two years, and is often chalked up to "that's just the way he is." Isolation, self-esteem issues, and constant fatigue are hallmarks. The person gets up, holds a job or goes to school—maybe not optimally, but he does these things. A *joie de vivre*, long-term outlook that spawns action is missing, and instead this person remains passive.	This person may appear wounded of spirit, negative, irritable, with much self-doubt as well as problems making decisions and concentrating. Interpersonal relationships become conflicted, and this persons lacks the energy to improve. Addictions are often common.	Antidepressant medication helps, as does talk therapy with CBT, family systems, or solution-based components. If the issues date back to one's youth, more work regarding family of origin should be done. Behaviorally, this person can help himself via exercise, developing coping and communication skills, and improving diet, sleep, and other habits necessary for good health.
Disruptive mood dysregulation disorder (DMDD), a new descriptor for kids (ages six to eighteen) with severe, recurrent outbursts not consistent with age or development level, that occur three+ times weekly. The child seems irritable most days. These criteria must be present for twelve months (without a three-month or more interruption) and noticed before age ten. Irritability must occur in at least two settings, where the behavior isn't accounted by another mental diagnosis.	DMDD reactions are beyond typical expectations; the tantrums and irritability must occur outside of the child's home. The twelve-month marker eliminates some stressors (moving, new school, or transitions). Grouchiness remains between angry outbursts (at least three times per week). "Excessive" eruptions cause greater woes and result in the child feeling resentful and cranky and then easily losing his/her temper. Watch for crying, pouting, negativity, and meltdowns.	Treatment here is very individualized to the specifics of the child and family. There's no one size fits all. Counseling and often family therapy are needed. In some cases, a child may benefit from group therapy or social skills training. Medication addresses symptoms. This diagnosis stemmed from too many children being labeled with bipolar disorder. Irritability may lead to other diagnoses, so make sure careful assessment by a therapist and/or psychiatrist rules out other issues.

Depression Type	Anger Component/Symptoms	Treatment/Remedies
Bipolar disorder (used to be called **manic depression)** exhibits with extreme changes or elevations in mood, thoughts, feelings, and behaviors, plus periods of mania, extreme optimism, euphoria, energy, self-confidence, risk-taking, lack of inhibition, impulsivity, racing thoughts, pressured speech, marked changes in appetite, decreased sleep, and inability to focus. Often, there are peculiar thoughts and behaviors along with substance abuse. Depressive symptoms (previously outlined) then occur. Bipolar disorder can cycle quickly in some people. **Cyclothymic disorder** is a milder, chronic form.	With more than prickly, cantankerous, irascible anger, for those suffering from Bipolar I or Bipolar II (swings aren't so extreme, with hypomania) a frightening rage takes over. Garden-variety bad behavior flourishes over-the-top as sarcastic jokes become denigrating insults and everything the person has bottled up spews forth with dragon-force venom. Not surprisingly, that type of anger can cast ruination, or at the very least, much destruction in its wake. Anger becomes self-blame and a negative mind-set takes hold with "Why me?" or "What did I do to deserve this?"	This is another form of depression where medication is a must. Bipolar disorder affects brain chemistry; thus, patients must work together with a prescribing physician, preferably a psychiatrist trained with such medications, to treat the symptoms. Additionally, talk therapy supports the person to live a positive path with proper coping skills and encourages the patient to stay on medications and openly discuss any side effects experienced. Unpleasant side effects are oft-used reasons why people abruptly stop medication and thereby see the return of symptoms.

I'd just never wake up" to frequent, intense, lethal thoughts combined with a plan to commit suicide. Despite understood blessings in their lives, the depressed person still feels overwhelmingly sad and hopeless.

Though suicidal ideation can be transient, it's serious when you see a person do the following: stockpile medications; purchase or gain access to a weapon; isolate or harm themselves; give away prized possessions; express sudden interest in wills, insurance policies, or burial plots; make more permanent plans for child or pet care; take risks or abuse alcohol or drugs; or make statements such as "I wish I were dead" or talk of "ending it all." Especially if a close friend or family member committed suicide, or if the person has recently suffered a loss, serious torment, allegations, or investigations, it's important to monitor the depressed individual. A person with a previous suicide attempt is at very high risk. When chronic pain intrudes upon life, people can also become so overwhelmed by grief, panic, and anger that their risk for serious depression spikes, as it also does for those with heart disease or cancer.

Untreated depression worsens pre-existing medical conditions and doubles healthcare costs. Only about 51 percent of people, if that, receive treatment, and even fewer, 21 percent, receive *appropriate* treatment.[8] The rest self-manage or deny their symptoms. Researchers have linked sustained stress to an increased risk for depressive and anxiety disorders because of its impact upon brain chemistry. Depression can also be a side effect of medications administered for other maladies.

Early intervention is crucial (especially with children). Each subsequent major depressive episode increases the odds of a possible recurrence. In this era of discoveries, we know the biological links to depression and anxiety. Medication works on specific brain neurotransmitters and can certainly provide relief. Passive-aggressive patients, however, often remain stuck where they seek secondary gain through complaints and inactivity.

Pediatric bipolar disorder does exist, but other diagnoses may better account for a child's symptoms. Most initial bipolar diagnoses occur in early adulthood (late teens or early twenties). High-achieving and particularly creative people have a higher incidence of bipolar disorder. Genetic links have been associated with depression and bipolar disorder, but they are not a determinant in and of themselves. Environmental and lifestyle factors contribute to genetic vulnerabilities.

ANGER THAT AFFECTS EATING

At sixteen, Blake shares a room with her fourteen-year-old stepsister after dad remarried a woman with a daughter. Their closet serves as a constant reminder that Blake's size sixteen clothes hang opposite Megan's size six. To Blake, girls like Megan have it all—the body, the clothes, even the pearly whites. When their dentist pulled her stepmom aside to discuss Blake's eroded enamel, the family began to question her excusing herself after dinner, recent requests to buy clothes in increasingly smaller sizes, and their having to settle episodes of name-calling when Blake vents upon

Megan. Blake lets loose on Megan infrequently, but it's enough to wreak havoc at home.

Blake exhibits signs of an eating disorder, which sometimes involves hidden anger components. Both anorexia nervosa and bulimia are physically harmful and potentially life-threatening conditions, and those who succumb are sensitive to rejection, need approval, and feel resentful. While these eating disorders often affect women, particularly adolescent girls, they also affect men. You'll also find eating disorders in those who must maintain an ideal body weight, such as models, dancers, gymnasts, and racing jockeys.

There are two main types of eating disorders—the restricting type and the binging/purging type (bulimia nervosa). A hallmark of anorexia nervosa is that the person weighs below 85 percent of normal body weight. Those who restrict their diets tend to be compulsive, introverted, fairly passive and dependent, and have low self-esteem. They also may resent parental control over their lives, craving independence. With bulimia nervosa, the diagnosis meets similar criteria except that the person's weight doesn't necessarily fall below 85 percent of normal body weight. Many bulimic patients induce vomiting and abuse laxatives or diuretics in a secretive manner. Here, we see the indirect personality style and hidden anger manifest. Bulimia sufferers tend to avoid conflict and live stressful and negative lives that are out of control. Harming themselves through binging and purging restores their feeling of self-control, at least in their minds. There is a growing body of evidence linking genetics to increased risks for eating disorders (though this is not causal). Future research will grant greater insight into the complex causes, but eating disorders mandate immediate medical intervention.

Psychologically, those suffering from eating disorders need to acknowledge the passive-aggressive role they play in refusing assistance from authority figures. Like many who conceal their anger, they desperately seek acceptance and lack problem-solving skills, assertive and expressive openness, and relaxation. They improve more if they jettison perfectionism altogether, become comfortable with a healthier body image, and acknowledge their hunger as well as their anger. Family counseling and a positive environment, along with individual therapy and medical treatment (a must), can restore good health to those afflicted by eating disorders.

SELF-DIRECTED HARM

Another destructive behavior that has risen dramatically is cutting or other self-afflicted bodily harm. While this behavior is seen mostly in adolescent girls or adult women besieged by emotional turmoil, stressed by life situations, and conflicted about their body image, a growing population of boys has turned to self-mutilation. All cry out for help by cutting, bruising, or burning themselves because they cannot articulate their thoughts, feelings, and need for love and acceptance.[9]

The behavior develops until it becomes a person's primary outlet for dealing with life's frustrations. Many who self-injure want to blunt their emotions and relieve bottled-up psychological pain. They report being much calmer and at peace once the body's natural opiates release upon bodily injury. Clothing conceals the wounds, inflicted where others won't readily discover them. Sadly enough, this relief is only temporary and doesn't solve the true problems, which surface again in the absence of effective therapy.

Proper treatment of self-inflicted harm is multifaceted, often focused on treating an underlying depression or anxiety disorder while using behavioral interventions to control the self-mutilation. By learning to express one's anger, shame, guilt, or other intense emotions, the individual can regain lasting, healthier control over life. Michael Hollander, PhD, details the many myths surrounding this growing problem in *Helping Teens Who Cut*. Hollander reports that fewer than 4 percent of adolescents cause deliberate self-harm in order to achieve attention and that teens rarely injure because of peer pressure but may choose friends who do share in this behavior. With suicide as a leading cause of adolescent death, self-harm should not be taken lightly; however, Hollander writes that self-harm is generally not a deliberate or halfhearted suicide attempt. He suggests that most clinicians today can differentiate between self-injurious behavior and the intent to die, and yet admits that moods change rapidly with teenagers. It's always better to err on the side of caution and seek help when in doubt.[10]

ANGERED BY INATTENTION

Joel, two years out of graduate school, has become angry over the corrective action plan he received at work. Simply put, Joel resembles disorganized chaos, with papers strewn about his desk and with projects still on his computer's hard drive because he's never quite finished them or didn't turn them in. Through school, Joel struggled. He's not stupid—in fact, he's far from it, with an IQ in the gifted range—but his tendencies to put things off and to anger easily have finally gotten the better of him. Joel has ADHD, diagnosed much later than most cases, but he's fortunate. His diagnosis and treatment will not only save his career but become a personal epiphany as he taps his strengths to overcome his weaknesses.

SIGNS OF ATTENTION-DEFICIT/HYPERACTIVITY DISORDER (ADHD)

- Difficulty paying close attention to details; makes careless mistakes
- Difficulty sustaining attention and organizing tasks/activities; easily distracted by extraneous stimuli
- Doesn't appear to be listening when spoken to; doesn't follow through on instructions/duties
- Often forgets or loses things; disorganized
- May appear not to be present emotionally; silent
- Often avoids or dislikes tasks that require sustained mental effort
- Impulsive or hyperfocused at times; fidgety; "on the go" a lot
- Needs much stimulation; seeks conflict (such as arguments)
- Interrupts; impatient; trouble delaying gratification
- Talks a lot; processes verbally
- Gets stuck in thinking; holds strong opinions; appears uncooperative
- Intrudes into or sometimes takes over what others are doing

---

Attention-deficit/hyperactivity disorder (ADHD) refers to a set of behavioral symptoms that usually begin in childhood, when it's often first diagnosed. About half of all children with ADHD show symptoms into adulthood. A Centers for Disease Control and Prevention report released in 2015 revealed that 11 percent of children ages four to seventeen have been diagnosed with ADHD at some point, compared with only 7.8 percent ten years prior. Boys are three times more likely (13.2 percent) to be identified than girls (5.6 percent). Adult figures (4–5 percent) are less reliable because many cases were not confirmed in childhood.[11] A child's diagnosis frequently uncovers adult cases. Since more children have been diagnosed in recent decades, their parents have thought, "that sounds like me."

How can this remain hidden? Because the symptoms weren't intense or frequent enough to cause academic or social impairment, or if they did exist, the person found coping strategies that worked well enough to get by. Teachers may have treated it as a behavior problem, and partners dealt with the behaviors without understanding the root causes.

Accurate diagnosis of adult ADHD follows a paper trail of lackluster grades, poor driving records, or behavioral difficulties with friends, siblings, parents, or peers. It often presents when adults hit an impasse. Their résumé looks choppy, with six jobs in four years, or their reactive or inattentive behavior lands them in trouble (a wrecked car, an unplanned pregnancy, racking up debt). Their performance at work can appear erratic, such as the top salesman on the road who is terrible sitting down with follow-up paperwork. Not every child with ADHD appears hyperactive, and that contributes to its being overlooked until adulthood. With adults, hyperactivity (if present) takes on the appearance of quick, rash judgment, poor follow-through, and a short temper. Marriages succumb when one tunes out of the relationship or takes an impulsive, risky leap into poor choices (financial decisions or sexual liaisons). Failed businesses or career goals wreak havoc upon finances and family goals. Without awareness and strategies to prevent or mitigate the fallout, many are left with a primal protective anger that keeps other emotions at bay.

Russell Barkley, MD, author of ADHD *and the Nature of Self-Control*, believes that the biological component of ADHD makes anger difficult to process. His book is filled with the brain-based neuroscience of these mental processes, explaining why the ability to contemplate the past to understand the present and future gets scrambled.[12] Those with ADHD must work harder to orient themselves to the future because their condition puts them squarely in the here and now. Barkley sees ADHD as a self-control problem largely because the person has difficulty modulating angry experiences and feels overwhelmed much of the time. Procrastination, avoidance, and brooding abound because it's hard to let matters drop. Most of us use coping strategies when we're annoyed. Something tells us to count to ten, take a deep breath, walk away from the conflict, or use imagery to soothe ourselves. That same something doesn't alert the person with ADHD as fast, and sometimes not at all. The result can feel like a flood of unwanted stimuli turning frustrations into battles.

When a person has a hard time focusing, anger management strategies are challenging to implement. This explains why some children with ADHD may appear passive-aggressive, as if they have the tools or knowledge to deal with whatever is challenging them, because teachers and parents know darn well that they have taught them, and they have even seen the kids use those skills before. Spouses get angry because after asking their partner with ADHD to clean up after a meal, for instance, they'll still spot crumbs. Here, too, the ADHD person must first notice the crumbs to wipe them away; those without ADHD assume this lack of attention is done on purpose. When there's no follow-through, the person with ADHD seems defiant.

In adult relationships the non-ADHD partner feels more responsible, reminds, and cajoles. The imbalance, over time, becomes burdensome. When a person with ADHD first falls in love, the novelty provides constant stimulation. He thrives on the newness and tends to hyperfocus on his love object with much attention, flowers, wine, and romance. When love settles, the person's interest or focus appears to wane, and not surprisingly, leaves the one accustomed to being wooed perplexed when a birthday or Valentine's Day goes forgotten or a promise feels unfulfilled. Acrimony erupts.

If the adult with ADHD doesn't pick up on social cues that other people recognize more readily, she may be drawn to the wrong kind of mate, failing to realize it's a poor match. She could find herself in shouting matches because she's drawn to such stimulation, which as we indicated, could include risk-taking extreme sports, simply driving too fast, or corporate deal making. It's easy to overlook the true neurological condition as being the culprit, and yet, neurology is no excuse either.

THE UPSIDE

There honestly *are* positives with ADHD: authenticity and spontaneity; humor; taking life not so darn seriously; creative energy; just plain energy, period; exuberance and innovations that a mind with a fast brake pedal would have possibly stopped at original inception; and the ability to take risks that are necessary for advancement.

Having ADHD can work well in some professions (but can be a detriment in others). In a job where movement is required, the hyperactive type is helpful to have. An emergency-room physician would thrive in a fast-paced, constantly changing environment. A brain surgeon, on the other hand, requires hours of careful concentration and the ability to shut out all distractions.

The worker with ADHD may shine if given flexible hours so that he can work when he is most alert or if given a job that breaks up deskwork with tasks away from the office. As one's career progresses, the help of a good assistant or staff is invaluable. Medications lessen symptoms by stimulating the brain's frontal lobe, home to executive functions that channel attention, making it easier to learn skills, to focus, and to be organized. With medication, life may settle down, mood often improves, and study or work becomes more efficient. Though medication improves concentration, the person with ADHD still has to overcome years of inefficient habits learned by default. Many with ADHD use cognitive-behavioral therapy to help with anxiety, impulse control, managing their emotions, and organizing their lives. Counseling can also teach how to reframe things and work with strengths. For that, many creative and successful people have had ADHD. You may be the next! Keep blazing new avenues toward your goals and let your vocabulary reflect that with positive phrasing. Rather than admit that your notes are scattered during a meeting, say, "I work best if I use a tape recorder to ensure I capture all the important details," or "if it's okay to stand, I do my best thinking on my feet."

HELPING THOSE WITH ADHD

Rather than lob an inaccurate passive-aggressive label, here are tips to manage anger in children and adults who have ADHD:

- Remain consistent. Structure and consistency go much farther than waffling or ambivalence that may give children false hopes. The child with ADHD may persist to get his or her way, and if you're not careful, your indecision or lack of backbone may set up poor outcomes over time.

- Monitor getting a balanced diet, enough sleep, and exercise, and limit too much exposure to electronic stimuli, especially with children. Promote meditation and other means of calming the mind to improve mood and focus.

- Invite the person with ADHD to join you in a relaxing activity. It's often hard for them to settle down. Children, especially, have a hard time turning off their switch from active play to passive activity. If you take the lead and teach relaxation, you will perhaps calm anxiety and anger, and limit impulsivity as well.

- Encourage the person to stick with things, because the person with ADHD has a penchant to quit and give up on a sport, subject, or task.

- Set realistic expectations. Many people with ADHD are bright and intelligent, but they've had their disappointments and obstacles. Ask things of them that tap into their strengths, and don't set them up for failure by insisting that they accomplish something that you know is not a strength of theirs. Remind the adult with ADHD of his numerous strengths, because he may easily ruminate solely on negative self-talk when things don't go so well. Suggest that he find and practice strength-related habits, as this boosts self-esteem so that negativity doesn't set in for the long haul.

- Calmly remind them when household requests or other tasks remain incomplete or unattended. Don't belittle the adult with ADHD or accuse her of bad intentions.

- Break tasks into parts rather than presenting one huge job. Write down steps to processes or keep track of lists in writing.

- Refuse to allow ADHD to be used as an excuse for laziness or lack of personal responsibility. Adults with ADHD must show up for work and academic programs and take part in home life

continues —

— continued

and parenting. They cannot push their responsibilities onto others. Spouses can quickly lapse into a "mothering" role, but that can lead to an unequal distribution of responsibility.

- Don't discriminate. Plenty of famous, inventive, and successful people have had ADHD. Having the diagnosis does not suggest lack of intelligence. While the Americans with Disabilities Act protects their rights, many are reluctant to disclose their condition for fear of stereotyping, stigma, or judgment.

- Educate yourself about the condition. *ADDitude* magazine features insightful articles. CHADD (Children and Adults with Attention-Deficit/Hyperactivity Disorder) offers meaningful support and a magazine called *Attention*.

- Understand the role that hormones play in conjunction with ADHD. Teen girls may experience difficulty with academics, aggression, and depressed mood, and are more at risk for substance abuse. Because girls tend to internalize while boys tend to externalize, symptoms in girls may go undiagnosed. By a woman's forties and fifties, when estrogen levels begin to drop off, fuzzy thinking and memory lapses may seem more pronounced.[13]

- Don't allow the condition to split you as a couple. Just as the person with ADHD must find her way to success, so the two of you can find solutions for a rewarding relationship. *Delivered from Distraction,* by Edward M. Hallowell, MD, and John J. Ratey, MD, contains this and other good tips.[14]

OPPOSITIONAL-DEFIANT DISORDER

According to CHADD, 40 percent of those with ADHD also have oppositional defiant disorder (ODD). A lesser number of children may experience conduct disorder, in which more extreme anger and aggression surfaces.[15]

ODD involves a perpetual pattern of negativistic, hostile, and defiant behavior that includes arguing with authority figures and defying their requests; frequently losing one's temper in conflicts; deliberately annoying and testing people's limits; and blaming others for mistakes or misbehavior. Also reported are low self-esteem and low frustration tolerance;

precocious use of alcohol, drugs, or tobacco; and acting stubborn, touchy, angry, resentful, or vindictive.

Sound similar to passive-aggression? It is, though ODD is exclusive to children and adolescents. This behavior is more prevalent at home, but it may impair social, academic, or occupational functioning as well. Experts believe that biological factors (neurotransmitters, co-occurring mental illnesses), genetic details (family history of mental illness or personality disorders), and environmental influences (dysfunctional families, inconsistent/harsh discipline, disrupted caregiving or mental illness/substance abuse) contribute to this behavioral condition.

Cognitive-behavioral therapy and, sometimes, family counseling can help to remedy an oppositional pattern in kids. To be effective, one has to actively build the child's trust and encourage the child to openly but responsibly express negative, hostile thoughts. Adults need to model respectful behavior, reframe complaints into polite requests, and explain "Here's why this rule is in place . . ." instead of resorting to an authoritarian "No, that's the way it is." The problem is that kids with ODD are often exhausting to be with.

WHEN PASSIVE-AGGRESSION PERSISTS

The term *passive-aggression* was invented during World War II by an Army psychiatrist to describe difficult soldiers who essentially followed orders with ever-present hostility.[16] When there's smoldering resentment with both purposeful resistance and antagonistic compliance it may fit what researchers have dubbed the passive-aggressive personality, which in the 1980s added interpersonal conflict as a descriptor because there was often waffling between the polarities of dependence and independence, passivity and activity.[17]

Scott Wetzler researched the topic in the early 1990s, claiming that passive-aggressive behavior was the number one source of men's problems in relationships and at work. "I don't think it strikes men more than women, but it's that men are clumsier about their passive-aggression," Wetzler told us. "They call attention to it, and it can be more irksome to those around him."[18] Martin Kantor, a psychiatrist, further expanded the professional literature in 2002, identifying paranoid, narcissistic, affective (depressive, hypomanic), obsessive-compulsive, histrionic (teasing, creating drama, using lots of body language), and sadomasochistic (delighting in misery, driven by spite) variants.[19]

CAN PASSIVE-AGGRESSION BE DIAGNOSED?

The answer is yes, it can, but like any disorder, it's complicated. In 1994, researchers added the word "negativistic" to the description, and the DSM-IV committee allocated passive-aggression to the psychiatric tome's appendix for further study.[20] It became a provisional diagnosis with seven specific criteria.

For passive-aggression to be more than behaviorally noted (meaning diagnosed), people must meet this general personality disorder criteria: enduring behavior that deviates from expectations (taking culture into account) with patterns in thinking, mood, interpersonal relationships, and self-management (impulsive leaps to anger) that manifests in personal, social, work/school settings, and causes significant distress or impairs getting along with others. All this dates back to adolescence or early adulthood, so it has endured and been impervious to change. Lastly, it can't be better explained by another diagnosis. A person with all of this, plus a specific constellation of traits, can be diagnosed with passive-aggressive disorder.

New criteria says that for a personality disorder to be diagnosed in an individual younger than eighteen years, the features must have been present for at least one year, with the exception of antisocial personality disorder (where it's conduct disorder).[21]

Situational episodes of such behavior do not count. A person might meet these descriptions, but if there is no impairment or distress, then they don't fit the criteria. In addition, if the patterns look odd to someone from a Western perspective, but they are perfectly understandable in that person's culture, once again, it is *not* a personality disorder.

Thus, while passive-aggression doesn't appear in the DSM-5 as a listed personality disorder, the book does give professionals the ability to use the diagnoses of "other specified personality disorder" or "unspecified personality disorder" when:

- the general criteria of a personality disorder has been met
- the person exhibits traits from existing DSM-5 personality disorders and/or
- the individual is considered to have a personality disorder that is not included in the DSM-5 classification (e.g., passive-aggressive personality disorder).[22]

PASSIVE-AGGRESSIVE PERSONALITY DISORDER (NEGATIVISTIC PERSONALITY DISORDER)

A pervasive pattern of negativistic attitudes and passive resistance to demands for adequate performance, beginning in early adulthood and present in a variety of contexts, as indicated by four (or more) of the following:

1. Passively resists fulfilling routine social and occupational tasks
2. Complains of being misunderstood and unappreciated by others
3. Is sullen and argumentative
4. Unreasonably criticizes and scorns authority
5. Expresses envy and resentment toward those apparently more fortunate
6. Voices exaggerated and persistent complaints of personal misfortune
7. Alternates between hostile defiance and contrition
8. Does not occur exclusively during major depressive episodes and is not better accounted for by dysthymic disorder.

Source: *Diagnostic and Statistical Manual of Mental Disorders, 4th ed., Text Revision (Arlington, VA:* American Psychiatric Association, 2000), 789–791.

What the average person can take away from this: Difficulty ahead! If you deal with this type of anger, you can't go it alone. Enlist the services of a mental health therapist or a psychiatrist to help you. We've listed additional resources at the end of this book to assist you in learning about these characterological problems.

CONSTANTLY CAUTIOUS AND WARY

There are two major categories of mental health that we haven't yet included but will in the next chapter: anxiety and alcohol/substance abuse disorders. Suffice to say here that when you're dealing with difficulty, you worry. You live on edge. Sometimes you panic. That's anxiety.

Furthermore, many people who do not seek an accurate diagnosis or treatment self-medicate their angry moods by drinking alcohol in excess or abusing drugs or recreational substances.

WHEN ANGER COMBUSTS AT WORK OR HOME

Shocking headlines broadcast the lone gunman's barrage of bullets fired upon innocent people, a car intentionally crashed into a workplace, students lashing out at classmates, and domestic arguments that turn into deadly standoffs. These tragedies leave us all stunned. How do we predict that a person may commit such violence? Several factors have been identified that increase the likelihood of internalized anger turning explosive:

- People who have committed violent acts before and threaten to do so again. Though rare, workplace violence can occur in any setting.[23]
- Certain demographics and occupations increase the risk—for example, nurses and correction officers who have experienced violence against them.[24]
- Perpetrators being refused a service or request.[25]
- Some personality disorders (borderline or antisocial), severe depression, and alcohol/substance abuse heighten the risk of domestic violence incidents.[26]
- Maladaptive and destructive coping strategies. As reported in a 2006 study in *Violence and Victims,* "85% of domestically violent men referred for treatment meet the criteria for some personality disorder including passive-aggressive, aggressive or aggressive sadistic profiles" on psychological tests.[27]
- Childhood influences such as a lack of nurturing relationships, abuse in the family of origin, and alcohol and drug abuse have been seen as predictors of domestic violence.[28]
- Displaced frustrations taken from home to school/workplace, and work/school to family/home settings frequently telegraph

intentions through social media. Writings and speech may depersonalize others, referring to a role, for example, "the mother of my children." These may be narcissistic rants that focus on how others do not understand or are not worthy of them. The writings surface resentment of the others' success, a lack of empathy and insight, a deep harbor of contempt, or someone completely overwhelmed by financial difficulty, caregiving, or other strains. Often, the person reacts to others because someone reminds them of a troubled personal relationship.

Whenever a person threatens to hurt herself or another, take it seriously. Employers should take clear and decisive action by calling police when there has been a threat. If someone has suffered from stress, has an existing diagnosis, or behaves oddly, the person should be taken to the nearest emergency department for evaluation. Provide what you know of the person's psychiatric history. Withholding this simultaneously prevents appropriate treatment and endangers others. If you sense potential workplace violence, protective measures are warranted, including requesting the presence of security officers or locking down a building, providing limited access and requiring identification.

IN SUMMARY

Don't be too dismayed with the specifics here regarding deeper disorders and toxic behavior. We realize some of this chapter is technical, but we also know that our readership includes physicians, mental health professionals, and others in healthcare as well as the lay reader. The real message here is that if you don't take care of your hidden anger, life may forever seem defeating.

Reflect upon your struggles. Strategies that blunt emotional pain in unhealthy ways or mask your anger probably haven't worked so well, correct? If you're the cause of your own anger, that's okay. At least you can do something about it.

Getting help through the right therapy spells hope. It's like when you are driving and you get lost for a while. First, you must recognize that you're lost. Next, you may try looking at a map. And if that doesn't get you where you need to be, then you may ask someone who has been there before for better directions. In essence, that's what therapy is like—a new direction and better routes to your destination. Keep reading, as we have some road maps and maybe a few shortcuts to offer for that journey.

ten

People Pleasing and Tolerating Crap

A T FORTY-FOUR, CAMERON SINGLE-HANDEDLY RAISES ZOIE, HIS sixteen-year-old daughter, who some days seems more like a pre-teen. They fit the definition of a troubled family—Zoie's mother had abused drugs and died of an overdose when Zoie was in preschool. Ever since, Zoie's had a history of problems at school. Cam has navigated her special needs, his car mechanic business, and his own life as a single dad. On July 4th, he closed his shop to hang out with their relatives and field everyone's well-intentioned questions.

"No, Zoie hasn't applied for a summer job," "I do know there's SAT prep," and "no, don't need the money, thank you . . . just hired an assistant and a night shift." Cam uttered none of this, even when Aunt Roberta launched into "You know what you should do. . . ."

If Cam tried to change the topic and grab a beer, Roberta would try track number two: "You really need to stop babying that girl. When I was her age . . ." A slow, long swig would keep him from going off on his meddling aunt, especially when he heard the word "enabling."

In this chapter, we'll help you to respond when others harangue you with benevolent, albeit negative sermons that cop superiority . . . if you let them, that is. Since all situations are vastly disparate, there is no one-size-fits-all guidance for modern tough-to-take scenarios.

WHEN DOES HELP CROSS THE LINE?

Whether Aunt Roberta understood the full scope of Zoie's neuropsychological profile, how she processed things slower than her peers and lagged behind them in social skills, is immaterial. Cam knew he was lucky if he made it to the many school meetings and if Zoie remembered her lunch for YWCA camp. Few sixteen-year-olds still went to the camp; they were more into boyfriends, skimpy tank tops, and everything Zoie hadn't discovered yet. Zoie's computer stayed locked in layers of parental controls, and with high school boys eyeing his daughter, Cam knew she couldn't be home alone this year. It was another milestone that could meet unsolicited advice.

Have you ever felt criticized, guilted, or perhaps judged over your choices or prior mistakes? Cam's wife had battled addiction. If people in his life remember only his past denials of this and disregard strides Cam has since made, we can understand his frustration.

WHO ENABLES?

Merriam-Webster's definition of *enable* is to make something able to do or be something, to make something possible, practical or easy, and to cause something to be active or available. In a sense, it's very close to what we explained as the indulging pattern that can occur in families.

Enabling and *empowering* are subtly different in meaning. When we lend a hand to help others accomplish things they couldn't do alone—teaching them to complete their homework or fix their broken car—we empower. In the psychology world, enabling means making excuses for an addicted person's poor actions and self-destructive habits. Lending money that will be misspent—not on rent, but on drugs—is enabling a struggle with substances to continue while removing active incentive for the addict to right his own choices.

Within recent decades, the term has meant assistance that perpetuates rather than solves a difficulty. Parents who clean teens' rooms and do every load of laundry so that their kids can enroll in more classes and study after sports and attend student council meetings may think they're empowering their kids. Another viewpoint is that they are limiting their kid's learning of life skills and are portraying servitude. Future employers inherit workers who are perhaps intelligent but are ill-equipped for adult responsibilities.

What about extenuating circumstances, such as physical illness, a mental health struggle, a learning disability, a trauma? Does assistance offered equate to enabling? If it's okay to render help one minute but allow individual freedom in another, then where is the distinct, clearly demarcated line?

When people judge others as enablers, unleashing lectures with their strong opinions, they typically annoy the recipients. If you are that recipient and you allow their projected anger or identify with part or all of it, should you stop? See if any of your rendered assistance fits these categories:

The gullible: This group trusts that others will do or say things with kindness. Thinking positively is fine, but one also needs a healthy sense of skepticism to protect one from harm. We need to see the darker side of human nature as well as the good. If you find yourself being naïve, easily fooled, or fleeced because of your innocence, you might believe a passive-aggressor's alibis, excuses, or twists of the truth, thereby enabling the person's behavior. If you're the victim of another's nasty barbs, you might fume because no one else witnesses them quite like you do, or at all. Tolerating them can enable that person. At the office, you might see an employee who says, "I'm trying my best" rather than working to produce the best. He wants *you* to change and for you to judge him based on his motives, not on his results. If you buy into this, you're enabling him.

The caretakers: Who can find fault with a person who always takes care of others? Let's say that your father always takes the family out on the town each New Year's Eve, but one time, you wish to ring in the New Year in your own home. Only, you're afraid of Dad's reaction and the sarcastic shower that will drench you later when you fail to follow his wishes. This isn't an isolated incident—you know how he'll react. Here, he has taken care of you in one sense, and your reluctance to stand up to him, stifling your own emotions, takes care of him. Your silence may only enable more "gifts with strings." It could also lock you into a more dependent role when you're striving to be your own person.

The needy: Do you rely on other's approval, to the point where you feel taken for granted or used? Do you find yourself stepping in, doing more, or shielding others from unpleasant consequences? Low self-esteem, trying to prove yourself worthy, loneliness, or being in a vulnerable spot invites this. Needs lead you to overlook increasingly poor behavior because the payoff is your honest hope that this time you'll obtain something (like acceptance).

The peacemakers: When people know that you'll go to any lengths to smooth over tension and avoid conflict, you become a safe dumping ground for another's hidden frustration because you swallow the anger for them, rather than bring it to anyone's attention. We know the negative health consequences of harboring your own anger over time, let alone how detrimental it can be if you take on more than your share. When you take the scorn or verbal lashings to save someone else, you reinforce the behavioral link telling them that anger gets results.

The guilt-ridden: "Don't you want my birthday to be special by doing this one little favor?" Or "Look how you made me feel" followed by "You always (never) _____." These manipulative phrases push guilt buttons—buttons that the manipulator may even have installed. This puts the recipient in an awkward spot, feeling uncomfortable, embarrassed, maybe even mortified. He has to follow through on the person's expectation or request, because if he doesn't, he will feel remorse. One boss kept overlooking missed deadlines. His aide told him that it would look bad if she got fired. Knowing she had a point, the boss's only recourse was to make finding a new job her idea so that he could avoid firing her.

Have you accepted excuses like the gullible? Stepped in with action for the idle person like the caretaker? Provided the shoulder to the whiner or clinger, the ear for the lonely heart because you need her as much as she needs you, while neither of you gets your lives together? Have you been the doormat for the abusive one, avoiding conflict, but seeing the situation get dirtier, like a carpet after more muddy shoes? Or, have you overlooked behavior hoping to offset any forthcoming guilt that would make you squirm?

It's not altogether uncommon to find someone who fits into more than one of these categories of enablers. We're challenged to deal with angry people or situations. Helping in a pinch is one thing; recognizing a pattern is quite another. Indeed, we teach people how to treat us by what we put up with and what we refuse to tolerate.

RARELY NO AND OFTEN TOO NICE

When you're asked to render assistance—even in a civic situation for a cause that you support—are you ever fearful of saying what you really would like to convey, such as "I'm sorry, I just can't take that on"? Instead you squash the inner voice that's reeling, thinking "are you kidding me?" and outwardly express "Well . . . I guess I can possibly fit that in." Write down your phrases. Find qualifiers—wigglers such as *maybe, probably, I guess, just this once, I think I can, perhaps, in all likelihood, I suppose,* or *most likely.* What has the request put you up against? In other words, what will it cost you to say a definite, but kindly delivered, "No"?

People end up unhappy, and frequently resentful, when they agree to things or act in ways that they would really rather steer clear of, and it so often brings to mind the multiple times they've conceded themselves and their choices in the past (adding layers of buildup). If you do this, not surprisingly, you may burn out, meltdown, or implode. Your childhood training may have steered you to suppress your own needs in favor of the wants and desires of others. Or, perhaps you were told repeatedly what you *should* feel instead of having others listen and accept how you *did* feel.

Next time you find yourself stressed with choices you are reluctant to make, think about this: Every single person under stress or with difficult choices has before her three paths: (1) she can explode (you get what this looks like); (2) she can implode (you're reading the book on this); and (3) she can take a measured, thoughtful stance where she calmly states what she can or will do *and* declares what she cannot (won't) do.

Focus on that last option. If taking a position for yourself makes you squirm, is that because it involves saying *no* or out of fear someone will not like you or your answer? If it's either one or both, maybe highlight this chapter.

Too often people pleasers have permeable boundaries. When you can execute this last option matter-of-factly, without justifying your choices or loading on the apologies, you're much closer to assertiveness.

PUTTING YOURSELF OUT THERE IN ALL THE WRONG WAYS

You just learned how to avoid outward or inward anger and take the one healthy route, which means taking a stance for what you believe. Take heed of how you present yourself to others as a people pleaser. When you are asked to do more (accept more, be more), you shouldn't be terribly surprised by your own remorse, especially if you have:

- Hung around people who exploit your weaknesses—install then later push your buttons.
- Received questions that you wanted to confront because they seemed like sly attacks, but kept quiet instead.
- Overlooked remarks that insinuate you shouldn't have fun because you were afraid to upset the person.
- Consistently put your own needs, plans, and priorities on hold in deference to another's agenda and goals.
- Lied, withheld information, or told half the story to cover for someone else's misdeeds.
- Offered your time/talents when they were not recognized or appreciated . . . yet you still kept offering.
- Shifted blame to another, or took it yourself, rather than allow the real culprit to take responsibility . . . because you would "hear about it" later.
- Experienced somatic affects (headache, insomnia, stomach upset) as a result of someone projecting their misery and culpability onto you.
- Made excuses for someone's drinking, drug use, or other abuses when there's a bona fide addiction.

If you see yourself here, perhaps you've set yourself up for mistreatment. Being persistently reactive or negative leaves you vigilantly on the defensive. Each subsequent people-pleasing act will stairstep more enabling and further misery. Ultimately you avoid interactions out of fear that they won't go well. If you have collected passive-aggressive or anger-concealing people at home, at work, at school, or in life, you will need to carefully consider how to act differently from now on.

JOURNALING TO DISTINGUISH PASSIVE-AGGRESSION

James Pennebaker, a psychologist, found that writing twenty minutes a day for five consecutive days helped to improve both mental outlook and physical health.[1] Take twenty minutes now and write down negative experiences, deep-seated feelings, what happened, how you felt, and what led you to feel that way. Keep the words flowing without regard to grammar, spelling, or punctuation. Consider journaling a gratitude list, as it often helps you to feel positive.

By now, you may have a good sense of whether someone's behavior fits with our descriptions. It's not always easy to assume motive or intent; in fact, it can be dangerous to cast behavior as anger unless you know for sure it is. If in doubt, we suggest that you write the situation down from the other person's perspective. This helps to spot a person's righteous anger or maybe take his culture into account as the reason for his indirect demeanor. List what happened, when, how, where, and whoever else was affected. Include what led up to the incident and how it was taken care of. This last part helps you to determine any role you play in fanning the other person's anger. Be as specific as possible and write your sentences or phrases using "I" statements.

To journal "He made me mad" tells you very little of what actually transpired; "I felt used and taken for granted as if my feelings didn't count for very much" details much more. Describe the person's non-verbal behavior as well as spoken comments or actions. Capture the dialogue. Your secondary gain: if the situation with the angry person gets troublesome enough that you seek counseling, this journal will provide handy insight into these interactions.

RESPONDING TO CRITICISM AND GOSSIP

Angry people need to express themselves, but they need to do so when it's appropriate and find ways to surface their frustrations without venom. They need to give others feedback without attacking them. New perspectives, when offered with positive intent, foster growth, exploration, intimacy, and problem solving. Most importantly, people who conceal anger must control their dysfunctional emotions, cultivate answers, and get to an end point. Frequently, they don't, and criticism springs forth.

WHAT IS CRITICISM?

Criticism is the total opposite of feedback, often stemming from an angry mind or heart. That kind of anger never stands alone. Something triggers it—jealousy, loss, revenge, shame, regret, embarrassment or humiliation, low self-esteem, self-hatred, deeper depression, or lack of self-control. The bottom line is that whoever lobs the critical remark first feels bad, squirms with those bad (sometimes mad) emotions, and then mistakenly feels better because someone else (perhaps you) became the dumping ground.

YOUR RESPONSE

Knowledge is power, and the more you understand the dynamic behind the criticism, the better able you'll be to prevent it or escape from it.

Instead of getting equally annoyed, angry, self-doubtful, or confused, it's quite useful to develop coping strategies to ward off these negative side effects of criticism. For instance, stay focused on your goal. Here are some other strategies or perspectives to consider:

1. **Check if the criticism has validity:** Is there even a morsel of truth to what the angry person said? Was it lobbed indirectly with hostility? Or did it emanate from righteous anger? Could it foster your own growth? Unfortunately, criticism and develop-ment are not mutually exclusive. Instead of "I'm tired of doing the laundry for you" (criticism), try "we need to work out a plan of sharing the laundry" (solution).
2. **Does the criticism have nothing to do with you?** Let's face it: people can become ticked off just by the way you walk into a room. You can often see it in body language, and you can cer-tainly detect hidden resentment or jealousy by speech, which projects thought and mood onto a situation or denial of any particular plight. Watch how secretly annoyed people take lit-tle responsibility. They use rare "I" statements, many accusatory

"You make me feel _____" or "You did _____," followed by the defensive-inciting question "why." When someone feels threatened, she feels she doesn't "measure up." Rather than sit with that sense of insecurity, she casts it off. Sometimes, conscientious, goal-achieving people become the most convenient targets for the passive-aggressor. The passive-aggressive person who struggles with appropriate self-expression may not be able to sit with the anxiety your presence or your achievements stir. It may seem as if it's about you, the angry person may say or shout that it's about you, their nonverbal behavior indicates it's about you, but guess what? It's about them. The next criticism you hear, watch to see if the person might actually be criticizing himself. The need to put others down reflects low self-esteem or being stuck in a situation. Often the only way the critical person can think well of herself (or in the circumstance) is to make someone else feel worse.

3. **Don't fan criticism; defuse it:** Ignoring often takes away the power of such a putdown. That's so pivotal when dealing with passive-aggression and hidden anger, but sometimes, you can't ignore it. Know, however, that your reaction either spawns more criticism (anger) or eases into something more positive, such as a solution, an understanding, a connection or bond, or progress toward a goal.

4. **Recognize that criticism builds:** Self-fulfilling prophecies are mostly setups. Critical people heap negative thoughts or emotional insecurity and end up saying or doing something that produces responses to confirm these beliefs and/or insecurities.

   For instance, twenty-year-old Gwen, the only girl in her family, finds that her older brother Jason got engaged to Emily. This is going to take some getting used to! If Gwen reframes her threatened feelings, she acknowledges thoughts about her shifting status. Sounds good, but openly expressing anxiety like this requires a hefty dose of self-awareness. Passive-aggressors lack self-awareness; they usually sweep away true feelings and fears, even from themselves. They disconnect in order to avoid dealing with anything unpleasant.

5. **Deal with criticism directly:** Tell the critical person, "I can learn more from you if you teach me rather than criticize me." If someone tells you what you're doing right, you'll repeat those things because they guide you. Otherwise, you remain locked in fear, afraid to act. You wait it out, and then you get criticized again. The pattern repeats if you don't take care of it. In Gwen's situation, Gwen needs to deal with her insecurities and jealousy. She needs to welcome Emily, not attack her. But if she's not aware of the jealousy, her actions will undermine Emily's appearance and imply that Emily is not good enough for her brother.

DEALING WITH GOSSIP

Though it's indirect, criticizing requires a small amount of confrontation. If the fear of confrontation mounts high enough, the passive-aggressor may unload his frustrations on a third party through gossip. Of course, this triangulates the situation. What's more, it's often coupled with hidden anger that further distorts the truth, embellishes minor incidents, plays victim, or undermines the person being talked about so that she loses stature or gets annoyed. The truly angry person can't bear to feel the angst directly.

> Tell the critical person, "I can learn more from you if you teach me rather than criticize me." If someone tells you what you're doing right, you'll repeat those things because they guide you. Otherwise, you remain locked in fear, afraid to act.

In our previous example, if relatives ask Gwen where Emily and Jason are registered for wedding gifts, and Gwen lies and says that they're not registered, she can secretly smile inside as Jason and Emily open seven toasters or things they absolutely don't need. But since a façade usually doesn't last, Emily might eventually catch Gwen and call her out. This gives Gwen all the convincing evidence she needs: "I always knew Emily was a trouble-maker!" Voilá: a self-fulfilling prophecy! Gwen set in motion a series of events that built upon themselves, and a dynamic stemming from insecurities eventually came full circle.

A self-fulfilling prophecy happens frequently in stepfamilies, when children often resent the intrusion of a stepparent; in schools with new students facing existing cliques; at work with a new employee; or, as we've seen, in almost any situation when a new member joins the group.

Dr. Murphy researched self-fulfilling prophecies for his doctoral dissertation and found that teachers who operated from certain beliefs about students' personality traits tended to treat the students differently in ways that then enhanced those traits.[2] The same goes for families, friends, and the workplace. We can become what others try to make us by praise or bullying. But life doesn't have to be determined by how we're treated. When we refuse to own the prejudices placed upon us, and instead rise up with confidence, we can change the direction of our own lives for the better!

Hanging on to anger creates an illusion of control. Gwen feels things happening to her family that are beyond her influence, which causes her discomfort. When trying to regain her balance, her anger gives her ego a false boost. This gives her an illusion of control. Temporarily, Gwen met her goal. If others buy into her gossip, they enable Gwen. On the other hand, if they call her out on it right away by saying, "I kind of like Emily," "I don't see it that way," or "It just doesn't matter to me," then they stem the angry gossip. In the long run, Gwen's anger creates more problems, even for Gwen herself. Her angry thinking and actions provide no lasting satisfaction. That's the way life plays out for many passive-aggressive, negativistic people, yet the pattern can indeed end.

CHOOSING YOUR REACTIONS

How would you have reacted if you were Emily—or Jason—to Gwen's being mean-spirited? We advocate against fanning the flames of criticism but encourage you to learn from it and defuse it. Anytime you react quickly, especially in a less thought-out, knee-jerk fashion, your response may attack back as a defense. "Well, you made me mad" or "There you go again" almost guarantees that your conflict will escalate. Sometimes no matter which way you turn, it's a poor choice. Passive-aggressors are skilled at placing people in double binds or no-win situations. If Emily or Jason calmly stated their hurt and disappointment, that too would play right into Gwen's setup. With a more collected reaction, the anger doesn't flare as much.

You are no one's doormat. There are times when you need to assert your position or confront a person's remarks or behavior. If you do it all the time, you look reactive and serve up another platter of buttons the passive-aggressor can push. You enable them. Rein in your reactivity and choose what you do carefully. Let some remarks, innuendos, or harmlessly stupid actions slide. Save your energy for the things that matter most. Here's another scenario with choices:

> When your family gathers, your older cousin, who has no children, undermines your authority when you appropriately discipline your daughter. Your cousin makes thinly disguised comments about "today's parents." Last time the clan gathered, she showed everyone embarrassing pictures of you from high school. Before that she criticized the casserole you brought, and another time she came late when you hosted the holiday. How do you respond?
>
> a. Ignore her and walk away.
> b. Overlook her behavior because you understand the pain of her being childless.
> c. Offer up something embarrassing she did as a child.
> d. Demand, in front of everyone, that she stop treating you this way.
> e. Take her aside and tell her that you won't tolerate disrespect, especially in front of your child. Tell her that if it continues, you'll leave the gathering early.
> f. Remember all the times you teased her as a child and remind yourself how it's fair payback.

If you chose *e*, taking your cousin aside, you are correct. Ignoring her might be appropriate if it's an isolated incident; our scenario indicates otherwise. Meeting her hidden anger by taking a cheap shot at her only puts you on her level, puts her in a weak spot (which she'll loathe), and plays her game (thus enabling her). Understanding her pain is one thing, but plenty of people have regrets and don't discharge anger because of them. The option of overlooking your cousin's behavior based upon her pain is perhaps the most enabling one in our list. Believing in fair payback compares childhood to adulthood, akin to comparing lemons to watermelons.

Though telling her what to do is exactly what she resists (and she might keep it up out of spite), clearly communicate what is and isn't acceptable to you. By keeping the focus on your boundaries, you can convey to her what she's done, what you expect, and what the consequences of any continued action will be. It also gives her a choice—the independence that these folks crave. Be specific and follow through if you offer ultimatums (which should never be the beginning of the discussion but can be added if someone doesn't respond or attacks back). Make sure that whatever you promise you can enforce. Otherwise, you walk away weak and malleable. And once again, you enable.

POOR COMMUNICATION TRAPS

When choosing your reactions, don't condemn the person's character. Kids often make the mistake of attacking, and unfortunately, adults do it, too. "You're a liar!" one might yell. "Like you're so honest. You couldn't tell the truth if your life depended on it!" Now *that's* disparaging character.

Becoming less reactive truly takes practice. Passive-aggressive people have graduate degrees in raising your blood pressure and anxiety. You can't impact their behavior. You may even feel emotionally drained being around them, but if you invest your energy in changing your own behaviors and reactions, you have a shot at turning around a covert dynamic—not a guarantee, but at least a shot. This is important, because essentially, this is the only real control you have: to manage yourself. And it's key—pivotal in fact—to stop you from enabling passive-aggression. At the very least, better reactions ease the momentary anger and avoid creating another buildup or spark. Sometimes it's best to put some space or time between the problem and your response.

To learn from your mistakes, take note of how you've responded to a troublesome person in your past. Ask yourself what you stand to gain by any action and whether it meets your goals. If you do nothing else, make a conscious effort to respond in a totally positive way. Remember that we tend to rehearse (and reinforce) negative patterns; for example, "So I said (insert your nasty comment here) and I showed him!" Instead, we need to mentally rehearse the positive (repeatedly) to break the negative habit. Insight isn't enough. Deciding to change isn't enough either. You must move from poor reactions to positive ones. You must rehearse the better response, so you don't fall back into an old habit of a bad reaction.

If you've been reactive before, stay cool this time. Listen, rather than attack. Reflect what the other person has said rather than offering your own interpretation. Use empathy, not frustration. Model the assertiveness and respect you'd like to see instead of passive-aggression. Don't talk to the other person's anger. Talk to the resolution.

Get him to say more when you can't stand him? Yes. Use empathy? Yes, even though deep down you know these people are way out of line, in order to turn the tables on this irritating behavior, you need to appreciate their emotion—which is best done by being empathic in as even a tone and temperament as you can muster. You'll ruin it if your body language sends an incongruent message. Softly couch what you have to say. Be direct.

Take the information in this small section and craft a script for yourself. Rehearse what to say and how you'll say it (including body language). Practice responding to reactions that the other person might have so that you aren't surprised. Here's another example and chance to test what your reaction might be:

Rick, Jodi, and Ed all report to the same project manager, out of the San Francisco headquarters, while they're stationed in Connecticut. Though three on a team forms a triangle, this crew has worked supportively, preparing important presentations for a product rollout. Funds have gotten tighter, however, and their manager informed them that the budget allows only two of them to attend the big event. As the last hire, Rick will be left behind.

Time runs short. Rick left around noon to fetch everyone's sandwiches. At 12:45, Rick was nowhere to be seen. The team had a 1:00 phone conference. At 12:58, Rick sauntered in with two lunches. "Where's yours?" Jodi asked, knowing she'd only be able to nibble a few bites. Rick replied that he wasn't hungry, and while starved, she and Ed put their food aside for the important call. Later, Jodi noticed a red ketchup stain on Rick's shirt that hadn't been there in the morning. Not hungry, huh?

The next morning, Ed searched the office for a vital report, then desperately re-created some of the contents only to later find the document buried in Rick's in-basket, where it didn't belong.

What do you think is happening here? Take a sheet of paper and write down possible phrases you could use to confront Rick, because with such an important work event approaching, the team isn't working efficiently.

It's a good guess that Rick is acting out his conflicted feelings without ever openly acknowledging them, or he's very aware of them but thinks about his coworkers, "If you're getting all the glory, do all the work yourself." Of course, his reaction only shows his immaturity, which will hold him back from any chance of traveling next time (if there ever is a next time).

If your list contains "Rick, why are you acting this way?" the buzzer just sounded. "Why" will only put Rick on the defensive. If you wrote, "Rick, we know you must be disappointed not going to the rollout, but we need you," you're getting closer. Rick may resent your assumption of how he feels. It could place you in a one up/one down position, and to save face, Rick may retreat behind his cubicle and emotions. If Rick is young and naïve, he might deserve such a learning-curve approach, but he also needs to know his behavior has been unacceptable and that he cannot do it again.

If you started soft, something akin to, "Rick, we were working so well together, and your contribution has been tremendous. Lately, though, I sense we're not the same team. Is everything okay?" you're much closer. Now, it's Rick's chance to talk, and hopefully he will, because you've used "I" statements, praised him, and shown concern. Rick's in a much better position to apologize and admit his disappointment. You could follow up with "You've got a point about that, Rick. You've worked so hard, and I wish everyone could attend. When we're not working together though, we all risk failing and facing the consequences if this product launch doesn't go well."

Placing yourself in a situation with "we" rather than "you" softens things. Phrases such as "I agree with you," "you've got a point," or "tell me more about that" are good approaches because they align people. Asking open-ended questions also encourages angry people to express what they've stored inside.

Yet empathy only goes so far. If you're the coworker or boss, it's helpful to see some things as misunderstandings since everyone is entitled to a bad day, but you also need to set clear limits.

If Jodi and Ed had both voiced their concerns, Rick would feel two up/one down, it would triangulate things, and the conflict would be frozen in place. The closest path to a person is a straight line—a more direct, more personal approach at least as a first course of action. Letting off steam or name calling might feel good momentarily, but it's bad for long-term relations. Business has a bottom line, and if their project loomed, it is highly likely that Jodi and Ed would communicate about this. If that happened in a situation for you, you would need to be extra cautious not to jump on a bandwagon, because your own anger could gain momentum and color your reaction and complicate things.

Remember, anger-concealing people have been trained not to show true emotions. They're scared, jealous, frustrated, selfish, or mean. They need to talk, and they need for you to listen. Don't go around them; go to them. Even if they are disrespectful, you should set a respectful, nonconfrontational example.

> If you do nothing else, make a conscious effort to respond in a totally positive way. If you've been reactive before, stay cool this time. Listen, rather than attack. Reflect what the other person has said rather than offering your own interpretation. Use empathy, rather than anger. Model assertiveness and respect instead of passive-aggression. Don't talk to the person's anger. Talk to the resolution.

Gently easing information out of them sure beats doing battle. Each situation is different, but sometimes humor disarms and softens anger; respectful, not mean-spirited humor, that is. It's *usually* safer to poke fun at yourself. Indeed, if you work with any angry person, doing so at the very first sign of passive-aggressive behavior might make future interactions much more positive.

SPECIFIC REACTIONS

Focusing on what the passive-aggressive person frequently fears or avoids and the behavior frequently seen, here are additional ideas to alter your reactions.

Reacting to Control

Certainly, we all should listen well and extend empathy to the controlling person. It's a skill to use with all secretly fuming people. Equally important to the person who avoids being hurt and fears failure is having people "on their side." Next, be direct and very specific as you communicate what you need or want to achieve through calm confrontation. If you can help the controlling person to feel successful, or at the very least not diminish his or her sense of competency, you'll achieve more harmony. Where control manifests in a truly unhealthy pattern, encourage the person to seek treatment. Otherwise, refrain from enabling.

Reacting to Manipulation

Since the manipulator skillfully pushes your buttons and sometimes plots to do so as "get back," it's important to rein in your own reactivity and not seek revenge yourself. Set firm boundaries and define the consequences while remaining vigilant. This type of passive-aggressor doesn't easily admit to problems. Coping with someone else's needs or concerns? That's difficult, too. Accept no excuses when the person shirks responsibility. Also, hold firm to your beliefs, make direct requests, but be willing to cooperate and even show how to solve problems. This creates win-win situations (countering the "my way or the highway" attitude). Because the person fears being discovered or confronted, tackle any lies, distortions, illogical thoughts, or harmful motivations with calmness—model problem solving. Reject the behavior, not the person. Remember to praise more, criticize less, and of course, use empathy. When necessary, act decisively, because the manipulator may thwart your goals. When the going gets rough, avoid the bandwagon, coalitions, and triangles altogether and always deal directly.

Reacting to Childlike/Immature Behavior

At the core of the immature passive-aggressor is a strong need to recreate parts of childhood and receive acceptance. These people feel dependent, yet they yearn for freedom. With fears of losing favor, never being able to "get it right," and being loved conditionally, they look for others to take care of them. In one word: *don't.* Focus on the here and now, and unless the person is indeed a minor, gently remind them of their adult independence, responsibilities, and choices. Their aches, pains, and ailments, many times communicated in a whimpering fashion, may annoy, and it's oh-so-tempting to step in and lighten that load. This only enables them. Instead, demonstrate how they can shift from problem-focused to solution-focused thinking . . . and action. If you explode at them, you become just one more person who doesn't understand. Say perhaps "I'm sorry you don't feel well. Please understand how hard it is for me to hear you focus on your limitations when I know you have the strength to figure this out (improve things, etc.)."

If you remind them that they are accepted—faults and all—and that they have what it takes to express themselves appropriately, plus make their own decisions, you lead them down a more mature path. Encouraging all people who conceal their anger to appropriately assert themselves is not only wise, but very much needed. When assertiveness was often prohibited in one's childhood, refusing to learn the skill perpetuates passive-aggression.

Reacting to Self-Absorption

Revisit our tips in other chapters regarding the self-absorbed. With their passive-aggression mixed in, those who are self-absorbed easily confound most people. Refuse to be too impressed by them, because if you are, you feed their ego. When your hopes are too high, you believe in the favors they promise, or you become star-struck, you'll be that much more disappointed. You'll be equally struck by their lack of empathy, by the special rules they design for themselves, and by the mixed messages when their words don't match their body language or actual behavior.

These folks yearn for attachment, security, and happiness (which was often lost years before), and they continually create situations where others will notice them. You'll see exquisite discomfort with competition because they're hypersensitive. Irrational fears lead them to see competition as stage stealing.

It may take time to experience the full effects of the self-absorbed person who gradually ingratiates herself. You'll sense that she feels she's always right, it's all about her, and the relationship seems off balance. If she forms triangles (to keep the stage lights on her), don't do likewise. Don't argue over who is right or who knows more. Ignore what you can. Calmly confront her attempts to show off at someone else's expense. Avoid becoming dependent when she believes she should lead and you should follow. Try to channel the vain person's strengths for everyone's benefit. However, if problems occur where the self-absorbed adult becomes emotionally abusive or cannot delay gratification, especially to look out for the needs of a child, run (don't walk) away. Mean, malignant, or entrenched narcissism requires professional support.

Reacting to Depression and Addictions

Each case of depression will be different, depending upon the severity. Rather than give advice, show through your own example how you can reframe negative occurrences to help the person feel more competent—the hallmark of good self-esteem. Reinforce brainstorming that reflects responsibility and action. Listen. If you do inquire, ask open-ended questions to facilitate the depressed person's sharing, and encourage them to seek treatment. If they request you accompany them to an appointment, this might alleviate their discomfort and provide insight that assists the counselor.

When someone chooses to self-medicate with alcohol, substances, or other vices, see this as a deeper problem and make your choices accordingly. Tell yourself that you deserve to direct your own path and that you can live a good life, free of such crutches, and the consequences of use. Redirect any energy you've put to hiding, denying, begging, or pleading with the addicted. When you no longer have to adapt your lifestyle around theirs or stop fearing that your possessions will be hawked for the latest drink or hit, you will breathe more easily.

EXIT STRATEGIES

When you're at your wit's end, you may lack the ability to set good boundaries for where someone else and their needs end and where your rights and your needs begin. Own that. There's absolutely nothing you can do about what has transpired in the past because it's relegated to history. However, a wise person learns from previous encounters. If it's truly difficult to cope with someone else's anger, you may need to seek help and devise an escape plan. Passive-aggressive people can send you into orbit through their behaviors. They delight in doing it. Sometimes, though, the helping path gets frustrating. One woman said, "I'm the one in therapy, but they have all the problems" as she recounted the long litany of nuisances she tolerated with her in-laws.

continues ——

— continued

How do you exit? Accusing with "you this" or "you that" is never the best option. Defenses kick in, and no one really listens after that happens. Instead, point out the results of the problem, how upset you get, how hard it is to enjoy time together, or how frustrating things appear. Remember that assertiveness can be a calm, respectful confrontation. If relationships get too dicey, workplace interventions or therapy are positive forms of triangulation, supported by people trained to mediate conflicts. The passive-aggressor may not feel as targeted or stigmatized in those settings.

If the behavior is well entrenched, however, your approach to the passive-aggressive person, hoping he will work through the problem or "get it," may be dashed—anger-concealing people can hide things even from themselves. From his point of view, there may be nothing to discuss. When the behaviors are simply too painful to be around, it's time to implement an exit strategy. If you can predict angry messes before you head into them, devise a signal among family such as "Honey, don't forget to check your voicemail." Yes, it's indirect; but if you can't extricate yourself with "gee, I think we had better get going," it's far better than lobbing a rather rude "I'm done" or "I'm outta here."

BUILDING POSITIVE INTERPERSONAL SKILLS FOR KIDS

Anger doesn't need to beget anger. It's not pretty when it does. Children who display passive-aggression deserve much empathy, yet their peers often reflexively respond through mirroring behavior when they, too, are sent over the edge. Teach them thoughtful alternatives.

Imagine how threatening it would be for the child of passive-aggressive parents to be direct. She fears reprisal, so she meets her parents' emotional level so as not to upset them by appearing happier when mom or dad is down, or by feeling sad herself because that may not sit well, either. Every child yearns to receive positive parental feedback, but when your parent hides anger, you never know quite where you stand. It's confusing and hurtful. Child and teen cultures today don't promote much interpersonal education. Computers, video games, handheld entertainment, and cell phones have spawned a generation brought up without the skill of calming and entertaining themselves through anything other than electronic stimuli. Text messaging doesn't foster social skills. Nonverbal communication doesn't exist when you're typing messages. No one sits with you in silence and listens unconditionally with eyes riveted and body turned toward you. The best prescription: turn off the electronic devices.

Children caught in angry tussles want things to improve. Teach them about positivity and hope and that they cannot change others who may strike out passive-aggressively; they can only change themselves. Role-play so that they understand the power of "I messages" and the destructive nature of "you" attacks. Model how to be appropriately assertive and how to take a position in a calm yet factual manner. And if they have tried repeatedly and see no results for their effort, teach them how to exit a relationship gracefully.

CLASSROOM MANIPULATION

How do you maintain your composure when one student defies your authority? "You can't send me to the office 'cause I'll tell the principal you threw a book at me!" Or in the university lecture hall, when an interrupting student picks apart your research or an online student tries to run the class? Teachers mask anger, too. In adult education, picture your instructor, joking with a group of students. Everyone tosses around a few tame remarks, and suddenly the instructor replies, "You don't have to be mean." Anger-concealing people take offense when clearly none is intended. It comes across as delusive and confuses others.

Well-hidden anger elicits reactions from subtle to strong. Students carry their reactions with them after the class is over. If you are an instructor and think you're dealing with disguised anger at school, try the following tactics:

- If you're dealing with immature anger, let them know straight up that if they'd like to be treated like a child, that's fine, but they will not have the more mature (teenage or adult) perks either.
- Be sure it's anger; anger is always attached to another negative emotion. Children with learning disabilities, ADHD, or sensory-processing concerns might appear angry and defiant when they are merely shutting down due to classroom challenges or the teacher's requests. A disorganized or slow

continues —

—— continued

child might have legitimate difficulties with attention and brain-based executive functioning but appear to be passive-aggressive, lazy, or oppositional. Investigate what else might be going on before labeling the behavior.

- Check on self-esteem. Hidden anger may really be a child's low self-concept, she may have slipped into a negative expectancy set; if you expect a certain behavior from the child, over time, the child gives you just what you expect. Pessimistic students often perform beneath their potential.

- Stay in control of the class by controlling your reactions. Any anger or attention you give to passive-aggressive behavior usually reinforces it. If the offending student looks for a stage upon which to perform, take away that platform by dealing with the child privately instead of in front of the group. Once you become annoyed, the situation resembles a power struggle, the student becomes defensive, you may respond more quickly with anger, and this becomes a cycle.

- Use your own feelings as a guide. After a stressful incident, how do you feel? Was it a struggle? Did you feel powerless? Confused? If your current methods aren't working, identify ones that will. Target the behaviors you wish to change without tackling too much at one time. Choose no more than one or two behaviors to address at first.

- Invite the sarcastic or cynical student to stay after class. When students show their egos, reacting with resentment and irritability, they often feel they haven't been heard. Listen to them. Do this privately so that other students aren't swayed by their cynicism.

- Tell students that you care about them and their performance, acknowledge their difficulty, and vow to get through it together. Don't use this as a time to lecture or threaten. Build a relationship first. Use a suggestion box by which you invite students to freely share so that they feel heard.

- If the angry student creates a distraction, acknowledge their struggle before the group to solicit peer support. "It looks like Johnny is having a hard time focusing on our work," you might say. "He's acting silly, but I know he wants to get a good grade because we've seen his good work. I wonder what we can do to help him."

eleven

Anger Antidotes

IDDEN ANGER SNEAKS UP AND ISN'T EASILY IDENTIFIED. WE HAVE recounted its many detriments. Systems thinking certainly drives this home.

"From the Bowen family systems viewpoint, anger is a substitute for dealing effectively with an important relationship," wrote Michael E. Kerr, MD, director of the Bowen Theory Academy.[1] "The high road to dealing with anger and its consequences is gaining the objectivity about the relationships that generate it," Kerr stated.[2] Dr. Kerr worked and wrote professional literature with the late Murray Bowen, MD.

What parts of this book have made you most uncomfortable? Is what drew you to this topic originally still an issue as you come closer to closing the back cover? If not, what has changed that? It may be useful to jot down the answers to these questions.

That you have stayed the course of these chapters shows that you're open-minded and willing to learn and grow, especially since we have driven home that though others' behavior may vex you, your power remains within yourself.

"This is not about giving up or giving in to the other person, but about changing one's part in the problem," Dr. Kerr offers us. "If a person can be more of a 'self' in a relationship, the anger disappears—not that it's repressed, it's just no longer needed. It can be as basic as overcoming a fear of rejection and saying 'No' to another person's unrealistic expectations."[3] Interestingly enough, while *no* is one of the most powerful words, it is also one of the most difficult ones to say. We'll provide help for this.

TOP FOURTEEN WAYS TO EASE ANGER AND BITTERNESS

Here's a quick take on anger-reduction strategies; see further recommendations in our list of recommended readings at the end of this book.

1	Mindfulness	Relaxed awareness of the present allows an openness of mind strongly correlated with well-being. It reduces rumination. Rather than fight or judge feelings, you pay attention to them, even their physical sensations. Gradually, your anxiety and depressed mood lessens or dissipates. Mindfulness-based stress reduction was introduced by Jon Kabat-Zinn at the University of Massachusetts Medical Center. The current trend of adult coloring books switches your brain from stress, focuses your attention away from anxiety to color, shape, and size, and creates calm as you replace negative images with appealing ones that you create.
2	New frames	By crafting a new cognitive reframe, you take a negative event, concept, or feeling and find the positive alternative. Frames are why two people can live through a harrowing incident and come out with two vastly different perspectives. Change your mental perspective and behavior—key catalysts to create optimism.
3	Values	A value is neither right nor wrong; it varies among cultures, religions, and families and deals with overarching concepts such as freedom, friendship, love, and more. Principles describe rules, standards, and truths, which anchor us. Both values and principles guide and direct us in a dilemma. Ambivalent fence-sitters have not determined their own values and principles (adhering to what's been decided for them); thus, they send mixed messages.
4	Happy rituals	Good habits shape us. Rituals connect people: coffee among couples, family movie night. If you fight traffic and arrive home cranky, de-stress with music or an audio book. The "Work & Family" column in *The Wall Street Journal* reported that even entering through the front door and stashing your briefcase out of sight could clear a bad mood.[4]

5	Empathy	*The Washington Post* explored lack of empathy as contributing to personal conflicts, communication failure, and conflicts.[5] Empathy is necessary when dealing with a passive-aggressor. Ask yourself what happened in the person's day (or life) to have created their behavior. See something from the other person's eyes or perspective; accept that you both can be right. How are you alike versus different?
6	Meditation and prayer	Meditation can reduce anxiety and depressed mood, increase pain tolerance, and improve quality sleep, memory, self-awareness, and goals. Over time, the benefits have also resulted in better emotional regulation and learning retention. Physically, meditation brings better blood flow to the brain, decreases blood pressure, and has been correlated with a stronger immune system. Some meditations reflect one's faith and belief in prayer for healing.
7	Friends	Social isolation has detrimental effects on emotional well-being, and that loneliness can turn on our pro-inflammatory genes and increase stress hormones. Social connections help stave off cognitive decline.[6] Once we feel lonely, we often perpetuate this state and may blame others for not reaching out to us. When you battle negativity, low self-esteem, and addictions, choose your peers carefully. Friendship builds trust, a sense of purpose in everyday life, and humbles you to not take yourself too seriously!
8	Praise and affirmations	For a job well done, compliments should be sincere and heartfelt. "You look fantastic," "I really appreciate that," or even "we all make mistakes" can go a long way to building connection and positive regard. An affirmation is a compliment to yourself. Write down positives in list form or cut them out onto strips of paper that you confine to a jar. "I really added to someone's day," "I am worthy and do good work," or "I'm creative and fun" are good examples. Revisit these or say them out loud daily.
9	Yoga and exercise	Yoga can reduce blood pressure, stress, and muscle strain at the same time that it improves mood, flexibility, strength, and stamina. Medical and counseling professionals promote exercise as self-help for worry, depressed mood, and anger. Consult your physician if you have physical limitations or haven't exercised in a while; you must build strength and stamina lest you injure yourself. The release of feel-good hormones will improve your outlook, help to restore better sleep, and promote physical/mental well-being.

continues —

— continued

10	Laughter and smiles	Appropriate, shared humor stimulates the brain's reward center (the amygdala, which in turn releases dopamine). The jokes, of course, cannot be at someone else's expense or they become passive-aggressive. Laughter and genuine smiles become contagious and are universally understood. The face uses far fewer muscles to smile than to frown, which contorts and exhausts those muscles. A smile motivates and inspires, aids your career, and with its "halo effect," helps us to remember happy moments more vividly.
11	Hobbies	What do you do to break from the daily grind and relax? Read a good book, paint, complete a jigsaw puzzle, play an instrument, or build a plastic brick creation? Hobbies are as diverse as people, taking them outdoors, into the sunshine, placing them into groups (book clubs, sports teams), out on the water (sailing, fishing), or merely helping to pass the time (needlepoint, writing). It's hard to stay angry when distracted by an activity, which then has positive cognitive benefits as well.
12	Reflective listening	How many times do you feel as if someone is not really attending to you but merely figuring out what they will say to defend or fight back? When you listen for meaning in order to paraphrase, you really . . . well, listen! You catch more content with fewer interruptions. Your eyes focus on the speaker; when it's your turn, you get the chance to say, "What I heard is ___. Is that correct?" Or "You feel . . . because I . . ." The original speaker can acknowledge that you understood or clarify if you misunderstood. Either way, people feel good when they are heard.
13	Touch	Sue Johnson wrote *Hold Me Tight* about her emotionally focused therapy (EFT), which aims to bring a corrective emotional experience to couples. Touch is one of the most basic methods that connects all humans.[7] A handshake, a fist bump, even a high five counts. Those with deeply seated anger may have experienced bad touch (abuse or harsh discipline, which only perpetuates anger). Healing contact occurs with a needed hug, a hand that reaches out to rest on top of yours in a moment of need or grief. Touch often does what words simply cannot.

| 14 | Forgiveness | Being stuck in anger keeps your adrenaline high, which ricochets destructive effects to your immune system, among other things. When you forgive, you sleep better, stress less, and frequently require fewer medications. People resist forgiving because they may not wish to forget what grievance befell them. Using cognitive-behavioral therapy (CBT), the injustice can still inform your thinking (in order to avoid peril in the future); but when coupled with relaxation, forgiveness can alter your thoughts and behaviors. (See appendix for additional information.) |

TEACHING KIDS TO WORK THROUGH A PROBLEM

In 2007, *The Washington Post* outlined how students in Montgomery County Public Schools in Maryland were taught to deal with a situation when they deemed that other kids were bugging or pestering them unnecessarily.[8] Using a handy mnemonic with a five-part process, counselors and teachers taught the children the following:

> **D**o ignore
> **E**xit or move away
> **B**e friendly
> **U**se firm language
> **G**et help

This simple method works for both children and adults. Many perceived injustices don't have to be acted upon, and we'll show you how to check if your assumptions are even worth worrying about at all. Simply moving away from the problem often empowers you. If this is someone trying to honestly communicate, walking away (or sulking) equates to stonewalling. But if you've tried before or you think the situation is going to escalate rapidly, take a reprieve. A simple "Please stop . . ." often takes care of the issue. If not, assertive language with a more serious tone may work. Sometimes repeating your words helps. If all this fails or if you see the situation as unproductive or getting out of control, seek help. Children should find the recess monitor, lunch aide, teacher, parent, or other grown-up. Adults should move up the chain of command at an office or seek therapy for a problem that continues despite their best efforts.

ABOLISH PROCRASTINATION

What makes you put off one job but enthusiastically tackle another? Researchers have found that time plays a pivotal role, as does your ability to process distractions; for example, people may be more prone to begin a task that has a distinct deadline, such as within a month or by the end of the year. Some proceed better if they chunk a deadline down, dividing work into smaller, incremental steps, each having its own distinct deadline. Visualize your payoff or reward. Post where you can see it the grade you may receive at project conclusion or a vacation scene you're saving for as you make your own coffee or pack lunches to cut expenses.

COMING TO TERMS WITH DIFFICULT FEELINGS

Many of the feelings in the "Building an Emotional Vocabulary" box aren't easy to admit.[9] Collecting injustices and ruminating over grudges harms you. When you embrace letting these go, you won't be locked into your grievances and resentments, and will be much less likely to mismanage your anger again.

Sometimes knowing what you don't want can also help you become more contented. Having felt isolated and lonely, you might become more accepting and tolerant. Knowing what it's like to be silent may help you to finally assert yourself. Use frustrated energy for your own betterment. If you have failed to take any action, vow to comply or cooperate. Two critical tools—productive, open expression and problem-solving skills—will make the way much easier.

BUILDING AN EMOTIONAL VOCABULARY

Sometimes merely labeling negative feelings removes the fear of expressing them. Do any of these words or phrases ever apply to you when you're angry?

agitated • alarmed • ambivalent • apprehensive • ashamed • at a loss • belittled • bossed around • burdened • cautious • conflicted • confused • controlled • culpable • cut off • degraded • demoralized • desperate • despondent • devastated • disappointed • discounted • disgusted • distant • down • drained • edgy • enraged • exasperated • exploited • exposed • foolish • frustrated • guarded • guilty • helpless • hesitant • horrified • imposed upon • incompetent • indignant • inept • insecure • insignificant • intimidated • intruded upon • jealous • jittery • left out • let down • lonely • miffed • mischievous • mistreated • misunderstood • nauseated • neglected • needy • obsessed • overlooked • overwhelmed • pessimistic • picked on • pressured • provoked • put down • reluctant • repelled • resigned • resistant • restless • run down • seething • shamed • shocked • smug • sorrowful • stuck • suspicious • tearful • threatened • timid • tired • turned off • uncertain • unwanted • unwelcome • used • vulnerable • wary • worried • wounded

ENCOURAGING OPEN EXPRESSION

If the family you grew up in discouraged strong emotional expression or your parents easily brushed away your anger by saying things like "you're not really mad" or "now, now . . . that's not how you feel . . ." then using descriptive words to share feelings won't come easily. You'll perpetuate this unless you convince yourself to communicate well. Since family process trickles down the generations, your children will learn to mask their true feelings just as you did. They may gain power by being clever or oppositional, empowered one minute, demoralized the next, as they are dishonest or pull the wool over *your* eyes. You and they can both achieve comfort with ordinary, garden-variety anger by using these techniques:

Know what you can change: Define trigger emotions with specific words. A feelings chart or poster[10] assists kids to broaden their vocabulary as they point to a vast range of smiling or frowning faces. Get comfortable identifying various emotions, and build the new words into daily use.

Review your leadership style: If it's authoritarian, with the need to rule, it discourages honest expression. Indulging or permissive, indifferent or disengaged styles aren't optimal either, for they never teach. An authoritative style allows you to exercise control but in a warm, responsive, encouraging way. This invites discussion and builds bonds as opposed to closing down communication and pushing others away.

Extinguish shoulds, musts, and oughts: Whenever you find yourself thinking, "I *ought* to be silent," "Good people *should* smooth it over," "I *must* keep the peace at all costs," realize it's your inner critic speaking. Stop her. Express the thought you were about to squash, or, if the moment is inappropriate, respectfully wait for the right time to speak up and do so then. Yes, there are some things we all should do in this world, such as "I should be nice to other people" or "I should follow the law." However, self-imposed, impossible rules that put us into a spiral of neurotic shame, such as "I must always be perfect or else I'm a failure," are simply not true or valid measurements.

Let occasional mistakes slide: We all have bad days. Especially with children, berating people only adds to their sense of helplessness. Shame keeps the anger churning. Belittling shuts down communication, and when communication is lost, so is any influence you may have had. With no means for honest expression, people hide their feelings and become dishonest.

Practice open, positive, and helpful verbal expression to turn around anger that might have gone underground years ago. Give it time and patience, and these new patterns will form different habits.

ANXIETY OFTEN ABOUNDS

Blame and projection, the two most prevalent defense mechanisms used by those who suppress anger, spark annoyance. You feel exasperated. Occasionally you feel incensed. Very often, you are anxious and apprehensive of what's going to happen next.

Anxiety Type	Symptoms	Treatment/Remedies
Adjustment disorder occurs during external stress or life transitions—good or bad—that prove stressful, bringing anxiety and depressed mood or both. This can impair all aspects of life. Clinicians often use this diagnosis for garden-variety stress when people come in because they are bothered by another's or their own passive-aggression. It's the most basic code that's insurance reimbursable.	People feel overwhelmed, anxious, and restless. Adjusting to positive changes, there's worry nonetheless. A certain level of hypervigilance comes when dealing with someone else's shrewd, manipulative, and/or undermining behavior. One's mind may race with worry, affecting concentration and decisions. Emotional upset and feeling down in the dumps can accompany the worry.	Solution-focused, cognitive-behavioral therapy (CBT) and family systems therapy help to alleviate a person's fear and upset. Exercise, coping skills, and mindfulness promote anxiety reduction and better sleep. Prescribed medication reduces anxiety, improves depressed mood, and improves sleep. A therapist will determine if there are genetic tendencies toward anxiety. If the situation does not improve, another anxiety diagnosis may seem more appropriate.
Generalized anxiety disorder is excessive apprehension more days than not for six months in many situations. It can also describe hard-to-control anxiety. Other medical or mental health diagnoses cannot already apply. Children need only one symptom whereas adults must have at least three.	People exhibit being on edge, fatigued, and irritable and report difficulty concentrating, muscle tension, and sleep disturbance.	Genetics can influence one's anxiety. Understanding family systems and CBT can lessen or eradicate symptoms. Some cases need medication. Better coping skills, mindfulness and relaxation. Play and expressive therapies help, too.
Panic disorder describes recurrent, unexpected panic attacks with a surge of intense fear peaking within minutes, with four (or more) classic symptoms. The attacks occur with persistent worry about the panic and its consequences. Much avoidance stems from and perpetuates the disorder.	From a calm or generally anxious state, symptoms include abruptly accelerated heart rate, palpitations, or chest discomfort; sweating; shaking; shortness of breath; feelings of choking, nausea, dizziness, numbness, or tingling; feeling chilled or suddenly hot, as if totally "losing it" or detached.	Solution-focused CBT and family systems therapy work well in addition to medication management. But one should never rely upon pills alone, as some prescriptions are habit forming. Learn better coping skills and relaxation techniques.

> ### POSITIVE VERSUS NEGATIVE MENTAL ENERGY
>
> Martin Seligman, author of *Authentic Happiness,* teamed with Chris Peterson, a psychologist at the University of Michigan, to create the Values in Action Inventory of Strengths to identify a person's signature strengths. Knowing these, they say, makes it easier to achieve happiness throughout life.[11] Many psychologists and life coaches help clients play to their strengths, pointing out not-so-obvious mismatches between career or lifestyle demands that don't fit those core strengths. Adjust or remove these obstacles and you often remove misery, empowering people to action. If you feel competent in at least a few areas, this often compensates for those where you need improvement.

ASSERTIVE SELF-HELP STRATEGIES

When you solve problems and empower yourself, your anger slowly dissipates because you unlearn some of the patterns that have rendered you stuck. But in the heat of an irritating situation, you need short, specific, and easy-to-remember tips—a new menu of options.

Below, we break down some of those "stuck points" to help you select better alternatives and complete the work regarding hidden anger.

> ### CONTROL
>
> Now that you can look back upon things you needed as a child, or perhaps still do need, hopefully it's easier to understand why you're afraid of certain situations and veer to avoid them. Next time you feel yourself wanting to take charge, stop and think about what you've learned about control. Try a new strategy that's less liable to keep your hidden anger brewing.

Your Needs	What You Fear/Avoid	New Approach to Try
To have the upper hand	Taking chances, risks	Identify your payoffs or what you get out of being stuck: express these.
To be in control	Being hurt or blamed	Cooperate; solve problems.
Success	Fear of failure and competition	Work on your thinking; see the shades of gray in between all good and all bad.
Independence	Dependence and losing control	Commit to action, follow-through, and personal growth with new approaches where more risk and fear is involved. Seek treatment when stuck in a bad cycle.

When you go to great lengths to remain passive to control a situation, it may well be the moment you most need to act. Many disgruntled workers shut down their performance, hoping their boss will fire them. Unhappy spouses stomp off during an argument; put-upon teens "forget" to do a chore. These misuses of control reduce action. In a relationship, they counterintuitively reduce intimacy, and nothing gets resolved.

Parents and teachers come across as controlling if they adopt a "because I said so" attitude. Use phrases like these only when absolutely necessary, as in "run . . . the building is on fire!" Remember that an authoritative style, as opposed to an authoritarian one, allows you more room to operate fairly. You're still in charge, but not at the expense of good relations with your children or students.

MANIPULATION

If you've tried to exert pressure to force a particular outcome before, these new tactics may work far better, because they take into account what you need, what you're afraid of, and what you have tended to avoid when angry.

continues —

— continued

Your Needs	What You Fear/Avoid	New Approach to Try
To complicate life via fence-sitting and/or shutting down	Uncertainty	Focus on solutions, not obstacles.
To manipulate or control the outcome or the process	Having to cooperate, give and take; having to deal with others' expectations, needs, or concerns	Assert, rather than demand. Be a team player, acknowledging others' opinions as equally valid as your own.
To win, have fun through fighting/hurting	Authority, perceived or real	Cooperate; be willing to meet halfway.
To push people's buttons, exact revenge	Confrontation	Listen; let others speak for themselves.
To set agenda	Being found out	Count to ten; take deep breaths; relax.
To hide true emotions	Intimacy, dependency	Halt knee-jerk, immediate actions.
To blame, find fault	Guilt, self-blame	Increase your frustration threshold.
To be intentionally ineffective, independent	Admission of the problem or any anger	Keep your eyes on the problem so that you're not swayed by "getting back" at the person.
To keep responsibility at bay	Responsibility	Take responsibility for problems you created or put off. Match thoughts, feelings, and actions.

The need to manipulate the outcome is very similar to the need to control; both stem from an internal pressure to win at all costs, born out of fear and what one often avoids. Pat seemed to engage in battle for the sport of it, more so when he lubricated his emotions at the local bar. A divorced dad with a twin boy and girl, he took great pleasure in evoking reactions from his ex-wife Olivia, discovering one of the easiest ways was to refuse to cooperate as a co-parent; he refused to comply with ordinary expectations most any dad encounters—dropping his son off at little league or his daughter to a softball game and purchasing toiletries for his children. By complicating things, Pat essentially crafted Olivia's response: most Monday mornings he'd find an email reading him the riot act for being so damn difficult. "I'm not angry . . . you're the one upset," Pat would typically reply, yet nearly every weekend with his children, Pat dug deeper into this type of resistance, manufacturing the outcome.

Sometimes, "conflict avoidant" is an apt description, because those who need to control the outcome shy away from the uncertainty that open expression brings. Olivia's response to Pat's action was almost guaranteed (the certainty that Pat needed), and crafting the situation for it was easier than the work of being a co-parent. Little will turn this around until one of them changes the dynamic—Olivia becoming less reactive or Pat voicing his concerns directly to her.

CHILDLIKE/IMMATURE BEHAVIOR

We are creatures of our past; thus, unmet needs in childhood often drive our adult behavior. When that happens, try to recognize the source, acknowledging what you fear or avoid. Try out a new strategy to move you forward.

Your Needs	What You Fear/Avoid	New Approach to Try
To re-create earlier experience in childhood	Being loved conditionally	Take responsibility for your own issues.
To be seen as the "good boy" or "good girl"	Losing rank in family	Believe in yourself.
Independence, yet feels dependent	Powerlessness	Overcome learned helplessness.
To meet others' expectations	Never getting it right	Practice decision-making skills; be decisive.
Growing up and facing maturity	Responsibility	Practice relaxation techniques when you feel anxious.

Recalling our Fort Lauderdale family at Thanksgiving, nothing seems to suit Franny, and her list of injustices stretches wide. These reactions catapult Franny and family into the unbalanced dysfunctional dynamics of their youth, which now impact nieces and nephews as Franny has unrealistic expectations of them. Albert, the oldest, isn't very mature, mocking their brother to bond their coalition. The joke had ceased being funny decades ago. At least Martha takes a stand against the fast-rolling criticism. Franny silences what really matters—her feelings—and as a result she relegates herself to martyrdom.

Why? Possibly to remain favored or to seek attention. People like Franny often long for closer family ties but set up self-fulfilling prophecies—launching a litany of snarky remarks and self-aggrandizement that robs closeness and peaceful memories. Moreover, Franny might feel quite liberated if she used her energy to motivate others rather than to grumble.

Defenses rooted in childhood might have been used to protect a person from unavailable, insensitive, unreliable, or possibly punitive parents. We don't know what happened exactly, but if Franny lived in Albert's shadow or perhaps lost any special status as Martha and Jim came along, it's time for her to unlock the hold of those childhood recollections. Maturity means cleaning up messy circumstances that still affect you—things you've avoided by being "too nice," both then and now.

SELF-ABSORPTION/VANITY

Next time you feel selfish desires come over you, recognizing what you really seek in any given situation is far better than acting out of anger. Acting differently might very well allay your fears, put an end to what you have previously avoided, and help you to find the attachment, attention, or security you quite possibly have wanted all along.

Your Needs	What You Fear/Avoid	New Approach to Try
Attention, often to be the center of that attention	Loneliness	Cooperate consistently; become less sensitive; laugh.

Security	Living or working without support	Recognize other people's right to shine.
Attachment	Unhappiness	Take an active interest in others and their achievements; offer praise and empathy.
Happiness	Failure	Live by the rules; deal honestly.
Self-advancement	Losing	Respect other people's boundaries; realize everyone gets a turn.
To be loved	Responsibility	Stop faulty, negative thoughts.
		Work on being less sensitive; laugh.
To escape with alcohol and drugs	Facing the world; withdrawal	Seek treatment for addictions.

In our example of Pat, the divorced dad, his selfish need to get back at Olivia took precedence over his children, who avoided negatively charged weekends with him. When they said, "We want to be with Mom," he blamed Olivia. Pat should seek help for his drinking because it stands in the way of being a parent. Had Pat dared to get close to his kids, he could have found the attachment, attention, love, and security he craved. For many, lessening sensitivity and lightening the mood with laughter might establish close connections as well.

Vain people feel they know what's best for others. Being so self-assured often lands people in lonely places. Some inflated self-worth is normal for teenagers (part of maturing is working to modify it). With less understanding of the world and their place in it, they focus on themselves, often to the exclusion of others. Book titles like *Get Out of My Life, but First Could You Drive Me and Cheryl to the Mall?* elicit knowing laughs from parents. Maturity will surface, but in the meantime, get kids to do some volunteer work so they can better understand the world beyond their myopic vision. If you see them belittle others, rather than ground them to their rooms, have them write a short essay on a greater problem (e.g., bullying).

DEPRESSION

Everyone feels down about life and their specific circumstances some of the time. Very often, with positive thinking and other action steps, we can alter our mood, tackling our fears and meeting needs that have led us to a blue mood. Try these strategies, and if you still feel stuck, seek help from a qualified professional.

Your Needs	What You Fear/Avoid	New Approach to Try
Connection, understanding	Loneliness	Focus on the positive; reframe negatives.
Hope, support, security	Living or working without support	Use exercise and positive mood-boosting strategies.
Optimism, positivity	Unhappiness, difficulty	Seek treatment for addictions.
Self-worth	Failure, rejection	Use positive self-talk and relaxation techniques. Be proactive in life.

When self-esteem and self-confidence wane, especially with losses, anger often lurks behind passive, negative, and depressive symptoms. A helpful technique called reframing—mentally turning negatives into positives—can remedy this.

Stairstep to self-confidence by acting "as if" you are already self-assured. This may move you beyond your comfort zone, but it may also take you beyond the limits that keep you playing it safe.

ASSERTIVE THINKING AND PHRASING

Being assertive means that you act in your best interests without violating others' rights. It's the belief that everyone is equally worthy with the same opportunity to agree or disagree. Assertiveness equates to being firm but tactful, and it conveys openness, problem solving, compromise, and negotiation. You can recognize an assertive person by their comfortable posture, firm handshake, appropriate eye contact, and voice intonation. When you hold firm to your values, that's being assertive, and so is maturely taking responsibility for yourself and your actions.

There is no one right way of being assertive. If you struggle to become more assertive, practice these lines to short-circuit that critical inner voice. Use these when you're tempted to blame or drop hints instead of speaking up.

Assertive Thought or Phrase:	Instead of:
I would like to _____.	You should _____.
I'd appreciate your understanding that I'd like ____.	If you don't _____, I'll _____.
Everyone has a unique contribution.	It must be done this way.
I will improve my performance.	It's the teacher's fault.
It's _____ that bothers me, frankly.	Oh, everything is just fine.
Let's review this now and see what we can do.	"It's done . . . too bad . . . you lose."
I want to weigh all the information before I decide.	I don't have time now. Or [silence]
I know I made a mistake. Here's how I'll correct it.	People are out to hurt me.
Deciding has been a problem for me. It might help if we could sort it out. Could you help me with that?	Give me a break. I just can't do this.
When I don't know where you are, I get worried.	You were supposed to call from your friend's house. You're just so darn irresponsible.
I can see that. I should think about it. I'd like until tomorrow to get back to you.	I don't know. Whatever. [shut down from pressure]
I know I haven't been myself, that I've been cranky and critical lately. I just want you to know that it's not you. I'm doing the best that I can right now.	Look what you've done to me. You make me so angry!
I'm sorry I didn't come to you sooner. I should have.	Well, you would have gotten upset. I know it.
The human resources office can help us resolve this.	You should go for counseling.
I'd really appreciate your spending Saturday with me as it's my birthday, and I'd love to get together.	Doing anything this weekend?

twelve

When and How to Seek Help

Q UYNN FACED A LONG WORKDAY, WITH CLIENTS AND GROUPS EFFEC-
tively planting her at the therapy office until almost nine at night. Her
boss wanted progress notes and insurance claims filed before she left.
Amid the morning mail with business-sized envelopes, Quynn spotted a
small square one.

"Dear Miss Quynn, It's been years since I saw you, but I really wanted
to send this. I just got married! You were so right that if I made myself a
priority for once (instead of pleasing everyone else), I might find myself at
an entirely different, happy place. I worked my plan. So here I am. Thank
you for encouraging me to be . . . well, me!"

Quynn recognized her former client's name as she closed the note with
gratitude. It proved her client's hard work and validated to Quynn that people could grow and make their own destiny much brighter.

This therapist's story makes us smile, too. It is why we entered this field.
We wrote this book to inspire people that their efforts matter and that counseling can jumpstart, and often maintain, their progress.

WHEN THE SEETHING DOESN'T SUBSIDE

You've read many chapters with examples backed by research. You've seen the symptoms. For the person on the receiving end of passive-aggression, anxiety is huge and hypervigilance primes for further occurrences. If you feel that you hide your own anger for self-shielding, protective purposes, there comes a time when staying bottled up is simply too painful to perpetuate. Maybe you've held feelings inside to your maximum limit. Still, how can you become more candid and content without jeopardizing your progress?

Defeating your inner struggles with independence versus dependence, support versus resistance, cooperation versus refusal, passivity versus active management of your life, well . . . it can seem daunting. You're to be congratulated for giving it a try!

Anytime you embark upon change, it helps to have the support of family and friends. Being direct with them—perhaps using some of the phrases we've offered along with your own variations—may elicit their encouragement. Hopefully, you arrive at this juncture of your own accord, not at the behest of a spouse, an employer, or someone else. Resisting change keeps you stuck. You've got to be squirming, somewhat uncomfortable with the status quo, to give change a try. Predictably, when you make that commitment yourself, not for someone else, you get much, much more out of the process.

DECIDING ON THERAPY

Some people manage their struggles without therapy, but many decide to give counseling a try. A good therapist can help you determine what keeps your faulty thinking blocked and how you limit your actions. This person can hopefully nudge your reactions out of defense mode. By working with a caring, knowledgeable professional, you learn about how to halt your anger without causing emotional unrest and to visualize what a happier, less angry or anxious life would look like.

Those who begin often see the process as a useful opportunity to re-parent themselves, particularly if they can connect some of their lingering anger to their childhood. Viewing therapy this way causes many to become less self-critical and self-sabotaging, to actually commit to counseling as a journey of self-exploration. A counselor, for instance, can show you that expressing yourself yields far better results than walking out on a coworker or girlfriend, that your old default reasoning of "it's no use" sets in motion a self-defeating cycle, and that your not wanting to feel difficult emotions stems from messages that were perhaps instilled long ago. Role-playing conflict empties the fear out of it. With practice, even the most conflict-avoidant person can become comfortable with being challenged.

Does stigma stand in your way? Society has made great strides to acknowledge that people need occasional counseling just like they need occasional medical support. Yet many people still taint their choices with pejorative phrases such as "going nuts" or "needing a shrink." Toss stigma out the window where it belongs. Depending on your culture, you may have also been told that you shouldn't talk to outsiders. Indeed, you can and should attempt to work things out individually, through reading, or counsel gained from trusted clergy who offer insights into your faith. While confidants may lend an ear, many do not have mental health training, and others have no training at all. Friends may tell you what you wish to hear, not what you need to hear. They may also confuse their own problems with yours. Sadly, some friends or family, while well intentioned, unwittingly do more damage in their efforts to assist. Trained mental health professionals provide objective, supportive guidance.

Countless people go to counseling throughout their lifetimes. Most say it was refreshing, that they, surprisingly, discovered more strengths than they first thought they had, and that the experience overall was positive. Just as you may not relate well with a primary care doctor, the same goes with therapists. So, if you've had a prior experience that didn't live up to your expectations, don't let this deter you. Another professional relationship may click quite easily. Keep trying until you find one that does.

If you're using your health insurance to cover counseling visits, check with your plan for in-network providers, but if you are able to pay out of pocket, you significantly broaden your choices. Certainly, if you require very specialized help, you may need to search beyond your insurance network. When you find a clinician with the precise knowledge to help, don't be surprised if that specialization is not covered by insurance. For instance, locating a therapist who sees individuals or families is one thing; finding one with concurrent expertise to resolve long-standing hidden anger, eating disorders, broken relationships, sexual addiction, trauma, and the like can be arduous. Many would rather use their valuable time and talents helping people solve problems than pushing paperwork, which costs them more . . . and renders them less remuneration.

There are community mental health agencies that offer general therapy on a sliding scale if cost stands in your way. Contact mental health organizations for referrals. You want a counselor who can help you feel comfortable yet also effectively challenge you in order to move you beyond being angry and stuck. For children, school counselors can be helpful as an initial go-to person, and therapy groups may exist to sort through specific problems.

What type of professional you see is an individual choice determined by supply and demand. If you require medication, a psychiatrist is a medical doctor who is best trained to diagnose mental health conditions and write specific prescriptions plus monitor those medications for effectiveness and side effects. Today, over 70 percent of psychotropic drugs are prescribed by someone other than a psychiatrist, and this seems to work out just fine when mild medications are used for smaller problems.[1] However, medication errors delay or interfere with proper care. Also, occasional adjustments in medication levels are often needed as you progress through treatment, rendering psychiatrists the top choice because of their specific training with psychotropic pharmacology.

You will often work with another type of professional for talk therapy or group counseling. Psychological testing allows you to learn as much as possible about yourself; thus ask if the provider is qualified to administer such assessments. Psychologists (with a PhD or PsyD) test more than other providers. Otherwise, licensed clinical professional counselors (with an LCPC or LPC), marriage and family therapists (with an MFT), or licensed clinical social workers (with an LCSW) have two to four years of master's level coursework, experiential training, and state licensure to help most people with lingering anger issues. Pastoral counselors add a religious perspective, with a similar experiential track.

WHEN COUNSELING BECOMES CRITICAL

Clearly if you have symptoms of depression, anxiety, or anger, struggling relationships, or a stalled career, therapy would likely forestall further decline and minimize frustrations. Given our anger topic, you may find counseling appropriate if any of these descriptions fits:

- People pleasers who have bolstered the well-being of others at their own expense, not just on occasion but by habit. If you're not doing things that are meaningful to you and well-suited to your interests and goals, perhaps it's time to take stock of where you are and where you wish to be.
- Those who take on more than they can handle, never utter "No" and need to learn how to, because they may be so invested in outside approval that they find it impossible to refuse requests and set better boundaries. The inability to say this dreaded word often stems from fear, rooted in insecurity; sometimes people who give in and say "Yes" do so as a misguided expression of loyalty and devotion.
- Victims of bullying (at school or in the workplace) and emotional abuse who would much rather see themselves as survivors and thrivers. Physical wounds can heal on their own or kinesthetically help you to learn and prevent reinjury; emotional wounds don't automatically give such awareness because being emotionally involved in a situation can blind you.
- Men, women, children, and adolescents who feel caught in family traps based in hidden anger, and worse yet, those sinking into the murky waters caused by a passive-aggressive divorce. Therapy may well be the anchor during these rising tides.
- Friends or family members who have had their feelings trampled by nasty negativity, criticism couched as constructive, and personality traits that have been so difficult to navigate that they indeed begin to wonder who is crazier—the errant parties or themselves. When you feel that you've been dropped into the twisted world that others have created, run—do not walk—to seek help.
- Anyone who has lost a sense of self. You know this if you're not living your own wishes and dreams, hopes and values. When someone else's choices rule, and your attempts at righting that

imbalance have fallen short, a good therapist can serve as a beneficial thinking partner.

- Those who have enabled to the point of being codependent upon a drinker, smoker, substance abuser, serial cheater, gambler, or anyone else not functioning in a manner that's productive and appropriate. We're talking about time and again smoothing things over or covering up someone's tracks, believing that you can change them. You can't. You can, however, change yourself.
- Couples who see one or more of Gottman's Four Horsemen of the Apocalypse—criticism, contempt, defensiveness, or stonewalling. Time to book an appointment! These are serious predictors of demise. And they are not exclusive to intimate relationships.[2]
- People who do know their needs, but are tongue-tied and unable to recall the right words or phrasing. Role-play and behavioral rehearsal that happen in therapy can improve communication and assertiveness.
- Students or workers who feel trapped in a passive-aggressive process that impedes their ability to learn, grow, and create the life direction they need because difficult others stand in their way.
- Members of any family system (including a dyad) who have seen prior therapy sabotaged may wish to return to sessions to see how the counseling experience could be improved. This can protect you from slipping back into the anger traps set by others.

WHAT TO EXPECT

After establishing rapport with your therapist, you'll hopefully establish goals. Therapy doesn't explicitly tell you what to do. Some types, however, are much more directive and provide some specifics and plans for change. Therapy affords you the space to come to realizations yourself. A good counselor will help you move from talking about how things were or are to how you feel. When you are able to move beyond mere facts, the therapy hour explores frustrations and how these play out. Those interactions—the process rather than the content—make up the real work of sessions. Your therapist will pick up on any uneasiness and will not move you faster than you can safely handle. You owe it to yourself to speak up and make sure this happens.

Therapists will respond differently toward you than others have in your past—that's the truly cool part! Feelings that may not have been allowed when you were younger will most assuredly be welcome here. If you're accustomed to being criticized or rejected, feedback in therapy will be different. The space you had to fight for among self-absorbed parents, siblings, or bosses will be all yours. There will be no need to overadapt. If you're afraid of feeling powerless, unsupported, or foolish, you needn't worry. You truly hold much power in this process. Just feeling an opposite dynamic often shakes up the faulty pattern that has prevented you from expressing yourself. So, too, if your emotions seem to justify your conclusions, then you may be using feelthink (emotions without facts), which is on our list of cognitive thinking errors (described in detail later in this chapter). Cognitive-behavioral therapy addresses this and more.

Expect your therapist to spot ambivalence, spark recognition, and help if you inadvertently paste someone else's face onto an innocent party due to pent-up anger. New reactions create changes in others who, in turn, change their behavior. Those very same mixed feelings can tempt you to quit when thorny feelings surface and you're afraid to rewrite your anger script. It's hard to clarify your own standards if you never had any firm foundation. Maybe your parents kept you guessing. Think about your therapy goals if ambivalence strikes—if you feel the temptation to stay as you are, avoiding change. You may find that beliefs that make you squirm—those that tempt you to exit therapy—aren't entirely accurate. Sometimes change is painstaking; it may cause you to lapse into denial or blame or project what you can't face onto someone else.

If you really are tempted to quit out of discomfort, ask yourself: (a) Is it what we discussed? (b) Are things moving to the truth too fast? (c) Is there something in the counseling method that doesn't feel right? (d) Does the therapeutic relationship seem off? (If it was fine before, it's probably points (a), (b), or (c)), or (e) Is the change I have to make in myself so damn difficult that the mere thought of it makes me run out on this fast or blame someone else?

Any of these items deserves discussion—a conversation that you should and can initiate. Scary? Perhaps. Afraid your therapist will reject you? That's highly unlikely. *The Bob Newhart Show* was fiction, but the infamous "Stop It!" skit ends with the client asserting herself.[3] Those in such TV portrayals rarely reflect reality, and when they do, their stories are still mixed with attention-getting entertainment. True therapy, that you choose, allows you to become a better "self." Stick with this journey, make it your own weekly program, to insure that your "ratings" rise rather than your ire.

SUPPORT IN DIFFERENT FORMS

Group Therapy: Group therapy can be particularly effective in treating substance abuse; other addictions; eating disorders; when overcoming losses such as a separation, divorce, or the death of a loved one; or when trying to improve certain abilities, such as social or interpersonal skills, or while wrapping up individual counseling.

Trained facilitators carefully select and work with members to foster cohesion. The leader may be your own therapist or another professional who has group training. The approach runs most effectively when your aim is to discover how you come across to others. Will, for instance, never felt too self-assured even after college. He'd gone to the university counseling center, but Will was still afraid to ask women out on dates or make new friends. His therapist suggested he try group counseling to discover his strengths and receive input from group members. The leaders encouraged role-play, and Will's confidence grew as he tested how to phrase things and respond within such an emotionally safe setting. Will became much less frustrated with objective, supportive feedback.

Group therapy is also a good place to work through some of the issues that originated in your family, because amazingly enough, those roles seem to be recreated within the dynamics of therapy groups. Confidentiality is key—what happens in group stays within group.

Some insurance companies reimburse for group therapy, but like much of managed care, the group reimbursement rates are paltry. You find fewer choices and more out-of-network practitioners, though overall, group coun-seling is less expensive than individual sessions.

Support Groups: Although therapy groups delve deeper into root causes of one's unhappiness and dysfunctional patterns than support groups, some of the same topics, such as addiction or the impact addictions have on fam-ily members, through Alcoholics Anonymous or Alateen, for example, are excellent places to connect with others and build skills. Counseling and education also become the focus around specific topics including (but not limited to) divorce, parenting, chronic pain, anger management, or cer-tain illnesses. Members offer each other different perspectives and mutual strength. Support groups are NOT social meet-up groups, and they aren't covered by insurance, but they generally have a low or no cost.

Play Therapy: Play is the communication and work of childhood. Unlike adults, who are much more verbal, children often express how they relate to the world using toys, art, games, and imagination. This is how kids learn to explore, solve problems, and redirect anger, fears, and thoughts toward objects rather than people as they master new feelings. With a therapist who has had training in play therapy, younger clients are able to better under-stand and express their emotions; become more empathic, responsible, and self-assured in their abilities; and improve self-esteem, respect, and social skills.

Art and Expressive Modalities: Art therapy has its roots in archetypes, symbols, and dreams, and it's become recognized for its calming and kinesthetic qualities. Whereas the ordinary person would perhaps focus on the art outcome (a child's sculpture), the therapist sees the process (smashing clay and molding it into a particular shape) as decidedly more important. For survivors of abuse, torment, or pent-up hidden anger, working through one's misery in order to master and verbally disclose one's feelings is pivotal. What a child may wreck one week, she might put back together in subsequent sessions, symbolic of her feelings and attempts to rehearse or redo behavior. Dance, psychodrama, poetry, and music therapy also involve feelings as well as artistic expression. They may be appropriate for someone who is particularly sedentary or when memo-ries and cognitive decline make talk therapy less effective.

Distance Counseling: Counseling via telephone or video can save time and reach out to people with limitations of geography, work travel, illness, disability, or life circumstance. It is best for those who need fairly straightforward, short-term, solution-based therapy or help with a life transition, and it's *not* recommended when anger has truly taken hold or when you're in crisis or feeling depressed or suicidal, because these situations require face-to-face work, with a secure, confidential environment to conduct sessions.

Video counseling allows the benefit of visible facial expressions and body language. Some employee assistance programs (EAPs) allow distance counseling without question, but third-party reimbursers (insurance companies) have been slower to see the usefulness. We hope this changes. Clinically reviewing the client's chart with insurance company personnel, providers are forced to justify why distance counseling sessions could be of benefit. Unfortunately, some providers give up due to the time-consuming process that often comes with a denial at the end. What's excruciatingly worse is that given these challenges, people in need of treatment give up or fail to reach out at all. We live in a transient and global economy. It's time to embrace some new ways of doing therapy.

Neurofeedback: Also known as neurotherapy, neurofeedback is a brain-based intervention that uses electroencephalography biofeedback to provide ongoing, real-time visual and auditory feedback to the brain about how it functions and where it works too hard and perhaps not enough. The brain uses that information to perform more efficiently, and it essentially increases self-regulation. Sensors (with a bit of cream to help them remain in place during the training) are placed on the scalp to measure the electrical activity and the measurements are displayed on video or computer equipment. As brain function increases, patients have reported decreased anxiety, depression, migraines, and sleep disturbance as well as increased emotional regulation. However, there's weak support from researchers, and few controlled studies regarding its use with ADHD.[4]

Outdoor Behavioral Health Programs: Often called wilderness therapy, programs based in the outdoors benefit those with behavioral problems, substance abuse issues, relationship complications, trauma recovery, or those "failure to launch" young adults who have underperformed or been non-compliant with treatment or school interventions. Whereas in a traditional setting the work of therapy occurs weekly (on average), here trained mental health professionals use whatever happens in the moment, in a natural setting. If a client has been saddled with resentments, a counselor might hike with him while the client carries rocks in a backpack. At the end, they discuss what they just did using the metaphor of carrying around grudges and how strength on the trail symbolizes finally facing one's anger. Be certain that a program is regulated by the Outdoor Behavioral Healthcare Council, which sets specific standards for this industry. Very often these programs are not eligible for insurance reimbursement and are private pay only.

If you have any concerns about these or other therapies, do some further research. More knowledge usually quells anxiety. If you remain skeptical, however, question that stance also.

Where minors are involved, therapy is more intentional than plopping a child in front of a board game. The motive is fun combined with talk as well as feedback. The outcome is the client's increased emotional awareness. With a child who has difficulty talking, playing a game or taking a walk together can get a conversation going. Sometimes an uninformed parent buys a board game to reveal personal emotions as an easier or less costly option than therapy. It's bound to backfire. There's a lot more to it than any game or therapeutic tool. Many teens will see this as a parent trying to force banter between them. That's not what you want. Leave the therapeutic modalities to those trained to use them. Be sensitive with where your child's mind is at the moment. Keep the dialogue going in small increments, and if you stumble along the way, it can be very helpful to ask for advice from an experienced counselor.

TIMELINES AND OTHER ANSWERS

Still hesitant? Think about treatment this way: when you have specific problems, you may need to learn new skills (communication, assertiveness, fair fighting) in order to address them; short-term counseling with solution-based approaches can teach you these skills.

Ongoing problems that last weeks, months, or years; that have a history of failed starts and relapses; that involve any risks such as high anxiety, depression, psychosis, self-harm, eating disorders, violence, or suicide must be dealt with in longer-term therapy with a licensed professional or with a physician who can prescribe medication. Bouncing around to many therapists won't work in these situations; sticking with one therapist that seems a good fit and tells you what you need to hear and learn very well may.

The length of treatment varies. When what brought you into counseling (presumably your hidden frustration) goes and stays away, or when you've met the goals you and your therapist set initially, you take stock of your progress. As a client feels better, has a good day, or finds that another person affecting her has calmed down, she may end therapy prematurely. Be aware: an angry person may effectively cycle through a honeymoon phase or calm before the next storm (explosion) all while continuing to implode. Over time—key to our original definition—you'll know if the changes are more permanent.

> It takes time to get us into our problems, and it takes time to rid ourselves of them. Realize that very few people who attempt change get it right the first time. It takes practice, but change is not only possible, it's probable if you learn from each setback, recommit yourself, set specific, short-term goals, and surround yourself with the right supports. In other words, if you keep at it, you're there!

You could schedule sessions less frequently—say every other week or monthly—before you phase out of counseling altogether. Ending therapy can be stressful because it's a parting, but with most therapists, the door usually remains open for check-in visits in the future.

COMPLICATED PARTINGS

Quynn, the therapist, took a fifteen-minute lunch and gathered materials for an art therapy group. Seven kids would paint six-inch metal cans, and later fill them with frustrating sentiments—a creative outlet for difficult feelings they needed to express to mom, dad, or siblings. These children lacked social skills.

Angelette was new to this Phoenix suburb. The heat was the least of her eight-year-old concerns. Kids picked on her, both parents worked long hours, and her only friend, her dog, ran off (and returned) recently. Her parents constantly bickered, and given Angelette's art, they had quite the beverage collection, most of it sedating. Group was the only place Angelette could talk about her "jungle of emotions"—through art.

At 8:45 p.m., Quynn clicked open one last e-mail, from Gerard, the girl's father. It read, "You ignored my wife's calls. Angelette was making trouble last night. Estelle came to talk to you before Angelette's group. You avoided them by not coming out until group started. And, our co-pay is $25, not the $75 we were billed. Angelette didn't go that night, and after last night, won't come back."

Drawing in a long breath, Quynn thought it best to address this after a good night's sleep. She rolled with language barriers, people who promised to pay next week, and seven sets of parents who wanted "just a minute." In this era of in-session-only insurance reimbursement, most concerns simply had to be brought up in another appointment. Quynn had no idea which clients arrived early. When badly needed therapy got interrupted with misunderstandings and misplaced anger, however, Quynn cringed inside.

We crafted this last scenario to give a glimpse of what hidden anger looks like from other sides. Quynn knew Dad questioned the value of "all those toys" and of treatment altogether. After Angelette proudly showed him a drawing she made, her dad had mumbled, "Can't you color something like that at home?" Tonight, Gerard had seen the charge for last month's missed session and was possibly angry at himself for forgetting. Now, running with feelthink, this dad pulled the plug on his daughter's only outlet for her true feelings and the only place she felt accepted by other kids.

Professionals of all kinds see passive-aggressive behavior. The physician sees prescriptions that aren't filled, or when they are, are stopped and started with nontherapeutic and sometimes dangerous consequences. The physical therapist easily knows by the range of motion whether the patient has completed her home exercise program. And attorneys can give sound advice to minimize or avert further troubles, but if clients don't heed that counsel, they create their own misery. There are times when most of us have fallen short of perfect compliance, but as consumers who can change our own lives in consort with paid providers, we get out of any service what we're willing to contribute to it.

PROVIDER PERILS

Therapists enter their field with curiosity about human behavior and a desire to teach people new skills and explore possibilities of what can be rather than what currently exists. Like other professionals, they establish a business side of their practice that permits the helping side.

Very often the business aspects vex even the most healthcare savvy of consumers. Until the Mental Health Parity and Addiction Equity Act (Parity Act) went into effect in late 2009, insurance companies could frequently limit the number of sessions their members were afforded for mental health and/or substance abuse disorders, or they could deny coverage altogether. Expenses (deductibles, co-payments and co-insurance) were at times incomparable to medical/surgical benefits. The Parity Act has improved matters. Providers report, however, that they experience clinical reviews or audits to determine medical necessity and a reluctance from insurers to authorize telephonic sessions in cases of medically-necessitated bed rest, family crises, or extenuating circumstances (highways closed for public safety or weather emergencies). If a family travels a distance, they cannot take advantage of time and proximity to conduct a back-to-back parent intake and a child's first session because insurers refuse to pay for two sessions within one day. The resulting inconvenience feeds any reluctance that may exist.

Furthermore, consumers are shut out from effective treatments; for example, *The Wall Street Journal* ran "No Joke: Group Therapy Offers Savings in Numbers" in 2009, in which it stated that group therapy offered on average a 50 percent reduction of costs but that it accounted for less than 10 percent of the outpatient market.[5] One reason is that insurance companies have sometimes allowed an aggregate fee of as low as $20 to $25 per session—the amount of some people's co-payments for traditional therapy. Including the member's responsibility, the total value it considers for this modality frankly deems it cost prohibitive for therapists to offer it. Yet, overall if group therapy were offered more often it would save insurance companies money compared with the higher cost of individual sessions. Go figure!

Groups require more (not less) effort, organization, sometimes expense (supplies), and preparation. The therapist must complete a progress note for each and every member. Factor in claim submission (multiplied by the number of clients) plus dealing with any approvals, and you can see why this cost-saving and truly advantageous form of therapy remains underutilized.

These hassles force some professionals to decide against managed care participation or even EAPs, because they don't receive remuneration that reflects their training, not to mention the ancillary tasks, including necessary discussions with other treating providers, case preparation, and documentation. Mental health providers historically do not have billing codes that pay for collaborating with a physician/provider or reading relevant reports or clinical assessments that could move a person's treatment ahead or shorten it.

BECOMING A SATISFIED CONSUMER

What can you do as a consumer to avoid healthcare hassles? Here are a few pointers:

- Carefully review your informed consent. This is a document that discloses policies/rights up front so that no uncomfortable surprises or charges arise later. Upset clients occasionally project their own frustrations onto others when they should have done their due diligence by familiarizing themselves with policies and by asking questions.
- Refrain from hasty therapy exits. You really *can* tell your therapist that you're frustrated, that you need to talk, that something seems unfair to you. If you signed a business document that doesn't allow you to wiggle out of your commitments (nor should it), your exit angst gives you and your counselor honest-to-goodness material to work with—far better than hypothetical scenarios where you can reframe frustration. Any working business relationship involves respect on both sides.
- Feel comfortable with a provider's background by doing your research and asking relevant questions upon your first meeting. Those who communicate well their education, experience, and how they facilitate change may put you more at ease than those who only put forth a name and title.
- When life happens, communicate. Missed appointments due to truly extenuating circumstances may be discounted or given a

one-time waiver; however, what's extenuating to some clients (the coach called another practice or they forgot prior plans) may not be extenuating for providers. A heads-up, however, may allow another client to use your appointment time so that everyone wins.

- Finally, the Family Educational Rights and Privacy Act (FERPA) was originally created to keep students' grades private, but it also prevented parents from hearing about mental health problems, even if school personnel knew that a student struggled. After tragedies, parents sued, citing the obligation to communicate with them and that withholding information contributed to these tragedies.

- Schools argued that FERPA laws prevented that disclosure. Tim Murphy, in his congressional role, introduced legislation to allow a family member to be informed when a student's safety is at risk. Colleges now require students to sign a contract declaring what information will be shared. If you are a parent, inquire into the university's policy. If the school has no trouble reaching you when tuition is due, but refuses to let you know when your child is in psychological trouble, there are hundreds of other schools to select. Suicide is the second leading cause of death among youth. One in twelve young adults have considered a suicide plan at some point, and one person aged fifteen to twenty-four dies by suicide every two hours.

FIXING YOUR FAULTY THINKING

We all fall into faulty thinking, at least occasionally. Lists of cognitive thinking errors are plentiful. Here is ours. See if any of these faulty thought patterns play out in your everyday life:

- **Feelthink:** Confusing emotions with thoughts and using feelings as the sole basis needed for understanding. "I feel it, therefore it is." The feeling is all the justification needed to keep anger brewing. It's the "I'm mad so you must have done something to make me mad" justification. Separate feelings from facts in order to make changes in your faulty thinking.
- **Quick Leaps:** Fast interpretations that bottom out your beliefs when there are literally no facts to support your quick philosophy

and poorly told fortunes. Ambivalent folks do this often as they avoid confronting others and therefore fence-sit longer than they often have to.

- **Dirty-Lens Thinking:** Viewing everything through a very negative filter, as if there is an inch-thick coating of dust on the window and that's how you see the world.

- **All-or-Nothing Thinking:** Everything is one way or another with no shades of gray in between the black and white. Job performance must be stellar or else it's terrible. Watch for "must," "should," and "ought" in your thinking. Life has in-betweens. So do many circumstances and situations.

- **Magnifying and Minimizing:** Here you make more of your problem or exaggerate the significance (negatively or positively) of any inadequacies or limitations. "I'll never succeed" or "It'll always be depressing here."

- **Overdoing-It Beliefs:** You see one event in your life as game-changing or predicting a defeatist pattern. *Always* and *never* are red-flag words that alert you to this faulty thinking.

- **Bag-the-Benefit Thinking:** Rejecting the good, embracing only the bad. This isn't a mere bad day but is a constant pushing aside of the positive. All you're left with is discouragement, and it takes hold, spawning negativity.

- **Taking It Personally:** When you personalize something negative, internalizing it so that you feel responsible, it's a sign that your mood is at a low ebb. Many chronically depressed or angry people resort to this thinking pattern.

- **I Know You Better Than You Do:** This occurs when a person makes assumptions, thinking they can predict that another doesn't like them or reacts poorly to them based solely on their own negative perceptions of themselves. Attempts at mind reading like this cause much difficulty.

- **Label Thinking:** Making a global assessment, typically a pejorative attack such as "He's a jerk" or "All stepmothers are witches," is quick and easy but also unfair. If you're perpetually sarcastic and lob such low remarks, you're labeling.

MINDFUL ADJUNCTS TO THERAPY

Mindfulness can be a technique that enhances healing when you incorporate it into your own anti-anger lifestyle. "There are times when life is overwhelming," write Stanley Block and Carolyn Bryant Block in *Mind-Body Workbook for Anger.* "Your head is full of urgent and pressing angry thoughts, your body is full of tension, and you can't see the light at the end of the tunnel." They call this the powerless self affecting your mental state and every cell in your body. "This powerless self leads to a reactive state with possible explosive outbursts and actions that are abusive and inappropriate," the authors add.[6] Their workbook is chock-full of journal prompts, questions to answer, graphic diagrams, and paper-and-pencil as well as kinesthetic exercises to lead you to resolve your inner conflicts in a building-block, gradual approach.

Not much into reading? Try *Manage Anger Daily Meditation,* available on CD and MP3.[7] "Anger grows when you fail to recognize your own nervous tension, stress, and worry," reports Gina Simmons, PhD, a therapist with Schneider Counseling and Corporate Solutions, which produces this product. "When your next stressful event occurs, you react from a higher state of nervous system arousal, and when you react from that, you end up regretting your behavior. If you take the time to sit quietly and settle your nervous system, instead of ignoring your feelings, you can better manage your moods and behavior."[8]

These two thirty-minute guided meditations will clear your mind as you gradually begin to feel a sense of contentment. The benefits of meditation accumulate over time. You will react to life events from a lower level of nervous system arousal and bounce back from stress with more ease and emotional balance.

Finally, for children, *Sitting Still Like a Frog: Mindfulness Exercises for Kids (and Their Parents),* by Eline Snel, contains text along with a useful compact disc. *Mindfulness for Teen Anger* by Mark C. Purcell, MEd, PsyD, and Jason R. Murphy, MA, offers workbook prompts that get to root causes and anger resolution.

FREEDOM AT LAST

We've come to the end of our journey. We hope that through reading about anger's self-reinforcing nature, you realize the false illusion it often creates of being powerful and in control of a situation. No one is condemned to remain angry. We've not met any person who changed his destiny by staying the way he was.

Research out of the University of California at Berkeley revealed that core traits defining a person do change throughout life.[9] And, next time you feel tempted to sweep away a powerful emotion, silence your anger, or stash it so that it won't easily be discovered, think about how you're using that frustration. Very often, it's to create this illusion of control.

Illusions aren't real. They're fleeting. Figure out what purpose your anger serves—because trust us, anger can serve very useful purposes. Anger isn't necessarily the problem; mismanagement of it usually is.

Keep your eyes on the prize. Overcome hidden anger for yourself, your loved ones, and your career. Do it for your children, raising "can-do" kids who take on challenges and never think less of themselves if they can't take on those challenges. Want to really master problem solving? Teach problem-solving steps to your children; anytime you teach a skill, you reinforce it within yourself.

You can change. Yes, life is tough. It's also very rewarding. Commit to personal growth. Becoming the best version of yourself on a daily basis will later lead you to reach higher-order goals. If you refer to this book—our tips and strategies, phrases to help you assert yourself, and explanations to understand confusing behavior—when you need an added boost or simply a reminder of a better way, it will support your path.

You've dreamed about better times. Take these how-to steps to climb to that last rung on the ladder and seize the life you deserve.

Hidden Anger in the Clinical Setting

W E DESIGNED THIS SECTION FOR THERAPISTS, NURSES, PHYSICIANS, dentists, physical therapists, and providers such as occupational and speech therapists in addition to career and school counselors. (It may even benefit veterinarians . . . since it's human behavior that may not comply with treatment for Fido!)

When you treat passive-aggressive patients, no matter what kind of health-care professional you are, people will often present with other symptoms. Those who camouflage their frustrations face heightened cardiovascular, immune, and stroke risks, increased weight gain and periodontal disease, cellular deterioration, and premature aging, as well as lots of aches and pains. We know that clients may schedule counseling because of ADHD, depressed mood, eating disorders, self-harm, general irritability, relationship loss, and career fallout, as well as anxiety and stress.

ADVANTAGEOUS TRAITS FOR HELPING PROFESSIONALS

Lorna Smith Benjamin, PhD, who retired from the University of Utah, has written about passive-aggression and other more intractable behaviors (and personality disorders). She confirms what many providers already know or suspect—administrative difficulty may be your first sign. She also maintains that identifying passive-aggression is important because these clients are prone to canceling appointments, showing up late, ignoring payment, forgetting important forms, and, in the worst cases, seeking other kinds of retribution. The passive-aggressive patient agrees to comply with demands or suggestions, but later fails to perform, even with the therapist.[1]

We alert you so that you can prepare yourself to cope better with your patients, who maintain rudimentary internal conflicts. Most eschew being aggressive yet struggle to properly assert themselves; they also usually have distinct fears and a tussle between doing things their way or your way.

Key traits to understand when dealing with passive-aggressive clients include the abilities to set consistent limits and maintain boundaries, communicate acceptance, and offer empathy. A tall order, especially in the face of a client's resistance, anger, dependence upon you, and the exasperation it may cause. It will help if you are comfortable with slow progress. Passive-aggressive clients may not follow through on your referrals for consultations, twelve-step programs, and financial or legal advice, and they often aren't very effective carrying out instructions for their own care (wearing braces, brushing teeth well, home exercise programs, journaling thoughts, or practicing new skills). You must manage the transference and countertransference that arises; interacting with anyone (possibly you) may trigger negative behaviors related to a person in their past.

Medical providers know that a good patient-provider relationship fosters patients following treatment regimens. Some patients need a more collaborative approach, however, while others benefit from a more authoritarian one.[2] If a patient's goal is to lose weight, but she fears a reprimand, as has happened with authority figures in the past, she may cancel and postpone appointments. Never underestimate the power of transference in these encounters. Tailor your approach to each client individually to enhance the therapeutic alliance. Pay attention to somatic complaints that could involve regression. A passive-aggressive patient with high-dependency needs may spark your own or your staff's countertransference if those needs seem insatiable. And while the self-absorbed patient may flatter you, beware—their flattery might mask subtle but belittling comments that may make you question your competence.[3]

With this knowledge, it's paramount to cultivate the person's responsibility in his own treatment, and encourage him to express what he really feels. In other words, ask him directly to tell you what you *need* to hear.

IMPORTANT CONSIDERATIONS FOR ALL PROVIDERS

We go into helping fields because we desire to remedy maladies with skills we've devoted years of training to obtain. As a client comes to that first appointment, we're ready to engage in the work, because that's our job, and most of our clients are willing participants also. Yet passive-aggressive clients may be there at the behest of another person. Offer them the support they need, but be careful not to overstep and support dysfunctional behavior. Know their stage of change (see Elements of Change on page 261).

These are clients who expect you to have many answers for them, but don't be surprised if they become too dependent, or in some cases, argue "right" and "wrong." As a provider, of course, you must point out the probable consequences of certain behaviors (self-medication with alcohol or substances, poor posture or kinesiology, smoking, or hiding anger), and when clients come to subsequent appointments, you will see if they have followed your advice. When they have not, it's best to accept these patients for who are. Remember: if you do accept them and provide the empathy and boundaries they need, it might be one of the first times in their lives they've experienced such unconditional acceptance!

> Remember: if you do accept them and provide the empathy and boundaries they need, it might be one of the first times in their lives they've experienced such unconditional acceptance!

Using motivational interviewing skills will help you to obtain the patient's buy-in, own their responsibility, and see the advantages of proper assertiveness. This approach is frequently used in treatment of addictions; it fosters a collaborative exchange to strengthen commitment and incentive to change. Use motivational interviewing to promote healthy behaviors: exercise, weight reduction, medication compliance, safe sexual practices, and diabetes management.

For example, at a patient's dental visit, it's very clear that if the thirty-year-old patient avoids flossing, he's headed toward periodontal disease. The dentist cautioned him about this six months ago when he noticed redness, irritation, and bleeding of the gums, not to mention the bad breath, barely stopped by the dentist's mask.

> PATIENT: "I floss when I can, but it takes too much time between work, tennis, and my girlfriend."
> DENTIST: "It does take time, I hear you. Once you start, it becomes easier."
> PATIENT: "I just don't like it. No big deal."
> DENTIST: (Thinking patient will like the pain plus expensive gum surgery, much less) "What do you do to relax before you turn in at night?"
> PATIENT: "I watch TV or talk on the phone with my girlfriend. You can't floss and hold the phone, you know."
> DENTIST: (chuckling along with patient) "Yeah, you'd sound all mumbled for sure." (pauses) "How difficult would it be to floss while you watch the eleven o'clock news, even during the weather?"
> PATIENT: "Well, I guess I could do it even during sports. I always catch that."
> DENTIST: "There you go. Much easier to floss than deal with gum disease, bad breath, or lose your teeth."
> PATIENT: "I don't think I'd like that. Sounds gross."
> DENTIST: "I'm guessing your girlfriend wouldn't either. Does she like how you smile?"
> PATIENT: "She said that's what first attracted her." (smiling wide) "Do you have samples?"

Here the dentist rolled with the patient's resistance and created motivation for a healthy behavior. While he could have immediately suggested how to solve the problem (floss!), he held back. Our dentist listened to what the patient told him and incorporated reflective listening as well as the patient's excuses (without calling them that) to further the conversation and join with the patient several times. Becoming the authority figure too quickly would have backfired. Acceptance of the patient brought the provider and patient closer to a collaborative solution. Further, this dentist didn't give the patient much to resist. Admittedly, a provider often must spell out consequences quite unpalatably.

Don't expect too much, too soon. Passive-aggressive patients have anchored themselves to their indirect style due to resentments and perceived injustices often spawned from authority. Though this is the patient's problem, it will quickly become yours if you provide services without adapting your approach. Thus, it is important to set goals together. This is one of several points that Aphrodite Matsakis, PhD, discusses in *Managing Client Anger*. Matsakis reminds, "It is always important to set long-range treatment goals; but with passive-aggressive clients, goals should be set for each session." Think short-term. Matsakis suggests that the clinician should wait until after goal setting to offer several means of achieving the goals. This way, clients will not only buy into and pursue the goals but later cannot accuse the provider of not listening, acting as sole authority, or imposing provider goals onto them.[4]

ELEMENTS OF CHANGE

In *Changing for Good*, James O. Prochaska and his colleagues identified stages that self-changers experience.[5] They explained that everyone who successfully effects change goes through: **Precontemplation,** where they aren't even aware of what habit/behavior to change until those around them draw their attention to the problem. **Contemplation** follows; here, they've identified the behavior and are starting to think about ways to alter it.

In the **preparation** stage, they plan to take action in the days or weeks ahead. During the **action** phase, they muster the most commitment to changing their behavior, expending much time and energy. **Maintenance** comes next, because successful changers sometimes take one step back to every two steps forward. But they persevere, monitoring their progress, sometimes for a lifetime. Think of those who constantly monitor their weight or keep from taking a drink.

The sixth stage involves **termination,** a phase almost everyone loves to achieve, where they've extinguished an addiction or faulty habit. It's gone for good. The chain-smoker never yearns for a puff, or the anger concealer doesn't lapse into sarcastic gossip, shut down with "Whatever," or put off a task that she really could accomplish.

It takes time for us to get into our problems, and it takes time to rid ourselves of them. Realize that very few people who attempt change get it right the first time. This can mean **relapse.** People may experience a "fall from grace" as they evaluate what triggered a relapse, reassess their motivation and any obstacles to change, and perhaps plan for improved coping mechanisms to use in the future.

continues ——

— continued

Change takes practice, but it's not only possible, it's probable if your clients learn from each setback, recommit themselves, set specific, short-term goals, and surround themselves with the right supports. In other words, if they keep at it, they'll get there!

No matter what the therapeutic approach, remember how important the client is in the change process, and remember that as life experiences change them, they may be more ready than at other times to receive help. They are ultimately the very best experts on themselves— this is the message that Fred J. Hanna, PhD, gives in *Therapy with Difficult Clients,* in which he's identified seven precursors for client change. "A sense of necessity for change will not emerge if there is a greater necessity to remain the same," Hanna writes. "That necessity is followed by a readiness to experience anxiety or difficulty, awareness, confronting the problem, effort or will toward change, hope, and having social support for change."[6]

MENTAL HEALTH TREATMENT

Every therapist has a toolbox that includes psychological theories that resonate within themselves and their practices. While graduate programs teach a vast array of theories, some professors decidedly insist that their students master one or two. Of course, no one theory works in all situations. "Adherence to one theoretical approach, with no adaptation to client differences, personality styles, and needs, can result in what appears to be resistance from clients," writes Clifton W. Mitchell, PhD, in *Effective Techniques for Dealing with Highly Resistant Clients.*[7]

Consider that solution-focused and reality therapy approaches may move too fast for many clients who mask their emotions, including anger. The Rogerian or humanistic approach, often central in counseling, will likely stall the passive-aggressive client if it's the only theory used. "Because of the collaborative emphasis, the cognitive approaches of David Burns and Aaron Beck are less inclined to suffer the pitfalls of Ellis's ABCs," Mitchell advised in his book. Empathy must be used when dealing with the profoundly emotional basis of why people create façades involving anger.

Tempered, active approaches may grant you more forward movement and creativity. Here are a few of our best picks for working with passive-aggressive clients.

Cognitive-Behavioral Therapy (CBT)

Many people who trip themselves up with ingrained personality traits commit cognitive distortions. With CBT, clients analyze automatic thoughts (built out of family of origin schemas), recognize cognitive errors, craft positive reframes, and behaviorally learn and practice new skill sets. The cynical and glass-half-empty automatic thoughts of passive-aggressors perpetuate their victim status. Skills that shift this include (but are not limited to): communication ("I messages"), assertiveness, appropriate expression of negatives (saying no) and feelings (a range of new words), boundaries (taking a position for oneself), and how to deal with conflict in a nonconfrontational but direct way. Role-playing allows clients to see another's position without criticism that they might have previously encountered.

As Martin Kantor, who in 2002 wrote *Passive-Aggression: A Guide for the Therapist, the Patient and the Victim,* pointed out, "Passive-aggressives often misinterpret cognitive therapy as critical, unsupportive, or even assaultive, doing so especially when it has undercut their protective, particularly their protective projective, defenses."[8]

Looking back on our case studies from Chapter 1, CBT may have helped Elena, the young woman who swore she sought jobs despite a recession. However, her parents Mateo and Marcela frequently found Elena sprawled on the couch, electronic gadgets in hand, her chores long forgotten. Elena externalized her behavior with blame-filled statements. If you're a therapist, where might you take Elena's case?

Key to using CBT, join with Elena and stick to the facts. You don't wish to come across as another authority (like her parents) trying to budge her off the sofa, but elicit factual elements that Elena herself confides in you to do just that. Also, if you read any motives into Elena's slacking or stagnation, she may well provide a backlash of arguments akin to "You just don't understand," "My parents are the ones who . . . ," or when you attempt to gain her insight, Elena may answer with "How would I know?" Worse yet, she could continue to rehearse her anger through further blame and projection, and become more resistant.

To assist clients in developing self-awareness, Ms. Oberlin has engaged them by using an active whiteboard exercise. She creates three columns: Stuff That Happens, My Mantra, and Better Reframe. Elena's language of "my parents want me to get a job," could be considered the stuff that happens. What Elena tells herself, that is, "I might not know the job or I might get fired" could be her current mantra that keeps her stuck or allows her anxiety to ratchet. The better reframe might be "I'd probably get some training or mentoring." The process might start with you asking Elena to write on the board, prompting her with an indirect style, such as "How could *someone* change that?" Gradually you could lead Elena to directly take responsibility with "Tell me what Elena/you could do?"

If Elena continued to externalize with excuses, you could use what she provides: "Okay, so the boss might not be helpful. That's an obstacle, so what's a solution around that?" Over many sessions, as Elena works the process through, you should point out the work she's done and encourage these behaviors. Psychologist Lindsay Gibson writes that clients are "firmly attached to the notion that things need to change in the outside world in order for them to be happy, believing that if only other people would give them what they want, their problems would be solved."[9] In a session with such a client, work against this self-defeating habit that disrupts forward movement.

Since CBT is very homework driven, the therapist must use this with great care. One idea for the passive-aggressive client is to find a new way to relax (such as drawing/coloring) and then use skills taught in session ("I messages" versus sarcasm) to express a feeling she would normally hide. Alternative homework could be to write down a precipitating problem or incident in a journal and then jot down true feelings each day about it.

COMMON ASPECTS OF THERAPY WHEN CLIENTS HIDE ANGER

As therapy begins, you often find yourself sitting with an anxious, irritable client who will benefit from your empathy and reflective listening and from learning some anxiety reduction skills as you get to know them and their concerns. Remember that these clients have often been subjected to conditional love and acceptance in the past;

therefore, in their minds, you may be no less judgmental. Work hard to accept all clients as they are, but in particular, accept a person who hides anger.

Motivate them to stay with therapy; they might not have come to counseling of their own choice or they may remain on the fence as to any potential benefit. Watch for them to work in therapy one session, and at the very next appointment, become demanding or ornery. Of course, what they say might not always reflect their true attitude, so be constantly vigilant in assessing congruence versus incongruence. Encourage them to make sense of their mixed feelings, as this will decrease their anxiety.

Provide ongoing support, yet resist doing too much for your clients. They'll develop a more secure self-image if they accomplish something on their own. Help them identify their past accomplishments. Remind them to use those strengths again to achieve a new goal or complete a task. Remember that what's a simple task to you may be monumental to a passive-aggressor. Encourage them to follow through on plans and become more direct.

Also, be on the lookout for their negativism to decompensate back into anxiety and sometimes a markedly depressed mood. You may need to suggest a medication consult if the anxiety or depressive features warrant. In the worst cases, clients might act impulsively and make a suicidal threat, which, of course, you must take seriously. Family members might even try to dissuade you into thinking it is mere drama that they have seen and dealt with before, but you will have to deal appropriately on a professional level, with an immediate referral or petition the client to the nearest emergency department. This referral in itself may become a reason for the client to argue with and/or turn against therapy.

Family Systems Therapy

Using a family systems framework, a therapist would see that a person doesn't exist in isolation, but within the context of a family where roles and learned interactions carry into other settings. In Elena's case, the counselor would elicit family information, drawing a three-generation genogram with Elena, to see how differentiated she is from Mateo and Marcela, what faulty patterns have transmitted from prior generations, and how everyone's behavior affects the others (circular causality). There's room here to explore where cutoff lies, what triangles get formed, and what reciprocal relation-ship patterns exist that aren't serving the family or the individuals in it very well (over/under functioning being one pattern).

Bowen family systems work may involve Elena alone or include her par-ents in sessions. While Bowen-based therapists allow theory to guide them rather than techniques, some meaningful interventions were brought to the field by other pioneers in the systems movement.

The therapist using strategic family therapy works actively in sessions, and very passive-aggressive clients may push back on this if it is not handled carefully. The focus rests on changing the family's daily environment so body language and repetitive interactions get explored, and all members participate (sometimes limited by availability). The therapist would iden-tify double binds and use paradoxical injunctions such as "prescribing the symptom." Let's say Elena, Marcela, and Mateo argue constantly. By pre-scribing them to argue at a set time daily, the family must forestall all dis-putes until that moment. Most families find that when the appointed time arrives, there's little to quibble about.

Narrative therapists break the hold that unhelpful stories have upon fam-ilies, as these often get externalized. Taking rigid and pessimistic versions of nodal events and creating room for flexible, more optimistic insights, clients rewrite their life narratives. Structural family therapists would join with the family, see how things are done, and begin restructuring alternative behav-iors and interactions.

Virginia Satir once said, "The certainty of misery is preferable to the misery of uncertainty," and this may describe Elena and her parents. Satir's work used humanistic and experiential elements, among others. Using Satir's work to influence treatment, a family systems therapist could help Elena's family examine their existing rules. Satir's iceberg metaphor, in which a family reviews the behavior that's above water followed by the thoughts, feelings, expectations, values, yearnings, and self-beliefs below the waterline, could help to visually drive home this message. Exploring roles, the therapist might help Elena's family to see that placaters cater to and enhance unhealthy passive-aggressive behavior with an "I'll do what-ever to please you, just please don't reject me" attitude. When family mem-bers had developed a stronger sense of self, they could assert what they need emotionally, offer to be a resource, while not giving up all essential aspects of themselves to where they feel unsettled or implode. Through actually moving about the room, the family could sculpt what their current and/or future dynamics would look like. The therapist who followed Satir's advice would strive to be authentic and present with their clients during these exercises.

Forgiveness Therapy

Developed by Robert Enright, PhD, at the University of Minnesota, this method of therapy confronts both people's very real injustices or those they perceive. Resentment, Enright found, stems from unfair treatment and/or a person's not receiving enough respect. This negative attitude can quickly degenerate into persistent ill will, which is what we find with ingrained passive-aggression. Forgiveness therapy offers four phases: uncovering (how a client was compromised and how that pain still festers), decision (where the client learns what forgiveness is and decides if he/she can commit to forgiveness based upon this understanding), working on forgiveness (where the client begins to cognitively understand and see the offender differently before exploring compassion and empathy), and deepening (gathering new meaning from whatever has befallen them and discovering new purpose in life).[10]

Forgiveness therapy involves a paradoxical approach in that clients try to see things from the other's point of view, asking how the person they resent may have been raised as a child or wounded at another time, and how that led to the problem they need to forgive.

Enright reports that forgiveness therapy has succeeded in more than twenty studies with therapy clients ranging from age six into their eighties. In his video interview, he points to one study with cardiac patients that had positive physical data as part of its outcome.[11] He admits that while minor problems may see treatment success in a few months, some offenses (such as sexual abuse) could take more than a year to see results. But he asserts that the outcomes may mean the difference between leaving a legacy of bitterness or a legacy of mercy.

Forgiveness does not equate to reconciling, and Enright gives a client (in his demonstration video) the individual choice to make regarding such clemency. This empowers and assures her that she is "an amazing person" already, based upon what she has endured, and she will equally be so if she chooses the forgiveness route.

Interpersonal Reconstructive Therapy (IRT)

Using Lorna Smith Benjamin's IRT, the therapist would make sense of the client's early attachment patterns and how they affect his behavior throughout his life. If early caregivers rendered a less than secure attachment, the client's interactions in the world may be maladaptive because he had to attach nonetheless. Hence, one or more of three copy processes play out: the client acts as the caregiver did, the client acts as if the caregiver still has the control, or the client treats himself as the caregiver did years ago as a child. Throughout marriage and family, passive-aggressive partners may ignore or discount spouses or children, keep them at a distance as if they themselves are still being ignored, or they merely neglect themselves. Even when parents (primary caregivers) have deceased, the client's old patterns persist as they strive to repair that broken relationship with the now internalized parent (or caregiver).

IRT helps clients to change self-defeating patterns in favor of healthier ones. It employs structural analysis of social behavior, a technique that Dr. Benjamin developed, to describe behavior according to a focus (on other, on self, or on self as if by other), affiliation (hate–love axis), and interdependence (emancipate–control axis). By using what Dr. Benjamin calls the "growth collaborator" that seeks new and different changes over the "regressive loyalist," or the part of self that adheres to the old and familiar, her five-stage approach also involves collaborating with the client, learning the origin and use of former patterns, blocking those old habits, enabling a motivation to change, and acquiring new patterns.[12] This type of therapy typically requires many months or years.

Art/Creative Therapy and Play Therapy

Play and art come naturally to children, and so they are effective tools for them to use for communication. Children do not have the mastery of words and vocabulary that adults do, so the nonverbal approach of these therapies is supportive for them; it allows them to explore personal problems using movement, sensory integration, and physical play. Creativity boosts serotonin and generally makes young clients feel good, thereby allowing them a better connection from which to eventually talk and share with a therapist. Creative modalities, which are not age dependent, include art and card decks to explore questions where answers get internalized for use in one's own problem-solving process.

The therapeutic coloring movement has also grown in adult spheres, though coloring in itself is not curative. It does help the mind to relax its high wall of defensiveness and rigidity (both key components in passive-aggression). The well-guarded person either takes the risk to drop that guard for relaxation and happiness, or maintains it along with misery. While the client busily creates, the counselor attends and can begin the talking component of therapy.

One art therapy device is the mandala, a symbolic image dating back to classical Indian Sanskrit, meaning "circle." Very simply, when you feel upset or angry and then color within a circle—whether a coloring-book image or one created independently—that outer edge provides a boundary for those artistic and emotional feelings. It's a useful metaphor to use with clients who implode or explode, because, as we know, their feelings tend to spill out into life. When clients work to contain but process those feelings adaptively, the resolution leads to a much more beautiful picture for their lives.

CBT-based work could have a person trace a handprint. On each finger, the person could list one negative thought that sweeps unpleasantly through their mind. On the other side, they could write the positive reframe of those negative thoughts or the evidence that those thoughts do or do not exist.

Wyatt, our I-don't-want-to-be-here child, had rehearsed a lot of anger. How might a therapist reach him with play or art—either individually or with other family members?

Each member could draw what the family looks like on a typical day and then compare perspectives to provide awareness of how in sync/out of sync they are with one another. If a drawing shows some members far away, what does this represent? Is it a sign that one or more members of the family try to distance themselves from the drama that hidden anger creates? Finally, the therapist could ask them to depict what their home life would look like without their hidden anger, identify what common themes each member portrays, and then discussing with them how they could create active change at home.

If the therapist met alone with Wyatt who was still reluctant to talk, he might answer a question for an "anonymous other kid" in a therapeutic board game. The therapist would gain insight just as one would using action figures or dolls. A child's play might show his or her need for strength and mastery, such as the child who erects a large fortress out of blocks (protection, security from feelings one cannot express), and hopefully, over sessions, may build a lower wall when perhaps there isn't as much fear of expression or reprisal.

When using art as a modality, therapists should be careful not to judge or guess at an image. Instead, they should ask the client to talk about it, paying attention to the color, size, symbols, and any repeated patterns. Art needs to be respected and kept as confidential as the rest of the client's file: resist the temptation to send it home or to hang it on display. Comparing later art with early art may help young clients who are more visual learners to understand their anger and see how they have grown from it, gaining a greater sense of the coping strategies they have learned in counseling.

Psychoeducation and Group Therapy

Being recommended to a group could evoke negative thoughts, as if it's akin to punishment. Frame it with the empowerment one can gain by opening up, receiving feedback, and offering and accepting empathy. Confidentiality must be addressed in group settings as well as in psychoeducational gatherings, but while you can insist upon privacy for what's said in group to remain in group, you also cannot 100 percent guarantee this. An inherent risk of group therapy is that one persistently negative person may undermine other members' work. However, with proper screening and by only admitting appropriate clients to a group, you can avoid this.

Group treatment employs some psychodynamic elements whereby members revisit in group some of the roles they played in their family of origin. Members can find that they project their most offensive traits onto others. Group may allow participants the opportunity to reduce expectations of others and give them a chance to see the cognitive mistakes they make (e.g., the vain person's tendency to personalize). Role-play might often result.

These days, psychoeducation may be just as convenient as your client's favorite electronic gadget. Most consumer magazines have tablet subscriptions and apps. For the reader or the Internet-driven client, occasionally suggest a relevant consumer-based article. For instance, *The New York Times* ran a feature on teenage eye rolling where psychologist Lisa Damour explained how adolescents especially don't like to be told what to do, thus the reflexive eye roll, even when it's a suggestion with which they may agree.[13]

Let's return to the circular causality in our family of four siblings. Let's say it's January in Fort Lauderdale. Franny finds herself overwhelmed, regretting how the holidays played out, but she remains resentful. It's not until she undecorates the Christmas tree by herself that Franny falls literally, twisting her ankle and her emotions. She's angry at Albert and Martha and at Jim, for his offer to take the tree down days after Christmas. Doesn't he remember that they keep it up until Epiphany? A lot of cutoff exists in this family.

Franny has picked your therapy office to come to with her complaints about her family situation.

> FRANNY: "I do so much for our parents. Albert and Martha live clear across the country, and Jim, if he'd just settle down, maybe his wife could help out?"
>
> YOU: (picking up on the crossed arms, fuming tone, and criticism) "It must be hard to be so overwhelmed. Tell me more about your family and your parents' needs."
>
> FRANNY: "Damned right it is. My parents are in their eighties. Dad fell a few years ago cleaning the gutters. He had surgeries, doesn't get around very well. He left the homefront to Mom, except she has early dementia. The police found her wandering, took her to the ER, and called me in Tennessee, where I used to live. That call changed my life . . . forever."

You: "That must have been frightening with a lot of redirection. Explain more about forever. What does that mean to you?"

Franny: "I moved to Florida to take care of them. In my job, I'm a case manager for an insurance company. I used to be a nurse. I work from home now. Sometimes, I travel or have a conference. But why do I have to do everything? Thanksgiving was awful."

You: "Well, let's think about that. How might Thanksgiving represent how you and your siblings get along in general . . . or over the years?"

Franny: "I don't know. They are just . . . so . . . annoying!"

You: "How does not knowing affect the hassles you told me about? Or your parents?"

Franny: "My mother gets upset, and my father tells us to get along."

You: "How important is that feedback to you?"

Franny: "Well . . . I want to make them happy, but Albert, Martha, and Jim could help, you know!"

You begin to describe common family roles, asking Franny who might fit where, and you find that, in this family, someone has usually been on the outside looking in. What is interesting here is that each sibling might feel on the outside. Jim may have tried to help but felt the replay of old dynamics where his brother and sisters stepped right in with their "better ways." Martha, as a busy parent, may feel isolated; as the oldest, Albert could feel it's his responsibility to do more, yet Franny is . . . fussy, by her own admission.

Clearly, there's much work to be done. This gives you merely a glimpse of how a therapist may begin to unravel the cords that tangle this family into their rigid roles and lingering resentments. See the recommended readings in our sidebar Treatment Planning Assistance and the appendix which follows if you're interested in following up this and other case outlines in our book.

TREATMENT PLANNING ASSISTANCE

Selecting Effective Treatments, by Lourie W. Reichenberg and the late Linda Seligman, is useful for its client map of diagnoses, objectives, assessments given, interventions, clinician characteristics, and treatment emphasis.[14]

Clinicians may also benefit from two American Psychological Association videos. One is *Forgiveness Therapy in Practice*[15] featuring Robert D. Enright, who has also written, with Richard P. Fitzgibbons, *Forgiveness Therapy: An Empirical Guide for Resolving Anger and Restoring Hope.*[16]

Interpersonal Reconstructive Therapy for Passive-Aggressive Personality Disorder features a video demonstration of Lorna Smith Benjamin working with a highly passive-aggressive patient.[17] In *Interpersonal Diagnosis and Treatment of Personality Disorders*, Benjamin says that passive-aggression often complicates other disorders, including intractable depression.[18]

Finally, *Cognitive Therapy of Personality Disorders,* by Aaron T. Beck, Arthur Freeman, and Denise D. Davis, provides valuable insights on how to work with passive-aggressive automatic thoughts and core, conditional, and compensatory beliefs.[19]

Benjamin writes that passive-aggressive patterns demand targeted therapy; otherwise, a therapist's interventions will prove useless.[20] This speaks to the careful treatment planning you must provide for these patients.

WHEN TREATMENT MEETS IMPASSE

Despite your best efforts, passive-aggressive clients may continue to confound you. There is no one-size-fits-all treatment. They desire to be nurtured and loved by a powerful, perhaps parental figure, but giving in to the idea of therapy and change may threaten their independence. You've calmed their fears initially. They gained a bit of tolerance and uttered fewer "always," "never," and "forever" statements. You used brief behavioral contracting to help them see themselves as competent, and you thought that gaining their motivation to stay the course over their ambivalence, teaching anxiety reduction measures, and role-playing some assertiveness in situations they brought into session actually worked. Until they didn't.

Indeed, it's frustrating when good momentum and the positive therapeutic relationship you feel you developed begins to fray. It can do so suddenly or over time. Inertia may set in when you least expect it, seeming to paralyze your client who had previously made progress. This often fits with the contradictory messages the client received in childhood. They were often good and bad parallel to when their parents were supportive then critical, affectionate then miffed and standoffish. Hence, a double bind again sets in because no matter which way they turn, these clients cannot find the right direction. Whatever you might suggest may seem to them as an unrealistic demand, or they may denigrate themselves for their lack of progress and give you a why-bother attitude.

Often when the work becomes too challenging, and their old defenses seem too difficult to jettison, passive-aggressive people may blame their lack of progress upon the therapist. Sometimes, in the case of a couple or any dyad, improvement in one party can result in the other person soon showing what looks like passive-aggressive behavior or other symptoms. The two often perpetuate each other's struggles. Stay attuned to this dynamic.

Frequently, and particularly with more resistant clients, you will want to hold back on some of the knowledge you may have or perceptions you gather. Is this withholding passive-aggressive? Not exactly. Your motive is good, you avoid resistance, and you don't wish to be the immediate authority figure. However, if your client regains motivation for sessions and shows behavioral work you've discussed, then you may feel more assured that expressing your knowledge serves a better purpose.

Robert Leahy suggests in *Roadblocks in Cognitive-Behavioral Therapy* that angry clients come to treatment to change others, vent about their unfairness, receive validation that others are still awful, and sometimes because they typically want some kind of revenge.[21] If you've tried many ways to overcome this mind-set, then you must remind yourself: it's not you, and it's not the therapy. It's them.

Unfortunately, those who hide true emotions may terminate treatment prematurely. Those in therapy may convince themselves that the therapist doesn't truly understand them, when in all likelihood the therapist does. Quitting becomes a way for this person to choose independence and continue deriving secondary gains from their behavior. And as we saw in our final chapter, clients often push back on policies and any limits that they have once agreed to but now cannot face. Where does that lead them? Often right out the door.

It happens. We all lose clients, and it's hard if we don't truly understand why. And then there are cases that seem best to refer out. Especially where perhaps the client has seen you for a long time (read: depends upon you too much), and you feel that you're more engaged in the client's work than she actually is . . . yes, you may be at a referral point.

It's always helpful to think about what you could have improved. If you find yourself confronting clients a lot, perhaps it's a sign of burnout or compassion fatigue, which we addressed in Chapter 8. A gentle startup to difficult topics could help in the future, for example, "I could imagine that if others observed this, that they might be thinking that. . . ." Is it indirect when your job is to model how to be direct instead? Sure, a bit . . . but the motive and outcome in any given situation are key. If your intent is to engage the client and the outcome is to keep them in much-needed treatment, this indirect tactic ultimately works for everyone.

It's not uncommon that those clients who cope with passive-aggressive behavior continue to attend sessions more frequently, but when you hold them to their role in the dysfunctional dynamic, the same challenge may appear. Incorporating assertiveness and boundary setting into your sessions is obviously paramount. Relaxation and mindfulness techniques aid these often anxious clients so that they do not implode as the passive-aggressor does. Much psychoeducation (and patience) on your part may need to occur if this client feels locked and dependent with a controlling partner or in an untenable work environment.

Thank you for joining in this quest to help people overcome unhappiness and behaviors that keep them entrenched in difficulty. If you would like to learn more about these topics, please follow this book on social media and reach out through Ms. Oberlin's website for potential continuing education and workshop opportunities at www.loriannoberlin.com.

Notes

CHAPTER ONE

1. E. Harburg, M. Julius, N. Kaciroti, L. Gleiberman, and M. A. Schork, "Expressive/Suppressive Anger-Coping Responses, Gender, and Types of Mortality: A 17-Year Follow-up," *Psychosomatic Medicine*, 65, no. 4 (2003): 588–597.
2. L. Huang, F. Gino, and A. Galinsky, "The Highest Form of Intelligence: Sarcasm Increases Creativity for Both Expressers and Recipients," *Organizational Behavior and Human Decision Processes*, 131 (2015): 162–177.

CHAPTER TWO

1. American Psychological Association, "Intimate Partner Violence: Facts & Resources," accessed May 6, 2016, http://www.apa.org/topics/violence/partner.aspx.
2. United States Department of Education, "Bullying: What You Need to Know," stopbullying.gov, 2015, http://www.stopbullying.gov/image-gallery/what-you-need-to-know-infographic.pdf.
3. American Psychological Association, "Health Care System Falls Short on Stress Management," February 7, 2013, accessed May 6, 2016, http://

www.apa.org/news/press/releases/2013/02/stress-management.aspx; and American Psychological Association, *Stress in America: Paying with Our Health*, February 4, 2015, http://www.apa.org/news/press/releases/stress /2014/stress-report.pdf.

4. P. Tyre, J. Scelfo, and B. Kantrowitz, "The Power of No," *Newsweek*, September 13, 2004, pp. 42–51.

5. G. Gutfeld, "Stop the Madness!" *Men's Health*, October 1998, p. 118.

6. E. C. Suarez, "C-Reactive Protein Is Associated with Psychological Risk Factors of Cardiovascular Disease in Apparently Healthy Adults," *Psychosomatic Medicine* (September 2004): 684–691.

7. J. E. Williams, C. C. Paton, I. C. Siegler, M. L. Eigenbrodt, F. J. Nieto, and H. A. Tyroler, "Anger Proneness Predicts Coronary Heart Disease Risk," *Circulation*, 101 (2000): 2034–2039.

8. J. F. Todaro, B. J. Shen, R. Niaura, A. Spiro III, K. D. Ward, "Effect of Negative Emotions on Frequency of Coronary Heart Disease," *The American Journal of Cardiology*, 92 (2003): 901–906.

9. C. Leineweber, H. Westerlund, T. Theorell, M. Kiyamäki, P. Westerholm, and L. Alfredsson, "Covert Coping with Unfair Treatment at Work and Risk of Incident Myocardial Infarction and Cardiac Death Among Men: Prospective Cohort Study," *Journal of Epidemiology & Community Health*, 65 (2011): 420–425.

10. National Cancer Institute, "Can Psychological Stress Cause Cancer?" accessed May 6, 2016, http://www.cancer.gov/about-cancer/coping/feelings /stress-fact-sheet#q3.

11. M. Moreno-Smith, S. K. Lutgendorf, and A. K. Sood, "Impact of Stress on Cancer Metastasis," *Future Oncology*, 6, no. 12 (2010): 1863–1881.

12. J. Denollet, A. Schiffer, and V. Spek, "A General Propensity to Psychological Distress Affects Cardiovascular Outcomes: Evidence from Research on the Type D (Distressed) Personality Profile," *Circulation: Cardiovascular Quality and Outcomes*, 3 (2010): 546–557.

13. M. Kerr, personal communication, November 6, 2015.

14. P. Kennedy and S. Fried, *A Common Struggle: A Personal Journey Through the Past and Future of Mental Illness and Addiction* (New York: Blue Rider Press, 2015), 354.

15. S. E. Browder, *The Power: 11 Ways Women Gain Unhealthy Weight and How You Can Take Charge of Them* (New York: John Wiley & Sons, 2000), 133–141.

16. K. Raikkonen, K. A. Matthews, and L. H. Kuller, "Trajectory of Psychological

Risk and Incident Hypertension in Middle-Aged Women," *Hypertension*, 38 (2001): 798–802.

17. R. B. Williams, D. A. Marchuk, K. M. Gadda, J. C. Barefoot, K. Grichnik, M. J. Heims, C. M. Kuhn, J. G. Lewis, S. M. Schanberg, M. Stafford-Smith, E. C. Suarez, G. L. Clary, I. K. Svenson, and I. C. Siegler, "Central Nervous System Serotonin Function and Cardiovascular Responses to Stress," *Psychosomatic Medicine*, 63 (2001): 300–305.

18. D. Lykken and A. Tellegen, "Happiness Is a Stochastic Phenomenon," *Psychological Science*, 7, no. 3 (1996): 186–189.

19. D. P. Barash and J. E. Lipton, *Payback: Why We Retaliate, Redirect Aggression, and Take Revenge* (New York: Oxford University Press, 2011), 5.

20. B. J. Bushman, R. F. Baumeister, and A. D. Stack, "Catharsis, Aggression, and Persuasive Influence: Self-Fulfilling or Self-Defeating Prophecies?" *Journal of Personality and Social Psychology*, 76, no. 3 (1999): 367–376.

21. Editors of Harvard Health Publications, "Exercise and Depression," In *Understanding Depression: A Harvard Medical School Special Health Report*, Harvard Medical School, Cambridge, MA, June 9, 2009, http://www.health.harvard.edu/mind-and-mood/exercise-and-depression-report-excerpt; and A. H. Y. Chu, D. Koh, F. M. Moy, and F. Müller-Riemenschneider, "Do Workplace Physical Activity Interventions Improve Mental Health Outcomes?" Occupational Medicine, 64, no. 4 (2014): 235–245.

22. A. T. Merchant, W. Pitphat, B. Ahmed, I. Kawachi, and K. Joshipura, "A Prospective Study of Social Support, Anger Expression and Risk of Periodontitis in Men," *Journal of the America Dental Association*, 134 (2003): 1591–1596.

23. L. Sabbagh, "The Teen Brain, Hard at Work. No Really," *Scientific American Mind*, August/September, 2006, pp. 20–25.

24. H. Rosin, "The Silicon Valley Suicides," *The Atlantic*, December 2015.

25. A. Harding, "Depression in the Workplace: Don't Ask, Don't Tell?" Health.com, September 20, 2010, accessed May 6, 2016, http://www.cnn.com/2010/HEALTH/09/20/health.depression.workplace/#.

CHAPTER THREE

1. T. F. Murphy and L. H. Oberlin, *The Angry Child: Regaining Control When Your Child Is Out of Control* (New York: Three Rivers Press, 2001).

2. F. M. Rogers, "A Point of View: Family Communication, Television, and Mister Rogers' Neighborhood," *Journal of Family Communication*, 1, no. 1 (2000): 71–73.

3. G. E. Vaillant, "Ego Mechanisms of Defense and Personality Psychopathology," *Journal of Abnormal Psychology*, 103 (1994): 44–50.

4. S. Wetzler, *Living with the Passive Aggressive Man* (New York: Simon & Schuster, 1992).

5. N. J. Long and J. E. Long, *Managing Passive-Aggressive Behavior of Children and Youth at School and Home: The Angry Smile* (Austin, TX: Pro-Ed, 2001).

6. E. Kubler-Ross, *On Death and Dying* (New York: Scribner Classics, 1997).

7. L. B. Silver, *The Misunderstood Child: Understanding and Coping with Your Child's Learning Disabilities*, 4th ed. (New York: Three Rivers Press, 2006).

8. M. Main and J. Cassidy, "Categories of Response to Reunion with the Parent at Age 6: Predictable from Infant Attachment Classifications and Stable Over a One-Month Period," *Developmental Psychology*, 24, no. 3 (1988): 415–426.

9. M. Millon and R. D. Davis, *Disorders of Personality DSM-IV and Beyond*, 2nd ed. (New York: John Wiley & Sons, 1996), 568.

10. Ibid., 555.

11. Ibid.

12. J. V. Caffaro, *Sibling Abuse Trauma*, 2nd ed. (New York: Routledge, 2014), 18.

CHAPTER FOUR

1. J. M. Gottman and N. Silver, *The Seven Principles for Making Marriage Work*, 2nd ed. (New York: Crown Publishing, 2015).

2. W. R. Nay, *Overcoming Anger in Your Relationship: How to Break the Cycle of Arguments, Put-Downs, and Stony Silences* (New York: The Guilford Press, 2010), 38.

3. B. LeBey, *Family Estrangements: How They Begin, How to Mend Them, and How to Cope with Them* (Atlanta, GA: Longstreet Press, 2001), 246.

4. Ibid., 29.

5. Ibid., 248.

6. M. Millon and R. D. Davis, *Disorders of Personality DSM-IV and Beyond*, 2nd ed. (New York: John Wiley & Sons, 1996).

7. W. J. Pietsch, *The Serenity Prayer Book* (San Francisco, CA: Harper, 1992), 3.

8. G. L. Greif, personal communication, March 22, 2016.

9. Ibid.

10. KidsPost, "Debugging the Situation: Students Learn How to Apologize and Ways to Get Along With Others," *The Washington Post*, March 6, 2007.

11. C. N. DeWall, J. M. Twenge, S. A. Gitter, and R. F. Baumeister, "It's the Thought That Counts: The Role of Hostile Cognition in Shaping Aggressive Responses to Social Exclusion," *Journal of Personality and Social Psychology*, 96, no. 1 (2009): 45–59.

12. J. M. Johnson, "The Impact of Cyber-Bullying: A New Type of Relational Aggression," paper presented at American Counseling Association Annual Conference & Exposition, Charlotte, NC, March 19–23, 2009.

CHAPTER FIVE

1. S. Reddy, "Very Little and Acting Mean: Children, Especially Girls, Withhold Friendship as a Weapon; Teaching Empathy," *The Wall Street Journal*, May 26, 2014.

2. See recommended resources in T. Ludwig and A. Marble, *My Secret Bully* (New York: Ten Speed Press, 2004).

3. S. Shellenbarger, "Wanted: A Best Friend," *The Wall Street Journal*, February 17, 2015.

4. Y. T. Uhls, M. Michikyan, J. Morries, D. Garcia, G. W. Small, E. Zgourou, and P. M. Greenfield, "Five Days at Outdoor Education Camp Without Screens Improves Preteen Skills with Nonverbal Emotion Cues," *Computers in Human Behavior*, 29 (2014): 387–392.

5. M. W. Gilman, "Family Dinner and Diet Quality Among Older Children and Adolescents," *Archives of Family Medicine*, 9 (2000): 235–240.

6. D. Pope, M. Brown, and S. Miles, *Overloaded and Underprepared: Strategies for Stronger Schools and Healthy, Successful Kids* (New York: Jossey-Bass, 2015), 167.

7. V. Abeles, *Beyond Measure: Rescuing an Overscheduled, Underestimated Generation* (New York: Simon & Schuster, 2015), 24.

8. American Academy of Pediatrics, Adolescent Sleep Working Group, Committee on Adolescence and Council on School Health, "School Start Times for Adolescents," *Pediatrics*, 134, no. 3, 1697; National Sleep Foundation, "2014 Sleep in America Poll: Sleep in the Modern Family," Arlington, VA, March, 2014.

9. Pope, Brown, and Miles, *Overloaded and Underprepared*.

10. Ibid.

11. C. Parker, "Stanford Research Shows Pitfalls of Homework," *Stanford News*, March 10, 2014, http://news.stanford.edu/news/2014/march/too-much -homework-031014.html.

12. University of Maryland research cited in "Do Your Kids a Favor and Assign Them Some Chores," *Seattle Times*, November 10, 2008, http://www.seattletimes.com/life/lifestyle/do-your-kids-a-favor-and-assign-them-some-chores/; S. Shellenbarger, "On the Virtues of Making Your Children Do the Dishes," *The Wall Street Journal*, August 27, 2008, http://www.wsj.com/articles/SB121978677837474177.

13. Rossman's research cited in L. Wolf, "The Value of Chores for Children," Parenthood.com, accessed May 9, 2016, http://www.parenthood.com/article/the_value_of_chores_for_children.html#.VskLnVKud-U.

14. J. B. Wallace, "Why Children Need Chores," *The Wall Street Journal*, March 13, 2015, http://www.wsj.com/articles/why-children-need-chores-1426262655.

CHAPTER SIX

1. L. J. Waite and M. Gallagher, *The Case for Marriage: Why Married People Are Happier, Healthier, and Better Off Financially* (New York: Doubleday, 2000), 64.

2. R. Combs, "Marital Status and Personal Well-Being: A Literature Review," *Family Relations*, 40 (1991): 97–102; J. K. Kiecolt-Glaser and T. L. Newton, "Marriage and Health: His and Hers," *Psychological Bulletin*, 127, no. 4 (2001): 472–503.

3. J. Bookwala, "The Role of Marital Quality in Physical Health During the Mature Years," *Journal of Aging and Health*, 1, no. 7 (2005): 85–104.

4. T. Loving, "The Orchid Effect: How Relationships and Genetics Influence Your Health," *Science of Relationships*, December 2, 2013, http://www.scienceofrelationships.com/home/2013/12/2/the-orchid-effect-how-relationships-and-genetics-influence-y.html; S. C. South and R. F. Krueger, "Marital Satisfaction and Physical Health," *Psychological Science*, 24, no. 3 (2013): 373–378.

5. G. E. Vaillant, "Ego Mechanisms of Defense and Personality Psychopathology," *Journal of Abnormal Psychology*, 103, no. 1 (1994): 44–50.

6. R. M. Gilbert, *Extraordinary Relationships: A New Way of Thinking About Human Interactions* (New York: John Wiley & Sons, 1992), 18–25.

7. H. Hendrix, *Getting the Love You Want: A Guide for Couples* (New York: Henry Holt, 1988).

8. J. M. Gottman and N. Silver, *The Seven Principles for Making Marriage Work*, 2nd ed. (New York: Crown Publishing, 2015), 1–24.

9. J. Gottman, "Is Dr. Gottman Really Able to Predict Whether a Couple

Will Get Divorced with 94% Accuracy?" accessed May 9, 2016, https://www
.gottman.com/about/research/faq/.

10. The Gottman Institute, "Four Horsemen of the Apocalypse," YouTube, posted December 2014, accessed May 9, 2016, https://www.youtube.com /watch?v=1o30Ps-_8is

11. J. M. Gottman and L. K. Krokoff, "Marital Interaction and Satisfaction: A Longitudinal View," *Journal of Consulting and Clinical Psychology*, 57, no. 1 (1989): 47–52.

12. D. H. Baucom, N. Epstein, L. A. Rankin, and C. K. Burnett, "Assessing Relationship Standards: The Inventory of Specific Relationship Standards," *Journal of Family Psychology*, 10, no. 1 (1996): 72–88.

13. R. M. Gilbert, *Extraordinary Relationships: A New Way of Thinking About Human Interactions*, (New York: John Wiley & Sons, 1992), 66.

14. Ibid., 67–68.

15. S. Wetzler and L. C. Morey, "Passive-Aggressive Personality Disorder: The Demise of a Syndrome," *Psychiatry*, 68 (1999): 49–59.

16. T. Millon, *Disorders of Personality DSM-III: Axis II* (New York: John Wiley & Sons, 1981).

17. J. Diamond, *The Irritable Male Syndrome: Managing the 4 Key Causes of Depression and Aggression*, (Emmaus, PA: Rodale, 2004).

18. N. Reichman, H. Corman, and K. Noonan, "Effects of Child Health on Parents' Relationship Status," *Demography*, 4, no. 13 (2004): 569–584.

19. S. L. Hartley and E. M. Schaidle, "Marital Quality and Children with Autism Spectrum Disorders (ASD)," Waisman Center, University of Wisconsin – Madison, 2010, http://www.waisman.wisc.edu/hartleylab/documents /bethinstitute.pdf; A. Abbott, "Love in the Time of Autism," *Psychology Today*, July 2, 2013.

20. M. A. Whisman, L. A. Uebelacker, and L. M. Weinstock, "Psychopathology and Marital Satisfaction: The Importance of Evaluating Both Partners," *Journal of Consulting & Clinical Psychology*, 72, no. 5 (2004): 830–838.

21. S. P. Glass, *Not "Just Friends": Rebuilding Trust and Recovering Your Sanity After Infidelity*, (New York, Free Press, 2003).

22. J. M. Gottman and N. Silver, *What Makes Love Last? How to Build Trust and Avoid Betrayal* (New York: Simon & Schuster, 2012), 56.

23. Ibid., 64.

24. S. Wetzler, *Living with the Passive Aggressive Man* (New York: Simon & Schuster, 1992).

CHAPTER SEVEN

1. M. Millon and R. D. Davis, *Disorders of Personality DSM-IV and Beyond*, 2nd ed. (New York: John Wiley & Sons, 1996).

2. J. B. Kelly and R. E. Emery, "Children's Adjustment Following Divorce: Risk and Resilience Perspectives," *Family Relations*, 52, no. 4 (2003): 352–362.

3. S. Schrobsdorff, "The Rise of the 'Good Divorce'," *Time*, July 23, 2015.

4. M. Just, *Divorce Decisions: Practical Ways to Protect Yourself, Your Child, and Your Wallet* (Sterling, VA: Capital Books, 2009).

5. G. Levangie, *Stepmom*, directed by C. Columbus (Columbia Pictures, 1998), movie.

CHAPTER EIGHT

1. American Psychological Association, "College Students' Mental Health Is a Growing Concern, Survey Finds," *Monitor on Psychology*, 44, no. 6 (2013): 13.

2. A. Robbins, *The Nurses: A Year of Secrets, Drama, and Miracles with the Heroes of the Hospital* (New York: Workman, 2015), 37.

3. Ibid., 137.

4. L. Curry, *Beating the Workplace Bully: A Tactical Guide to Taking Charge* (New York: AMACOM, 2016), 11–12.

5. D. Witters, D. Liu, and S. Agrawal, "Depression Costs U.S. Workplaces $23 Billion in Absenteeism," *Gallup*, July 24, 2013.

6. M. Blanding, "Workplace Stress Responsible for Up To $190 Billion in Annual U.S. Healthcare Costs," *Forbes*, January 26, 2015.

7. K. Rost, "Medical Care," *The Health Behavior News Service*, 42 (2004): 1202–1210.

8. B. Chapman and R. Sisodia, *Everybody Matters: The Extraordinary Power of Caring for Your People Like Family* (New York: Penguin/Portfolio, 2015).

9. L. Vanderkam, "Treating Workers Like Family: A Mixed Blessing," *Fortune*, October 30, 2015.

10. M. M. Hutter, K. C. Kellogg, C. M. Ferguson, W. M. Abbott, and A. L. Warshaw, "The Impact of the 80-Hour Resident Workweek on Surgical Residents and Attending Surgeons," *Annals of Surgery*, 243, no. 3 (2006): 864–875; and Agency for Healthcare Research and Quality, "Physician Work Hours and Patient Safety," U.S. Department of Health and Human Ser-

vices, November 2015, https://psnet.ahrq.gov/primers/primer/19/physician -work-hours-and-patient-safety.

11. P. Krill, R. Johnson, and L. Albert, "The Prevalence of Substance Abuse and Other Mental Health Concerns Among American Attorneys," *Journal of Addiction Medicine*, 10, no. 1 (2016): 46–52.

12. V. Frankl, *Man's Search for Meaning* (Cutchogue, NY: Buccaneer Books, 2006), 112.

13. Department of Health and Human Services, "Stress . . . At Work" [Brochure], National Institute for Occupational Safety and Health, Publication No. 99–101 (1999).

14. T. Gura, "I'll Do It Tomorrow: A Penchant for Procrastination Is Damaging Careers, Health and Savings Accounts of Millions of Americans," *Scientific American Mind*, December 2008/January 2009, pp. 27–33.

15. S. Stosny, "Manage Resentment or Fail," Compassion Power: Resentment-Free Workplace, Germantown, MD, 1995.

16. S. Wetzler and L. C. Morey, "Passive-Aggressive Personality Disorder: The Demise of a Syndrome," *Psychiatry*, 68 (1999): 49–59.

17. M. W. Brown, *Working with the Self-Absorbed: How to Handle Narcissistic Personalities on the Job* (Oakland, CA: New Harbinger, 2002).

18. A. A. Cavaiola and N. J. Lavender, *Toxic Coworkers: How to Deal with Dysfunctional People on the Job* (Oakland, CA: New Harbinger, 2000), 40.

19. M. Ferguson, "You Cannot Leave It at the Office: Spillover and Crossover of Coworker Incivility," *Journal of Organizational Behavior*, 22 (2012): 571–588.

CHAPTER NINE

1. W. B. Johnson and K. Murray, *Crazy Love: Dealing With Your Partner's Problem Personality* (Atascadero, CA: Impact, 2007), 132.

2. S. Donaldson-Pressman and R. M. Pressman, *The Narcissistic Family: Diagnosis and Treatment* (New York: Jossey-Bass, 1994), 23.

3. World Health Organization, "Depression," WHO Fact Sheet No. 369, October 2015, accessed May 11, 2016, http://www.who.int/mediacentre/factsheets /fs369/en/.

4. Division of Population Health/Workplace Health Promotion, Centers for Disease Control and Prevention, "Depression," last updated October 23, 2013, accessed May 11, 2016, http://www.cdc.gov/workplacehealth promotion/implementation/topics/depression.html.

5.   Pospartum Progress, "The Statistics," accessed May 11, 2016, http://post
     partumprogress.org/the-facts-about-postpartum-depression/.

6.   National Institute of Mental Health, "Men and Depression," accessed May
     11, 2016, https://www.nimh.nih.gov/health/topics/depression/men-and
     -depression/index.shtml?id=10.

7.   T. Millon, C. M. Millon, S. Meagher, S. Grossman, and R. Ramnath, *Per-
     sonality Disorders in Modern Life*, 2nd ed. (New York: John Wiley & Sons,
     2004), 179.

8.   H. M. González, W. A. Vega, D. R. Williams, W. Tarraf, B. T. West, and H.
     W. Neighbors, "Depression Care in the United States: Too Little for Too
     Few," *Archives of General Psychiatry*, 67, no. 1 (2010): 37–46.

9.   J. Kluger, "The Cruelest Cut," *Time*, May 16, 2005, pp. 48–50.

10. M. Hollander, *Helping Teens Who Cut: Understanding and Ending Self-
     Injury*. (New York: The Guilford Press, 2008).

11. National Center for Health Statistics, "Health, United States, 2014: With
     Special Feature on Adults Aged 55–64," Centers for Disease Control and
     Prevention, May 2015, http://www.cdc.gov/nchs/data/hus/hus14.pdf.

12. R. A. Barkley, *ADHD and the Nature of Self-Control* (New York: Guilford
     Press, 1997).

13. L. F. McCarthy, "Women, Hormones, and ADD." ADDitude, Spring 2009,
     pp. 42–45.

14. E. M. Hallowell and J. J. Ratey, *Delivered from Distraction: Getting the Most
     Out of Life with Attention Deficit Disorder* (New York: Ballantine Books,
     2005).

15. Children and Adults with Attention-Deficit/Hyperactivity Disorder (CHADD),
     "Coexisting Conditions," accessed May 11, 2016, http://www.chadd.org
     /Understanding-ADHD/About-ADHD/Coexisting-Conditions.aspx.

16. United States War Department, "Nomenclature and Method of Recording
     Diagnoses," War Department Technical Bulletin, October 19, 1945.

17. American Psychiatric Association, *Diagnostic and Statistical Manual of
     Mental Disorders*, 3rd ed., revised (Arlington, VA: Author, 1987).

18. S. Wetzler, personal communication, December 3, 2004.

19. M. Kantor, *Passive-Aggression: A Guide for the Therapist, the Patient, and the
     Victim* (Westport, CN: Praeger, 2002).

20. See http://bcs.worthpublishers.com/WebPub/Psychology/comerabpsych8e
     /IRM/COMER%20IR%20B1-B84.pdf.

21. American Psychiatric Association, *Diagnostic and Statistical Manual of
     Mental Disorders*, 5th ed. (Arlington, VA: Author, 2013).

22. Ibid., 761–762.

23. N. L. Piquero, A. R. Piquero, J. M. Craig, and S. J. Clipper, "Assessing Research on Workplace Violence, 2000–2012," *Aggression and Violent Behavior*, 18 (2013): 383–394.

24. Baum, N., Sharon, M., & Rahav, G. (2014). "Heightened Susceptibility to Secondary Traumatization: A Meta-Analysis of Gender Differences." *American Journal of Orthopsychiatry*, 84(2), 111–122. doi:10.1037/h0099383.

25. Scalora, Mario J., David O'Neil Washington, Thomas Casady, and Sarah P. Newell. "Nonfatal Workplace Violence Risk Factors: Data From a Police Contact Sample." *Journal of Interpersonal Violence* 18.3 (2003): 310–27.

26. K. Corvo and P. Johnson, "Sharpening Ockham's Razor: The Role of Psychopathology and Neuropsychopathology in the Perpetration of Domestic Violence," *Aggression and Violent Behavior*, 18 (2013): 175–182.

27. D. G. Dutton, "Patriarchy and Wife Assault: The Ecological Fallacy," *Violence and Victims*, 9, no. 2 (2006): 125–140.

28. B. M. Costra, C. E. Kaestle, A. Walker, A. Curtis, A. Day, J. W. Toumbourou, and P. Miller, "Longitudinal Predictors of Domestic Violence Perpetration and Victimization: A Systematic Review," *Aggression and Violent Behavior*, 24 (2015): 261–272.

CHAPTER TEN

1. J. W. Pennebaker, *Opening Up: The Healing Power of Expressing Emotions* (New York: The Guilford Press, 1997).

2. T. F. Murphy, "Self Fulfilling Prophecies and the Effects of Personality Testing Upon Children's Independence," PhD Diss., University of Pittsburgh, 1979.

CHAPTER ELEVEN

1. M. Kerr, personal communication, November 6, 2015.

2. Ibid.

3. Ibid.

4. S. Shellenbarger, "Go from Grumpy to Happy: Rethink the After-Work Routine," *The Wall Street Journal*, February 11, 2015.

5. D. LaBier, "Empathy: Could It Be What You're Missing?" *The Washington Post*, December 25, 2007.

6. A. Paturel, "The Ties That Bind: Staying Social Keeps the Mind Active," *Neurology Now*, December 2014/January 2015.

7. S. Johnson, "Hold Me Tight: Love Demands the Reassurance of Touch," *Psychology Today*, January, 2009, pp. 73–79.

8. KidsPost, "Debugging the Situation: Students Learn How to Apologize and Ways to Get Along With Others," *The Washington Post*, March 6, 2007.

9. Feelings Posters are available from Creative Therapy Associates, http://www.ctherapy.com.

10. Ibid.

11. C. Peterson and M. E. Seligman, *Character Strengths and Virtues: A Handbook and Classification* (New York: Oxford University Press, 2004).

CHAPTER TWELVE

1. J. Goodman, "Hints for the Prescription of Psychotropic Drugs by Non-Psychiatrists," *Psychology Today* blog, December 4, 2011, accessed May 11, 2016, https://www.psychologytoday.com/blog/attention-please/201112/hints-the-prescription-psychotropic-drugs-non-psychiatrists.

2. J. M. Gottman and N. Silver, *The Seven Principles for Making Marriage Work* 2nd ed. (New York: Crown Publishing, 2015).

3. "Stop It!" *The Bob Newhart Show*, YouTube, https://www.youtube.com/watch?v=Ow0lr63y4Mw

4. S. Srivastava, O. P. John, S. D. Gosling, and J. Potter, "Development of Personality in Early and Middle Adulthood: Set Like Plaster or Persistent Change?" *Journal of Personality and Social Psychology*, 84, no. 5 (2003).

5. K. Helliker, "No Joke: Group Therapy Offers Savings in Numbers," *The Wall Street Journal*, March 24, 2009.

6. S. Block and C. B. Block, *Mind-Body Workbook for Anger* (Oakland, CA: New Harbinger, 2013), 3.

7. *Manage Anger Daily Meditation*, CD or MP3 (San Diego, CA: Schneider Counseling and Corporate Solutions, 2014), available from http://www.manageangerdaily.com.

8. G. Simmons, personal communication, February 8, 2016.

9. M. Bink, I. L. Bongers, A. Popma, T. W. P. Janssen, and C. van Nieuwenhuizen, "1-year Follow-up of Nurofeedback Treatment in Adolescents with Attention-Deficit Hyperactivity Disorder," *British Journal of Psychiatry*, 2 (2) (2016): 107–115.

APPENDIX

1. L. S. Benjamin, *Interpersonal Diagnosis and Treatment of Personality Disorders*, 2nd ed. (New York: The Guilford Press, 1996).

2. W. M. Zinn, "Transference Phenomena in Medical Practice: Being

Whom the Patient Needs," *Annals of Internal Medicine*, 113, no. 4 (1990): 293–298.

3. P. R. Muskin and L. A. Epstein, "Clinical Guide to Countertransference: Help Medical Colleagues Deal with 'Difficult' Patients," *Current Psychiatry*, 8, no. 4 (2009).

4. A. Matsakis, *Managing Client Anger: What to Do When a Client Is Angry with You* (Oakland, CA: New Harbinger, 1998), 203.

5. J. O. Prochaska, J. Norcross, and C. DiClemente, *Changing for Good: A Revolutionary Six-Stage Program for Overcoming Bad Habits and Moving Your Life Positively Forward* (New York: William Morrow, 2007).

6. F. J. Hanna, *Therapy with Difficult Clients: Using the Precursors Model to Awaken Change* (Washington, DC: American Psychological Associations, 2002).

7. C. W. Mitchell, *Effective Techniques for Dealing with Highly Resistant Clients*, 2nd ed. (Johnson City, TN: Author, 2009), 146.

8. M. Kantor, *Passive-Aggression: A Guide for the Therapist, the Patient, and the Victim* (Westport, CN: Praeger, 2002), 137.

9. L. C. Gibson, *Adult Children of Emotionally Immature Parents: How to Heal from Distant, Rejecting, or Self-Involved Parents* (Oakland, CA: New Harbinger, 2015), 89–90.

10. R. D. Enright and R. P. Fitzgibbons, *Forgiveness Therapy: An Empirical Guide for Resolving Anger and Restoring Hope* (Washington, DC: American Psychological Association, 2015).

11. American Psychological Association, *Forgiveness Therapy in Practice with Robert D. Enright, Ph.D., Series IV-Relationships* DVD (Washington, DC: American Psychological Association, 2016).

12. American Psychological Association, *Interpersonal Reconstructive Therapy for Passive-Aggressive Personality Disorder with Lorna Smith Benjamin, Ph.D.*, Video Tape Series II (Washington, DC: Author, 1999),

13. L. Damour, "Why Teenage Girls Roll Their Eyes," *The New York Times*, February 17, 2016.

14. L. Reichenberg and L. Seligman, *Selecting Effective Treatments: A Comprehensive, Systematic Guide to Treating Mental Disorders* (New York: Wiley, 2016).

15. American Psychological Association, *Forgiveness Therapy in Practice*.

16. Enright and Fitzgibbons, *Forgiveness Therapy*.

17. L. S. Benjamin, *Interpersonal Diagnosis and Treatment of Personality Disorders*, 2nd ed. (New York: The Guilford Press, 1996).

18. American Psychological Association, *Interpersonal Reconstructive Therapy for Passive-Aggressive Personality Disorder.*

19. A. T. Beck, A. Freeman, and D. D. Davis, *Cognitive Therapy of Personality Disorders,* 2nd ed. (New York: The Guilford Press, 2004).

20. L. S. Benjamin, *Interpersonal Diagnosis and Treatment of Personality Disorders,* 2nd ed.

21. R. L. Leahy (ed.), *Roadblocks in Cognitive-Behavioral Therapy: Transforming Challenges into Opportunities for Change* (New York: The Guilford Press, 2003).

Recommended Resources

CHAPTER TWO   CONCEALED EMOTIONS PUT PEOPLE AT RISK

Barash, D. P., and Lipton, J. E. (2011). *Payback: Why We Retaliate, Redirect Aggression, and Take Revenge*. New York: Oxford University Press.

Hollander, M. (2008). *Helping Teens Who Cut: Understanding and Ending Self-Injury*. New York: The Guilford Press.

Kennedy, P., and Fried, S. (2015). *A Common Struggle: A Personal Journey Through the Past and Future of Mental Illness and Addiction*. New York: Blue Rider Press.

Williams, R., and Williams, V. (1993). *Anger Kills: 17 Strategies for Controlling the Hostility That Can Harm Your Health*. New York: HarperCollins.

CHAPTER FOUR   FRACTURED FAMILIES AND FRIENDSHIPS

Gibson, L. C. (2015). *Adult Children of Emotionally Immature Parents: How to Heal from Distant, Rejecting, or Self-Involved Parents*. Oakland, CA: New Harbinger.

Murphy, T. F., and Oberlin, L. H. (2001). *The Angry Child: Regaining Control When Your Child Is Out of Control*. New York: Three Rivers Press.

Richardson, R. W. (2011). *Family Ties That Bind: A Self-Help Guide to Change Through Family of Origin Therapy*. 4th ed. Bellingham, WA: Self-Counsel Press.

Sprague, S. (2008). *Coping with Cliques: A Workbook to Help Girls Deal with Gossip, Put-Downs, Bullying, and Other Mean Behavior*. Oakland, CA: New Harbinger.

CHAPTER FIVE   HOSTILE CHILDREN AND TEENS

Doherty, W. J., and Carlson, B. Z. (2002). *Putting Family First: Successful Strategies for Reclaiming Family Life in a Hurry-Up World*. New York: Owl Books.

Francis, S. (2015). *Disney PIXAR Inside Out Read-Along Storybook and CD*. New York: Disney Press.

Huebner, D., and Matthews, B. (2007). *What to Do When You Grumble Too Much: A Kid's Guide to Overcoming Negativity*. Washington, DC: Magination Press.

Peter, V. J., and Dowd, T. (2000). *Boundaries: A Guide for Teens*. Boys Town, NE: Boys Town Press.

The Fred Rogers Company: The Legacy Lives On. This website offers a variety of anger-management resources for children (preschool through elementary age), including DVD materials for childcare providers, books for children regarding life transitions using Daniel Tiger's Neighborhood, as well as the Mad Feelings Workshop and Challenging Behaviors Training Kit. http://www.fredrogers.org.

Wagenbach, D., and Mack, S. (2010). *The Grouchies*. Washington, DC: Magination Press.

CHAPTER SIX   SABOTAGED ROMANCE AND RELATIONSHIPS

Burns, D. D. (2008). *Feeling Good Together: The Secrets to Making Troubled Relationships Work*. New York: Broadway Books.

Haltzman, S. (2013). *The Secrets of Surviving Infidelity*. Baltimore, MA: The Johns Hopkins University Press.

The Gottman Institute: A Research-Based Approach to Creating Stronger Relationships. This website includes resources for couples and professionals. https://www.gottman.com.

CHAPTER SEVEN   UNDERHANDED BATTLEGROUNDS IN DIVORCE

Johnson, W. B., and Murray, K. (2007). *Crazy Love: Dealing with Your Partner's Problem Personality*. Atascadero, CA: Impact Publishers.

Oberlin, L. H. (2005). *Surviving Separation and Divorce: A Woman's Guide to Regaining Control, Building Strength and Confidence, and Securing a Financial Future*. Boston, MA: Adams Media.

Stepmom. (1998). Columbia Pictures. Starring Julia Roberts, Susan Sarandon, and Ed Harris.

CHAPTER EIGHT   SEETHING THROUGH THE WORK AND SCHOOL DAY

Carnegie, D. (1981). *How To Win Friends and Influence People: The Only Book You Need to Lead You to Success.* New York: Gallery Books.

Fitzgerald, L. (2004). *If at First: How Great People Turned Setbacks into Great Success.* Kansas City, MO: Andrews McMeel.

CHAPTER NINE   DEEPLY SEATED ANGER

Behary, W. T. (2008). *Disarming the Narcissist: Surviving and Thriving with the Self-Absorbed.* Oakland, CA: New Harbinger.

Children and Adults with Attention-Deficit/Hyperactivity Disorder (CHADD), 8181 Professional Place, Suite 150, Landover, MD 20785, http://www.chadd.org; (National Resource Center on ADHD, 1-800-233-4050).

Kreisman, J. J., and Straus, H. (2010). *I Hate You, Don't Leave Me: Understanding the Borderline Personality.* New York: Penguin/Perigee Books.

Mason, P. T., and Kreger, R. (2010). *Stop Walking on Eggshells: Taking Your Life Back When Someone You Care About Has Borderline Personality Disorder.* 2nd ed. Oakland, CA: New Harbinger.

Reif, S. F. (2015). *The ADHD Book of Lists: A Practical Guide for Helping Children and Teens with Attention Deficit Disorders.* 2nd ed. New York: Jossey-Bass Teacher Books.

Roth, K., and Friedman, F. B. (2003). *Surviving the Borderline Parent: How to Heal Your Childhood Wounds and Build Trust, Boundaries, and Self-Esteem.* Oakland, CA: New Harbinger.

Young, J. L., with Adamec, C. (2013). *When Your Adult Child Breaks Your Heart: Coping with Mental Illness, Substance Abuse, and the Problems That Tear Families Apart.* Guilford, CT: Lyons Press.

CHAPTER TEN   PEOPLE PLEASING AND TOLERATING CRAP

Levine, M. (2003). *The Myth of Laziness.* New York: Simon & Schuster.

Rapson, J., and English, C. (2006). *Anxious to Please.* Naperville, IL: Sourcebooks.

Richardson, R. W. (2008). *Becoming Your Best: A Self-Help Guide for Thinking People.* Minneapolis, MN: Augsburg Books.

CHAPTER TWELVE   WHEN AND HOW TO SEEK HELP

Annunziata, J., and Jacobson-Kram, P. (1994). *Solving Problems Together: Family Therapy for the Whole Family.* Washington, DC: Magination Press.

Edelman, S. (2007). *Change Your Thinking: Overcome Stress, Combat Anxiety and Depression, and Improve Your Life with CBT.* New York: Da Capo Press.

Honos-Webb, L. (2010). *The Gift of ADHD: How to Transform Your Child's Problems into Strengths.* Oakland, CA: New Harbinger.

Naumburg, C. (2015). *Ready, Set, Breathe: Practicing Mindfulness with Your Children for Fewer Meltdowns and a More Peaceful Family.* Oakland, CA: New Harbinger.

Nemiroff, M., and Annunziata, J. (1990). *A Child's First Book About Play Therapy.* Washington, DC: Magination Press.

Purcell, M. C., and Murphy, J. R. (2015). *Mindfulness for Teen Anger.* Oakland, CA: New Harbinger.

Snel, E. (2013). *Sitting Still Like a Frog: Mindfulness Exercises for Kids (and Their Parents).* Boulder, CO: Shambala.

APPENDIX   HIDDEN ANGER IN THE CLINICAL SETTING

Professionals who wish to continue learning about passive-aggression in the clinical or helping fields, please visit Loriann Oberlin's website for periodic updates on continuing education or other presentations offered. http://www.lorian noberlin.com.

Engle, D. E., and Arkowitz, H. (2006). *Ambivalence in Psychotherapy: Facilitating Readiness to Change.* New York: The Guilford Press.

McDaniel, S. H., Doherty, W. J., and Hepworth, J. (2014). *Medical Family Therapy and Integrated Care.* 2nd ed. Washington, DC: American Psychological Association.

Van Der Kolk, B. (2015). *The Body Keeps the Score: Brain, Mind, and Body in the Healing of Trauma.* New York: Penguin.

Acknowledgments

FIRST, I HAVE TO THANK Loriann Hoff Oberlin, my coauthor. Her knowledge, experience, and dogged determination to research, draft, and edit our first edition as well as this extensive revision were not only essential when my congressional and Navy duties demanded my time, but also went above and beyond conventional collaboration. She is a talented author, a dedicated mental health counselor, and a very hard-driving cowriter, as well as the key point person for this project. That dynamic influence and vital willpower has paid off.

While working on my mental health reform legislation, several psychiatrists and psychologists sharpened my professional psychology skills, even if they didn't have a direct hand in the manuscript. Physicians Michael Welner, Jeffrey Lieberman, Harold Koplewicz, E. Fuller Torrey, Sally Satel, and Alan Axelson are true leaders in their field of psychiatry, who taught me a great deal along the way. Psychologists Dr. Shannon Edwards and Dr. Tony Mannarino were incredibly helpful with their personal support and expertise in forensic psychology and trauma. All of these professionals are among the best in the field, and I thank them for their assistance even when they did not know they were helping.

The Navy is a team, and my shipmates in psychology and psychiatry deserve a real salute for their selfless work. Psychiatrists David Williamson, Colonel Geoffrey Grammer, and Jonathan Wolf and psychologist Johanna Wolf provide brilliant treatment for our warriors with traumatic brain injury and psychological wounds of war at Walter Reed National Military Medical Center at Bethesda. I'm honored and humbled to serve with them. Commander Eric Potterat, who created the Navy SEAL psychological selection test while also developing much of the resilience training for the Navy SEALs, and Commander Lloyd Davis, a Navy Reserve psychologist and veteran of several deployments, are both incredible assets for our nation's service members. I thank them both for their dedication, sacrifice, and true friendship. They all deserve medals for their work.

My work as a congressman is my priority job. As such, my constituents and legislative duties were the number one task each day. Writing this book occupied many a late night or weekend. My legislative focus on reforming our nation's broken mental health system required a massive amount of work in research and writing. Although they didn't work directly on the book, many people unknowingly contributed an anecdote here and there, and their friendships factored into my motivation to continue my work on the bill and this book. But primarily my colleagues deserve kudos for their outstanding leadership and support for mental health reform. The real list of colleagues who helped push reform would span well over one hundred members, but there are several who stood out by courageously and repeatedly speaking out. Eddie Bernice Johnson (TX), Fred Upton, (MI), John Shimkus (IL), Marsha Blackburn (TN), Renee Ellmers (NC), Mike Doyle (PA), Lee Terry (NE), Patrick Kennedy (RI), Jim McDermott (WA), Marcy Kaptor (OH), Earl Blumenauer (OR), Mike Kelly (PA), John Katko (NY), French Hill (AR), Tom Reed (NY), Mario Diaz Ballart (FL), and the House leadership of Speaker Paul Ryan, Kevin McCarthy, and Steve Scalise were among the biggest supporters. I also have to thank the House staff of Scott Dziengelski, Brad Grantz, Susan Mosychuck, Karen Christian, and Paul Edattel for their outstanding dedication and hard work.

Special thanks to Claire Ivett, our editor at Da Capo Press and Perseus Books, as well as the entire team there that has brought this book to its finished form, including John Radziewicz, Amber Morris, Kerry Rubenstein, and Raquel Kaplan and Jillian Farrel in publicity and marketing.

Finally, I have to thank my family. My wife Nan, our daughter Bevin, her husband Dan, and their beautiful children Thomasina and Luca are all blessings and a daily reminder of the importance of making our world a better place for the next generation.

Congressman Tim Murphy, PhD

BY MY COUNT, this revised edition is my tenth nonfiction book and twelfth overall. Back when Tim and I wrote the first edition, this was and still is the book I had always wanted to write. It's certainly a topic that most people, regardless of age, have encountered or will encounter when difficult relationship dynamics or personality styles entangle them. Previous readers have thanked us for providing them a framework in which to understand passive-aggression and other forms of hidden anger, and I'm gratified to have played a role in that.

On a professional level, our topic has evolved over the decades and lent itself to intriguing insights. This book forced me to immerse myself in the subject matter so that I could learn even more from researchers, other authors, and colleagues.

Speaking of whom, I'd like to thank Donna Troisi, LCSW-C, my very first clinical supervisor in this field, who greeted me with three questions that first internship day during my tenure at Johns Hopkins University. She stretched my thought process, and more importantly, made me recognize and think differently with family systems theory. Embracing that has been a true blessing in so many ways. Donna was and still is a fantastic sounding board, even as I researched this revision. She became a part of my original "office family," which included Christine Newell, PhD, and Robert Price, MS, LCPC. I love that I can still occasionally "think with" these and other colleagues as they offer insights, encouragement, and collegial friendship that I value so very much.

There are many people responsible for shaping this project into what you're reading right now, especially Claire Ivett, our primary editor, who first suggested that we might wish to revise this book because our first edition had sold so steadily. Claire, thank you for your patience leading up to the writing phase, and during it as two busy authors were often pulled away from the keyboard with other job responsibilities. Your understanding and your suggestions have been tremendously supportive. My appreciation also goes out to those at Da Capo Press/Perseus who helped to get this book started (Ashley Ginter and John Radziewicz), shape this text (Amber Morris as project editor), design the book (Kerry Rubenstein), and promote this edition (Jillian Farrel and Raquel Kaplan).

Many professionals were kind enough to lend their thoughts, opinions, and live quotes, especially Geoffrey Greif, PhD, Gina Simmons, PhD, Michael Kerr, MD, and Alan Zametkin, MD. I've known my coauthor Tim Murphy since the early 1990s when we were both freelance contributors to a regional publication. He sought my opinions back then on how to turn his professional path into print, and we've worked together off and on since. While we may have our bipartisan differences, I still recognize that 98 percent of everything he's taught me regarding psychology has been spot-on; the other 2 percent, I tease, is to keep him motivated to write and promote these concepts that so many would-be readers benefit from learning.

My good friends provided encouragement along the way, and certainly professors at Johns Hopkins University added immeasurably to my knowledge. To those who have shared their stories and challenges dealing with hidden anger, please know how much you have taught me about perseverance and the ability to grow through adversity.

Finally, it's not easy to have a spouse who often tries to pack thirty hours of work into a twenty-four-hour day, sometimes arriving late to the dinner table, aiming to complete that "one last sentence." My husband Bob has always accepted and encouraged my creative side. I love him for that and so much more. My sons, Andy and Alex, have known nothing else but that writing life, and I thank them for rolling with the joys of my work in print as well as the labor and long hours that it has often taken. They will always have my love, appreciation, and pride in them.

Loriann Oberlin, MS, LCPC

Index